Value of Design:
Creating Agency Through Data-Driven Insights

Dr. Andrea Chegut, Minkoo Kang, Helena Rong, and Juncheng "Tony" Yang

APPLIED
RESEARCH
+DESIGN

About the Authors

Dr. Andrea Chegut (1981–2022) was the founder and director of the MIT Real Estate Innovation Lab and the head of research and co-founder of MIT's DesignX venture accelerator. Her work centered on the financial performance and economic outcomes of change in the built environment, stemming from design, technology, and innovation. Her research identified product innovation with the aid of data science and machine learning techniques to measure how real estate and planning policy can be aligned across stakeholders to create more sustainable, healthy, socially inclusive, and intelligent real estate.

Minkoo Kang is the founder of General Partner Office, a real estate development consulting firm based in Boston. His practice is informed by his international design experiences and local development expertise. He started as a researcher of urban affairs at Strelka Institute in Moscow, then worked as an architect at the Office for Metropolitan Architecture (OMA) in Rotterdam, Doha, Hong Kong, and New York. He received his Master's in Real Estate Development from MIT.

Helena Rong is an urbanist, designer, and technologist, whose work leverages design and emerging technologies such as blockchains and AI to foster collective intelligence and resilience in the built environment. She is an Assistant Professor in Interactive Media and Business at NYU Shanghai, and the founder of CIVIS Design and Advisory, a design and research practice based in Boston and Shanghai that engages in multi-scalar and interdisciplinary projects. She received her PhD in Urban Planning from Columbia University, Master of Science in Urbanism from MIT, and Bachelor of Architecture from Cornell University.

Juncheng "Tony" Yang is a doctoral candidate at the Harvard Graduate School of Design and partner at CIVIS Design and Advisory. He conducts research at the Data-Smart City Solutions at the Harvard Bloomberg Center for Cities and is a Fellow at the Berkman Klein Center for Internet and Society at the Harvard Law School. His research focuses on the intersection of institutional arrangements and emerging technologies in "smart city" governance. He received a Master of Science in Urbanism from MIT and a Bachelor of Architecture from Rice University.

In Memory of Dr. Andrea Chegut

As we unveil the culmination of countless hours of dedication, we do so with bittersweet hearts, for we are compelled to acknowledge the profound absence of our cherished co-author, friend, and esteemed Director of the MIT Real Estate Innovation Lab, Dr. Andrea Chegut. In late 2022, the world bid farewell to a brilliant mind lost to a relentless brain tumor.

Andrea was more than a colleague; she was a visionary whose passion and dedication knew no bounds. Her intellect was matched only by her kindness, and her leadership inspired the best in us all. This book, one of Andrea's final and most significant contributions, stands as a testament to her profound impact on real estate research.

Our journey began with a shared vision. Andrea, despite not having been trained as a designer, had an open mind and interest in bridging the architectural design discipline with finance and economics. She sought answers to questions that no one had thought to ask in creative ways. What was fascinating about Andrea was that despite being an econometrician, she had the magic of attracting individuals from all walks of life and backgrounds, the three of us included. The lab Andrea has so carefully nurtured was composed of a wonderful mix of architects, designers, data scientists, engineers, entrepreneurs, real estate developers, and urban planners, who collectively shared the curiosity and passion for breaking disciplinary boundaries and asking questions that can only be answered in cross-disciplinary and collaborative ways. Before we knew it, the four of us, united by a shared passion for bringing more "agency" to design in the real world, had joined forces to write several peer-reviewed journal articles together, presented our work to academics and practitioners, applied for grants, and later partnered with AR+D to turn our lab's work into this book.

Although Andrea is no longer with us, her spirit lives on within these pages. Her keen intellect shines through our analysis, bringing clarity to our arguments and infusing hope into our conclusions. It was an honor to have had the chance to learn from and work with this inspiring individual. While she may have embarked on a journey without return, she has left behind a remarkable legacy—a legacy that we are honored to uphold and carry forward.

With heartfelt gratitude and love,
Minkoo Kang, Helena Rong, and Juncheng "Tony" Yang

Foreword

Professors Dennis Frenchman and Svafa Gronfeldt,
MIT Real Estate Innovation Laboratory, MIT DesignX,
Accelerator of Innovation in Design, Cities, and the
Human Environment

This book deals with the relationships between design and the value of real estate, a challenging topic among both developers and the architect-designers who work with them. Developers tend to think of their profession as based in hard numbers— costs per square foot of construction and financial market data. Many dismiss the designer's vision as pie in the sky, unrealistic, adding unnecessary expense for the sake of frills, or risky in the local market. As project designs evolve in practice, they are often subject to the painful task of "value engineering," at its worst, an exercise of stripping away distinguishing features or details of the design to get down to a simply engineered product; one that will stand up and enclose the required amount of space that at comparable rents for similar buildings will make the project financially feasible. The idea that those same features may increase returns on the project over its competition lies unconsidered in the absence of hard data on the value of design, which is difficult to objectively measure. If design is valued at all, it is more about the name of the architect, which can increase income from the building by enhancing its brand. Even then, there are often a lot of push backs on "starchitects" to add their secret sauce at no additional cost.

From the designer's perspective, there is an equal foreboding to attach financial value to design moves. In schools of architecture, students are often taught values that are best appreciated by other designers and critics, rather than the clients for their services. Listening in the studio, one can hear developers characterized as enemies of good design, interested only in the bottom line, not the subtleties of the art; and users as motivated by common tastes and desires. Given these perspectives, many designers are loath to have their work measured in financial terms, since it demeans the higher goals of the profession, preferring a rather fuzzy relationship between design and value creation, in hope that the client and potential users will "get it." This attitude among designers tends to devalue their own contributions, sidelining them from many fundamental decisions that affect their projects and the built environment as a whole.

Value of Design: Creating Agency Through Data-Driven Insights synthesizes perceptions about design from both sides of the aisle, in the belief that a better understanding of how it affects the performance of real estate will improve the quality of real estate products and of design itself, opening paths to innovation in the built environment. New approaches are desperately needed as we face increasingly complex development problems posed by global warming, unchecked urbanization, and resource depletion to name a few. The significance of design, encompassing both its financial and societal benefits, often goes unrecognized and under-investigated in real estate. This book aims to bridge the gap between design appreciation and financial evaluation by leveraging empirical studies and advanced urban data analytics to quantify design's impact on human behavior within New York City. Utilizing these novel data sources, the project seeks to establish a financial metric for design, advocating for its integral role in enhancing property values and addressing broader social challenges. By demonstrating design's tangible benefits through data-driven insights, these studies encourage the real estate industry to adopt a more integrated and holistic approach to valuing design, ensuring projects fully capture its qualitative and economic contributions. The research documented in *Value of Design* was initiated by Dr. Andrea Chegut, former research scientist and director of the MIT Real Estate Innovation Lab. Following her tragic and untimely death in November 2022, researchers in the Lab—Minkoo Kang, Helena Rong, and Juncheng "Tony" Yang—were determined to advance the work on the project and bring the vision to life. We are deeply indebted to these co-authors for their passion and commitment to the project.

This book asks some fundamental questions, such as: Do the design features of a building project affect its value in time and place? How can these features be defined and expressed in terms that developers and the wider community will understand? How do we account for unmeasurable values such as quality of life? For example: In the city of New York, characterized by rectilinear building forms—an outcome of the 1961 zoning code—is there value in developing a building with a diagonal footprint? (The answer is yes! It adds approximately a 12.4% premium per square foot compared to conventional designs.) In considering views from offices and apartments, what is a good or more valuable view? What about public spaces? Do the impressive, and unrented, spaces in modern office buildings—a signature of the Seagram building—live up to the heuristic that they will attract higher paying tenants?

(Again, the answer is yes, but the proportions of the space matter more than the absolute size.)

When presented with such findings, architects and academics are often highly critical, arguing that value depends on the holistic fit of a design to its context, and it's misleading to value individual features. The danger is that such knowledge will just cause such features to be added into projects without thinking, they argue. This may be a valid concern, but is it better not to know? We believe that in the hands of designers and developers, such knowledge will encourage creativity, enhancing the value of their work and the likelihood that they will be implemented. The authors of this book argue that the most valuable design aspects are those that add meaning and humanistic qualities to a project: diverse, articulated forms, pedestrian scale, connections to nature and local culture. In this way, the benefits of knowing what makes valuable design can extend beyond the building to the community itself, ultimately leading to a better quality of life. Conversely, ignorance about design value drives projects toward the lowest common denominator: a sterile, quantitative solution.

The work presented in this book is nascent. Nevertheless, it opens a window on the future practice of design and development in the context of growing data and artificial intelligence, where every aspect of the built world can be sensed and evaluated against performance goals. We can already see this transformation happening in the arenas of sustainability and community health, where the value of design has advanced exponentially in recent years, now recognized as central to resolving these challenges. The process and products of design will become increasingly important as other challenges to human habitation emerge in the future. Understanding the relationship between design and value in real estate is the first step toward maximizing this contribution.

Prologue   What is the value of design?

Through data-driven methodologies, we can reshape industry perspectives and advocate for a more sustainable and human-centric built environment.

In the context of architecture and real estate, the value of design—be it financial or social value—remains largely overlooked and inadequately researched in both academia and real estate valuation practices. By failing to acknowledge the potential of design, we miss opportunities to address the wide-ranging social and sustainability challenges at play today. This book acts as a platform to bridge the gap between design and finance, using empirical research to dissect design into measurable features through data-driven methodologies, with New York City serving as our experimental research site. Novel analytical tools such as artificial intelligence, machine learning, computer vision, and natural language processing, along with new forms of data like anonymized mobile phone mobility data, social media data, and image data, unlock new dimensions for gauging the impact of previously immeasurable design elements of the built environment on human behaviors. These novel measurements, when integrated into real estate valuation models, establish a financial benchmark for design, catalyzing a shift in the industry's perspective on the intrinsic worth of design and ensuring that future projects properly account for the qualitative impact of design on economic value and social benefits. By doing so, we seek to expand the conversation about the role of design in real estate from being an aesthetic afterthought to a critical, evidence-based component of project evaluation and decision-making processes.

As we uncover and quantify the inherent value of design, it becomes possible to persuade key stakeholders—real estate developers, investors, and policymakers—about the significant returns of thoughtful, sustainable, and human-centric design strategies. More importantly, this novel integration of design value within traditional valuation models allows for a greater understanding and recognition of the holistic impact of design. This approach not only champions the economic benefits but also emphasizes the social dividends and environmental sustainability that a well-designed built environment can bring. In essence, in this book, we aim to explore how the amalgamation of design and finance via empirical research and innovative data-driven methodologies can lead to a more integrated and holistic valuation practice.

Chapter 1

The introductory chapter describes the apparent dichotomy between the worlds of design and finance. Design, rooted in creativity and functionality, often struggles to quantify its value, especially in the face of the financial world's relentless pursuit of numeric precision. This tension has implications for the built environment, where design decisions must be financially justified. Traditional real estate valuation methods often overlook the nuanced contributions of design, leaving its value ambiguous. This chapter emphasizes the need for a more systematic approach to evaluating design's impact, especially as society moves toward data-driven decision-making. This chapter also highlights the importance of socially responsible and sustainable design, especially in the context of changing global dynamics like the aftermath of the COVID-19 pandemic.

Chapter 2

In the second chapter, we explore the history and context of New York City, positioning it as the primary research laboratory for our investigation. Commencing with a historical retrospective, this chapter traces the intricate relationship between design and real estate development within the borough of Manhattan. From the establishment of the Commissioners' Plan of 1811 to the con-temporary era, this chapter sheds light on the ever-shifting values placed on design, alongside the city's real estate development landscape, providing insights into the cultural and economic forces that have shaped Manhattan's unique urban identity.

Chapter 3

Here, we delve into into a data-driven approach to investigating real estate value, outlining the tools utilized to quantitatively dissect and assess various metrics that contribute to this value. The objective is to establish a novel framework that quantifies design value, surpassing traditional, often subjective, qualitative assessments. We complement this with an adaptable research methodology that caters to the complex nature of design value. Our aim is to deliver a nuanced understanding of design value, empirically grounded, using New York—with its rich development history, its diverse architectural styles, and real estate trends—as a testing and refining ground.

Chapter 4

Finally, the last chapter features a compilation of the research papers produced between 2019 and 2023 by the MIT Real Estate Innovation Lab under the umbrella subject of identifying the value of the design of the built environment. The research utilizes New York's commercial real estate (CRE) data from 2000. We have created a toolkit that deconstructs design into a series of measurable metrics and offers guidance for their assessment. In this chapter, we also present empirical evidence to demonstrate the value of design, focusing on selected features such as iconicity, physical design features derived from zoning requirements, daylight, views, green building technologies, street-level greenery, and work productivity. The terminology of buildings and design in the ensuing chapters is primarily framed within the context of commercial real estate, with a particular emphasis on office and residential applications.

The authors of this book are researchers at the MIT Real Estate Innovation Lab, who bring together decades of interdisciplinary experience in architectural and urban design, real estate development, urban planning, econometric research, and data science.

By establishing a financial precedent for the value of design, we can influence real estate development practices toward sustainability and human-centric designs. The goal is not only to pave the way for a more sustainable future but also to reshape our built environment in a manner that fosters health, resilience, and sustainability.

1 Introduction

There are two worlds that sometimes stand in apparent opposition with one another: the world of design and the world of finance.

1.1　The Wide Gulf Between Design and Finance

The concept of "design" is a modern construct. It is "a discipline of study and practice focused on the interaction between a person—a 'user'—and the man-made environment, taking into account aesthetic, functional, contextual, cultural, and societal considerations."[1] Unlike art, design is supposed to be functional and effective, an integrated amalgamation of utility and aesthetics. The purveyors of design embody the dual roles of creative visionaries and pragmatic engineers who synthesize creativity with utility. A recurring challenge for designers, however, regardless of the field and scale of design—from UX to industrial or architectural—is to position design as a contributor of value to projects. Measuring the value of design feels like an oxymoron: attributes of design that contribute to its overall effectiveness and appeal, from emotional relevance to psychological comfort, are deeply personal and subjective; it may, therefore, appear blasphemous to even think of quantifying the nebulous enchantment of creativity, as any such attempts seem to somehow risk tarnishing its essence, reducing the sublime to mere statistics and stripping away its ineffable charm. This dilemma is further complicated by the scarcity of tools that might enable designers to attempt quantifying their work.

The world of finance, on the other hand, similar to Jorge Luis Borges's described "Empire" infatuated with cartographic perfection in "On Exactitude in Science," is often absorbed in a quest for numeric precision.[2] As value cartographers, finance experts seek to delineate every subtle undulation and fluctuation of the market landscape with the aims of forging a one-to-one map of the vast empire of economic exchange and capturing each crest and trough of the financial terrain with the precise strokes of data. As the saying goes, you can't create and manage what you can't measure. Finance operates on narratives, a self-perpetuating practice and an artful science founded upon past empirical stories that can be measured, learned, repeated, and refined. The consequence of this way of thinking is that only things that can be measured are acknowledged as having value, while those which cannot

---

1　"What Is Design?," International Council of Design, n.d.
2　Jorge Luis Borges, "On Exactitude in Science," in *Collected Fictions*, trans. Andrew Hurley (New York: Penguin Classics, 1998), 325.

are relegated to the abyss of arbitration, whose worth is subject to the capricious verdicts of those who dictate the metrics.

1.2 The Built Environment and Its Dilemmas

This apparent clash of world views, between design and finance, has significant implications for the built environment—the very material world in which we live. In the realm of real estate development and architectural design, there exists an imbalance of power between those who devise design innovations and those who possess the authority to decide their value and whether to adopt these innovations, giving them their physical form.

Constructing a building is no small feat, necessitating substantial upfront investments and efforts. To offset these costs, each design decision needs to be financially evaluated by the real estate developer, who embarks on the risk-taking act of speculating the future sale price of the asset in order to justify its feasibility and worth. As finance interprets the world through numbers and spreadsheets, decisions are heavily built on financial precedents that serve to prove whether certain decisions will contribute value.

The Practice of Valuing Buildings

In conventional real estate development practice, a building's monetary value is assessed by a certified or licensed real estate appraiser. Commercial appraisals are often required for financing properties using conventional bank loans, as banks have specific loan-to-value thresholds that must be met before approving a loan. A valuation helps determine the asset's worth, enabling the lender to decide the size of the loan they are willing to provide. Local governments also conduct citywide property appraisals to determine and revise property taxes based on updated values.

Among diverse valuation methods, spanning from the sales comparison approach to the Net Present Value (NPV) rule, the direct capitalization approach stands out as the most commonly used.[3] This method estimates a property's value by considering its Net Operating Income (NOI), calculated by deducting operating expenses from the gross rent generated

---

3   The sales comparison approach in real estate compares a property to recently sold comparables with similar characteristics, ideally within a year in a competitive market. Also known as the market data approach, it's common among agents and appraisers. Net Present Value (NPV) in real estate is the difference between cash inflows and outflows, determining a property's value. Positive NPV indicates the asset is worth more, negative less, and zero equal.

by the building. This straightforward approach is widely adopted for its simplicity and effectiveness in evaluating a property's value.[4] By calculating the NOI and then applying a market capitalization rate (also known as the cap rate) derived from comparable sale data, the property's value can be estimated.

Property Value = Net Operating Income / Cap Rate

The appraiser will adjust the cap rate based on the building's condition and other property-specific factors, such as location, size, and building class. For instance, if a higher-quality building in a more desirable neighborhood than the subject building was recently sold for a 6% cap rate, the appraiser might use an adjusted cap rate of 6.5% or 7%.

The Discounted Cash Flow (DCF) approach is another common technique that necessitates a more detailed analysis. Most frequently used with rental properties, the DCF approach involves projecting net cash flows over a specified hold period. This technique requires an appraiser to make several assumptions about potential future cash flows, anticipated operational and capital expenditures, and the building's expected sales price at the end of the hold period. Both the DCF and direct capitalization approaches are commonly used by investors and developers, in addition to appraisers, to analyze potential deals.

In real estate finance, these conventional asset valuation models often overlook design as a relevant attribute that influences market pricing. Physical features of buildings that are included in the asset valuation charts typically consist of crude items such as age, number of floors, and renovation status—all of which are merely the programmatic prerequisites defined at the start of a project rather than the subsequent nuanced design choices made by designers.

As a result, the absence of financial precedents for design thrusts it into a precarious position of uncertainty, in which agency skews away from the designer and toward the financial arbiter, who can determine whether a design decision merits investment. All will agree that design delivers and should deliver value, but the exact mechanism through which it does so remains largely elusive. Architectural designers consider spaces that promote certain ethos and end goals—be it sustainability, spatial flexibility, sociability, health-promoting

---

4 Effective Gross Income (EGI) = Potential Gross Income (PGI) - vacancy - concessions Net Operating Income (NOI) = Effective Gross Income (EGI) - operating expenses - real estate tax

environments, or comfortability—that define the interaction and relationship between users and the built environment. However, the current practice offers few tools for designers to verify the worth of their works or to demonstrate the direct linkage between their designs and the value that is subsequently generated. For architects, whether a design proposal garners approval from the client—the ultimate decision-making authority—remains a complete enigma. Those who ascend to the deified echelons of "starchitects" might occasionally fare better in upholding their positions and values at a negotiation table with developer clients, but most practicing architects regularly grapple with the deflating behavior and indecisions of their clients, which is arguably inherent in the prevailing process of real estate investment and development wherein design lacks an authoritative, quantifiably legitimate voice.

The increasing fetishization of quantitative data, especially as we venture into the age of artificial intelligence, tilts our understanding and assessment of values further toward things that can be numerically counted, measured, represented, and learned. While digital advancements continue to offer exciting opportunities, there are obvious drawbacks to such obsession with quantitative governance. The most infamous example is the McNamara fallacy, named after the United States Secretary of Defense Robert McNamara (1961–1968) whose biased decision in the Vietnam War based relentlessly on quantitative metrics and oversight of apparently unquantifiable ones led to the debacle that characterized the involvement of the United States in the war.[5] However, it is also true that we now have more advanced reality-capturing apparatuses and data technologies that allow us to record and understand previously unmeasurable metrics, including those associated with the intangible qualities of design and subjectivity. While we do not attempt to uncritically subscribe to the pervasive trend of datafication in this book, we posit that there exists real opportunity in establishing systematic approaches to evaluate and measure design and to bridge the two worlds of design and finance. More importantly, the stakes of not doing so may be too high.

---

5   Robert S. McNamara, *In Retrospect: The Tragedy and Lessons of Vietnam* (New York: Vintage, 1996).

1.3 Defining Design

In the context of architectural design and commercial real estate, which is the focus of this book, design is characterized by its multifaceted nature, high level of specialization, and interdisciplinary approach. In contemporary practice, architectural work involves collaboration among diverse groups of experts from various social backgrounds, reflecting a trend toward more distributed and dispersed efforts. This shift emphasizes collaborative endeavors and is increasingly reliant on principles of knowledge-sharing and open-source methodologies. As the technology and methodology used in analyzing buildings advance, new types of design services continue to be innovated, underscoring the dynamic and evolving nature of the field.

Meanwhile, design offers far greater impact than mere aesthetic appeal. It has the potential to promote sustainability and minimize environmental impacts, bolster resilience against crises such as pandemics and climate change, stimulate health and well-being, cultivate social interactions, and foster community-building, among many other short- and long-term benefits. But the current lack of means to measure these attributes risks their marginalization to the point of irrelevance during real estate development processes that are becoming increasingly financialized. As such, we need tangible and assessable lessons rather than episodic and anecdotal narratives to give design its much-deserved agency, voice, and attention. Anecdotes often lead us to overlook the underlying statistical distribution and base rate. An attempt to demystify the creative magic inherent in design is by no means intended to discredit it but to help level the playing field between design and finance during the creation of the built environment in order to generate better products and solutions.

Past academic research has endeavored to bridge the gulf between the worlds of design and finance. Sporadic studies have attempted to quantify the economic value of design by associating real estate value with either an architect's accomplishments—using award recognition as a proxy for design quality—or through survey-based expert scoring of buildings. The underlying premise behind associating design with an architect's award-winning status assumes that the accolades received by architects are backed by valid reasons and that buildings designed by reputable architects or architectural firms must inherently possess higher design quality.

While this marks a commendable initial step toward recognizing the influence of design in contributing to a building's financial value and closing the gap between the two domains, it falls short in effectively pinpointing what exactly about the design contributes to that value. After all, designers vary their design strategies from one building to another.

What continues to be largely underexplored are the more nuanced physical and performative aspects of the elements, concepts, and principles that constitute the foundation of architectural design language, which require both qualitative and quantitative building information acquired at higher resolutions. In the discipline of architecture, several scholars have attempted to dissect architecture into its elemental features that are both tangible and intangible relating to materiality and historical meanings, but their interactions with the larger social world and their impact on values (whether economic, social, or cultural), remain an uncharted research terrain.[6] In this book, we extend beyond merely associating design quality with an architect's award-winning status in assessing their economic value, to dissect particular attributes of a building—encompassing both physical and performative aspects—into components that can be measured and evaluated using computational and data-driven techniques.

To this end, we propose a revised definition of design: a set of physical, aesthetic, performative, and functional considerations incorporated into the spatial organization of a building, which, through their unique combinations and arrangements, create a distinctive assemblage that influences the structure of a building, acting as an interface between occupants and the environment and shaping the overall experience and use of a building.

| Socially Responsible Design | As a discipline that requires both large amounts of initial capital investment and a willingness to adhere to localized policies such as zoning regulations, architectural design and real estate development reside at the intersection of sometimes conflicting private and public agendas. Design strategies that emphasize resiliency, equity, health, and wellness are often proposed without financial substantiation. This ongoing neglect perpetuates a bias that steers the production |

6   Mikkel Bille and Tim Flohr Sorensen, *Elements of Architecture: Assembling Archaeology, Atmosphere and the Performance of Building Spaces* (London: Routledge, 2016); Francis Ching, *Architecture, Form, Space & Order*, 1st ed. (New York: John Wiley & Sons, 1979); Rem Koolhaas et al., *Elements of Architecture* (Cologne: Taschen, 2014).

of new buildings toward bare financial returns for investors, rather than design innovations for the public benefit of their occupants. However, the field of architecture has experienced a perceptible shift in focus in recent years toward more socially conscious designs. Increasing attention has been dedicated to recognizing design that embodies the notions of economic, environmental, and social sustainability, as opposed to the more elitist notion that prioritizes iconicity. This is exemplified by recent laureates of the prestigious Pritzker Prize, such as Alejandro Aravena (2016) and Lacaton and Vassal (2021), whose works grapple with broader social issues of public significance.

In a post-pandemic world, it is increasingly vital for the private sector to identify sustainable investments that yield both social and financial returns, given that economic behaviors and market outcomes are deeply intertwined with social norms. The rise of environmental, social, and governance (ESG) criteria for financial investments over the past decade signifies a mounting obligation for investors to encourage corporate entities to embrace social and environmental responsibility, advancing beyond the earlier iteration of the perfunctory attempts at Corporate Social Responsibility (CSR) practices. Popularized in 2005 in a report by Freshfields, ESG is an institutionalized valuation system that integrates environmental, social, and governance considerations during investment evaluations. Non-financial data points such as carbon emissions, waste generation, fossil fuel dependence, biodiversity impact and management, board diversity, and so forth serve as indicators of sustainability when assessing a company's stocks. The underlying notion is that robust ESG performance cultivates both enduring environmental effects and financial returns for businesses.

ESG evaluation in real estate is far from being mature and developed. At present, ESG indicators in the field of real estate focus mainly on environmental and energy optimization as the key metrics to gauge a building's level of "greenness" and its translation into monetary values.[7] However, there are mixed and contradictory findings about how ESG impacts financial values due to a lack of standardization in ESG rating in real estate and asset management, along with a dearth of attention to the social dimensions of ESG. Across the board, there is a

7   Shirley Kempeneer et al., "Bringing the User Back in the Building: An Analysis of ESG in Real Estate and a Behavioral Framework to Guide Future Research," *Sustainability* 13, no. 6 (March 15, 2021): 3239.

pervasive emphasis on environmental sustainability in ESG evaluations and less focus on social sustainability. Existing health indicators related to buildings, such as indoor air quality, thermal comfort, and acoustics, can be readily captured and measured using sensor technologies. Yet, intangible qualities relating to human behaviors and perceptions, such as occupant movements, interactions, productivity, psychological and social well-being receive less attention, even though they are precisely the elements that thoughtful designs can influence. Research in environmental psychology shows that "biophilic" designs, which create connections between building occupants and the natural environment through elements of direct or indirect nature, can enhance occupants' visceral attraction to buildings and yield positive health benefits, such as stress reduction and improved cognition.[8] This heightened well-being of occupants could potentially translate into increased utilization of building facilities and improved productivity, which could, in turn, result in greater tenant retention and enhanced economic value.

Long-Term Resilience and Sustainability

Perceptual dimensions of design are not confined to the interiors of buildings but also extend to a building's surrounding urban context. Kevin Lynch was a pioneer in dissecting and identifying elements of the urban environment that shape human experience of cities in his seminal work, *The Image of the City* (1964).[9] Lynch distinguished five elements of the built environment—paths, edges, districts, nodes, and landmark—that aid individuals in forming mental maps of their surroundings. More recently, scholars Reid Ewing and Susan Handy operationalized numerous perceptual urban design qualities of the street environment in relation to the physical attributes of streets and their perimeters, namely imageability, enclosure, human scale, transparency, and complexity.[10] These nuanced and more subjective characteristics are associated with the concept of walkability and are suggested to test for associations between design qualities of the built environment with walking behavior of pedestrians.[11] A lengthy strand of

8   Nikos A. Salingaros, "Change the title to: Neuroscience experiments to verify the geometry of healing environments: Proposing a biophilic healing index of design and architecture," *Urban Experience and Design: Contemporary Perspectives on Improving the Public Realm* (2020): 58-72.
9   Kevin Lynch, *The Image of the City* (Cambridge: MIT Press, 1964).
10 Reid Ewing and Susan Handy, "Measuring the unmeasurable: Urban design qualities related to walkability," *Journal of Urban Design* 14, no. 1 (2009): 65–84.
11 Reid Ewing et al., "Identifying and measuring urban design qualities related to walkability," *Journal of Physical Activity and Health* 3, no. s1 (2006): S223–S240.

empirical research attests to the positive impacts of the built environment on active travel such as walking and bicycling.[12] This, in turn, engenders positive health outcomes such as lower Body Mass Index (BMI) and a reduction in obesity rates among the general public.[13]

Another critical aspect to bear in mind is the anticipated shift in our lifestyle and work culture following the COVID-19 pandemic. This book was largely written during this global health crisis, which brought with it enormous societal damage and altered how we live, work, and interact with one another. To curb the spread of the virus, cities around the world imposed lockdowns and businesses transitioned to remote work to maintain operations. A 2021 survey conducted by the Partnership of New York shows that remote or hybrid work was not simply a temporary remedy during COVID-19, but will become a crucial part of the future of work.[14] Office work benefited from the flexibility of work-from-home models, which indicates that hybrid or remote work will become a permanent feature in future operations, especially in industries such as technology, consulting, and accounting. As the demand for commercial office space declines and the need for expanded residential space increases due to changes in work culture, existing real estate products may no longer satisfy the needs of building occupants. This leaves room for both developers and designers to innovate and conduct research into evolving user needs to better accommodate the working population.

The post-COVID world underscores the critical role of design in achieving enduring sustainability across environmental, economic, and social dimensions. As we navigate changing expectations of the spatial qualities of the built world, we have the unique opportunity to shape cities that prioritize human well-being, catalyzing healthier lifestyles and fostering more vibrant and livable urban environments for generations to come. Empirical research into the value of design can provide significant contributions to the establishment of new standards for the evaluation and practice of design in real estate, urban development, and finance sectors.

12   Lance Freeman et al., "Neighborhood walkability and active travel (walking and cycling) in New York City," *Journal of Urban Health* 90 (2013): 575–585.
13   Andrew Rundle et al., "Neighborhood food environment and walkability predict obesity in New York City," *Environmental health perspectives* 117, no. 3 (2009): 442–447.
14   Partnership for New York City, "Return to Office Survey - June 2021," *Partnership for New York City*, June 2021.

1.4 Building a Design Database

In most current architectural design practices, research and analysis often rely on anecdotal and qualitative analysis of precedents gathered in unsystematic ways. More recently, research-driven architecture firms, such as Gensler, have begun to experiment with quantifying the design intentions and outcomes of their buildings in order to better understand the impact of their work. To bridge the need for designers to construct better measurable knowledge of their work and the current research tools and methods available, the MIT Real Estate Innovation Lab hosted a workshop with the global leadership at Gensler, entitled "The Value of Design: Leveraging Key Performance Indicators" on June 25, 2021, where we discussed the following set of questions:

– How do we currently demonstrate the ways in which design contributes to the asset value of buildings and workplaces?
– How can "financial precedents" be incorporated into our design proposals to align incentives between designers and financial stakeholders?
– What financial empirical evidence needs to be developed to deliver better design solutions in practice?
– How will design deliver value post-pandemic?

Our key concern is to leverage novel data-capturing tools to help find ways to establish a more systematic and forward-looking approach to data collection of design and to integrate such information with actual financial datasets that allow us to better understand the value proposition of design. The following takeaways help to lay out a broader platform of discussion for the need to construct a systematic design database for architecture practice.

COVID-19's Impact on the Commercial Real Estate Sector

The COVID-19 pandemic dramatically disrupted the way that people live, work, and play. These changes have had large effects on commercial real estate, particularly the office sector. The initial shift to remote work in the earlier days of the pandemic significantly reduced the demand for offices. Since our workshop with Gensler in mid-2021, new data on these changes has become available. A 2023 Pew Research Center survey revealed that approximately one-third of the U.S. workforce, in jobs compatible with remote work, are working from home all of the time.[15] Despite a gradual return to offices in early 2023, the national office vacancy rate remains at a 30-year high of 16.1% in Q1 2023, a stark increase from the pre-pandemic level of 11.4% in 2019.[16] In the first quarter of 2023, average office vacancies in 10 of the largest U.S. markets rose to 21.9%, marking an increase from the 19.4% recorded at the end of the previous year's first quarter.[17] Even offices currently under lease are far from full, signaling troubling implications for months and years ahead. According to security firm Kastle, these 10 markets witnessed an occupancy rate of merely 48% in 2023, indicating a potential future trend where tenants might opt for smaller spaces as their leases expire.[18] Zippia Research shows that 74% of U.S. companies are either already utilizing or planning to implement a permanent hybrid work model.[19]

Concerns about the downside risks of the CRE market were noted by market analysts and institutions. A May 2023 Financial Stability Report released by the Board of Governors of the Federal Research Systems highlights issues of weakened long-term fundamentals due to the prevalence of remote work, high valuation, and rising interest rates.[20] The report includes a comparison of inflation-adjusted CRE debt and CRE price index, showing a decline in CRE prices but stable debt levels, a disparity that may lead to solvency challenges and defaults due to fall in collateral values.[21] The resilience of the financial system hinges not only on the agility and innovation of financial regulations, but also the adaptability of building usage to meet the changing demands of the times.

Introducing Flexibility in the Building Stock

Although demand for office spaces is decreasing due to remote work, demand for living spaces is increasing. The need for additional space at home for remote office work has increasingly led office workers to relocate to suburban areas with larger properties, but it has also created a demand for new real estate

15 Kim Parker, "About a third of U.S. workers who can work from home now do so all the time," *Pew Research Center*, March 30, 2023.
16 Statista, "Quarterly office vacancy rates in the United States from 4th quarter 2017 to 1st quarter 2023," *Statista*, June 29, 2023.
17 Lyle Niedens, "Commercial Office Vacancy Rates Don't Tell the Whole Story," *Investopedia*, June 8, 2023.
18 Kastle, "Getting America Back to Work," 2023. https://www.kastle.com/safety-wellness/getting-america-back-to-work/; CBRE, "Office Buildings Hardest Hit by Pandemic Share Common Characteristics," *CBRE*, April 04, 2023.
19 Abby McCain, "30 Essential Hybrid Work Statistics [2023]: The Future of Work," *Zippia*, February 20, 2023.
20 Board of Governors of the Federal Research Systems, "Financial Stability Report - May 2023," *The Federal Reserve*, 2023.
21 Miguel Faria e Castro and Samuel Jordan-Wood, "Commercial Real Estate: Where Are the Financial Risks?" *Economic Research Federal Reserve Bank of St. Louis*, 2023.

products within city centers for those who chose to stay. In the case of New York City, according to listing platform StreetEasy, the current recovery in the residential market is primarily driven by high-end luxury tiers (top 20%) due to their provision of various amenities that would enhance the work-from-home experience for workers. As demands for different uses of spaces change, existing real estate products no longer satisfy the needs of occupants as traditional formulas for spatial organization no longer work. It is paramount for the industry to conduct research on user needs and prepare to introduce renovations in the real estate sector to better serve the working population.

Current discussions highlight the possibility of introducing flexibility in the existing building stock in metropolitan areas and considering converting excess office spaces into condos or affordable housing to reduce vacancy while meeting the growing needs for housing in the city. Office-to-residential conversions, a concept that has been around since the late 1990s when the office market faced significant pressures from vacancy, are becoming much more prevalent post-COVID to mitigate the dual problems of office vacancy and housing shortage. Past successful conversions are attracting the interest and attention of developers, architects, and policymakers alike. For instance, the "Icon," a 275,000-square-foot 1929 Art Deco office building situated in Center City, Philadelphia, was successfully redeveloped into 206 apartment units by Alterra Property Group in 2014, demonstrating a successful office-to-residential conversion for a prewar building. Modern office buildings, like 180 Water Street in New York, which boast much larger building footprints, have resorted to more intricate conversion operations, such as excavating courtyard spaces, in order to create spaces suitable for residential use and to meet daylight requirements.

In October 2023, the Biden-Harris Administration announced new actions to help facilitate the conversion of high-vacancy offices to residential use.[22] These actions, aligning with the White House Housing Supply Action Plan, include new financing, technical assistance, and sale of federal properties with goals of reducing housing costs, boosting supply, promoting fair housing, while addressing the climate crisis and reducing energy expenditures. The initiative leverages various federal tools, such as low-interest loans, guarantees, grants, and tax incentives to stimulate conversions. The Inflation Reduction

---

22 The White House, "ACT SHEET: Biden-Harris Administration Takes Action to Create More Affordable Housing by Converting Commercial Properties to Residential Use," October 27, 2023.

Act further brings more capital to conversions through the Department of Energy Loan Program Office's loans and guarantee programs and tax benefits.[23]

For both developers and architects, these ongoing market trends and policy guidelines signal uncharted territories for new value propositions, highlighting the need to leverage design to innovate in new real estate products that would cater to the changing needs of users and satisfy both changing demands for residential and commercial spaces in a post-pandemic world.

We Need Better
Design Data

Two types of data are currently missing in the financial assessment and valuation of building designs: (1) data that reflects the intentionality of design (i.e., attributes that designers embed within design decisions to achieve better performance outcomes); and (2) post-occupancy data that reflects feedback and usage of buildings from actual inhabitants. The lack of either set of data in the asset valuation of buildings means that the value generated by design is not sufficiently captured by current financial models, thus resulting in a lack of agency for design to effectively assert the value propositions it brings to stakeholders, who ultimately determine whether to invest in certain design products.

For architecture firms, the design data that highlights the intentionality of the designer already exists in the form of drawings and 3D models associated with each project. But this information is not systematically collected in current practice, and its outcome is thus not measured by developers in their financial assessments. Which design strategies, such as biophilia, have been chosen to enhance health? Which architectural elements or features—and in what quantities—have been employed to accommodate human needs for daylight and views? What are design interventions that address the need for sustainable construction through carbon reduction? And finally, how do we quantify these metrics, especially those that are more qualitative in nature? An industry-wide definition and standardization for design data collection is necessary, as it would mean that for the first time, we can capture the value-performance differential for different design strategies targeted at achieving better outcomes. Chapter 4.2 of this book catalogs a list of design features that can be described and measured from either physical or performative aspects.

---

23   The White House, "ACT SHEET", 2023.

On the other hand, understanding user expectations and the quality of their experience leads to greater insights of the drives behind occupancy and willingness to pay for different real estate products. Gensler is among one of the first architecture firms to begin constructing a design database that focuses on user-centered, post-occupancy experience of buildings. The Gensler's Workplace Performance Index (WPI^{SM}) is a pre- and post-occupancy survey tool that gathers employee input on workplace performance factors before and after a design project, which serves to both inform design decisions and to measure the success of design outcomes, with the goal of creating a comprehensive benchmark database to track design and business performance.[24]

The firm's more recent launch of the Gensler Experience Index is a research effort that attempts to identify and quantify the factors of design that impact the human experience. A key proposition of this work is that better design leads to better experience, which in turn leads to higher productivity and value propositions for businesses. This research relied on a nationwide survey of 4,000 respondents in the United States, which highlighted a range of factors that could collectively drive the quality of experience across retail, workplace, and public space segments, including qualities of expectation, interaction, and the aesthetics of space. These firm-led experiments with metrifying design exemplify ways for industry players in architecture to lead the effort of rethinking measuring design and building out a design database whose attention is not only focused solely on the intentionality of the designer but also the rest of the product life cycle that keeps track of feedback from real users during post-occupancy stages.

The challenge of creating standardized metrics is that there are many factors that depend on the local context, the individual client, and the multitudinal nature of the end users. For different segments, geographies, and types of clients and users served, there are different values that become highlighted and prioritized. The critical necessity for better design data thus calls for a concerted effort from the industry as a whole. Continued omission of design data in building valuation risks the perpetuation of a status quo where design's profound impact on economic, social, and environmental outcomes remains undervalued and underleveraged. In a world increasingly defined by rapid urbanization, climate change,

---

24 For a detailed study utilizing the Gensler WPI data, please see the section *Productive Buildings* in Ch. 4.

and shifting socioeconomic landscapes, the capacity to effectively quantify and integrate design value into financial models is not just desirable but essential. Ultimately, the quest for better design data is a call to action for architects, developers, policymakers, and researchers alike to collaboratively forge pathways that validate the intrinsic value of design, ensuring that our built environment can meet the complex demands of the 21st century and beyond.

2 The Case Study: New York City

New York City presents a rich tableau of real estate narratives and evolving architecture, offering a dynamic canvas to explore the intricate links between design, location, time, and market forces in shaping a city's ever-changing landscape.

"New York has never learned the art of growing old by playing on all its pasts. Its present invents itself, from hour to hour, in the act of throwing away its previous accomplishments and challenging the future. A city composed of paroxysmal places in monumental reliefs. The spectator can read in it a universe that is constantly exploding. In it are inscribed the architectural figures of the *coincidentia oppositorum* formerly drawn in miniatures and mystical textures. On this stage of concrete, steel, and glass, cut out between two oceans (the Atlantic and the American) by a frigid body of water, the tallest letters in the world compose a gigantic rhetoric of excess in both expenditure and production."
— Michel de Certeau, The Practice of Everyday Life[1]

Our research locus is New York City, an urban theater whose stage has been set by a tumultuous and constant flux of events that serve as the fertile seedbed for our empirical study. The city's bustling real estate activities—particularly in the commercial sector—offer a living archive of data that allows us to explore the nexus of architectural design, time, and market dynamics. Viewed from the Hudson River, Manhattan's iconic skyline is a physical manifestation of more than a century of compromising interactions and negotiations between different public and private actors shaping the city. In *Form Follows Finance* (1995), Carol Willis suggests that the city should be understood as a complex environment which commodifies location, space, and image. Manhattan's unique "vernacular of capitalism" is a product of comprehensive planning, local land-use patterns, municipal codes and zoning regulations interacting with speculative development and the impact of real-estate cycles.[2]

During such processes, design has served to negotiate between the competing interests of the public and private sectors while attempting to establish its own position about aesthetics, spatial quality, functional performance, and creative legacies. However, its outcomes have been under-evaluated, and its impact on financial and social values has been largely overlooked by both academics and practitioners. As a result, the disciplines of architecture and development are quickly heading toward a narrow focus of aiding the facilitation of

1   Michel De Certeau, *The Practice of Everyday Life* (Berkeley: University of California Press, 2011), 152.
2   Carol Willis, *Form Follows Finance: Skyscrapers and Skylines in New York and Chicago* (New York: Princeton Architectural Press, 1995), 19.

financialization and value capture of real estate driven by larger market currents. In the process, those who shape the built environment are losing sight of their ability to develop creative innovations for public good.

2.1   The Planning of New York City

With a history spanning over 400 years, New York City has consistently stood at the forefront of architecture and real estate development. Beginning as a small Dutch settlement named New Amsterdam in the 17th century, rapid transformation led it to become one of the world's largest and most influential cities. The cityscape was irrevocably shaped by periods of economic boom and bust, waves of immigration, and evolving architectural trends. Fig. 1

The rigid gridiron plan reigning the island of Manhattan north of 14th Street was the outcome of the Commissioners' Plan of 1811. The grid has often been hailed by its proponents as "legible, accessible, efficient, traditional, and perhaps, even egalitarian" and most commonly appears in centralizing or globalizing societies.[3] While feigning neutrality, the plan was in fact a device designed to maximize the value of real estate and to more easily divide the landscape into sellable lots because they facilitated the building of "straight-sided and right-angled houses that were the least expensive to build and most convenient to live in," according to the city commissioners who designed the now iconic grid.[4]

As a result, built structures in Manhattan were confined to generic rectangular lots along the gridded layout of twelve north-south avenues and 155 east-west streets. A handful of features, however, resisted and broke free from the harsh imposition of the grid. Namely, the Broadway thoroughfare—which predated the arrival of the Europeans and followed the Native American Wickquasgeck Trail—traverses the length of Manhattan from State Street at Bowling Green for 13 miles and cuts diagonally across the grid.[5] Not only a frustration for

---

3   Jill Grant, "The dark side of the grid: power and urban design," *Planning Perspectives* 16, no. 3 (2001): 219–241.

4   Paul Goldberger, "New York and the New Urbanism: Congress for the New Urbanism," Paul Goldberger, June 9, 2001. See also: Lewis Mumford, *The City in History: Its Origins, Its Transformations, and Its Prospects* (Boston: Houghton Mifflin Harcourt, 1961); and Peter Marcuse, "The Grid as City Plan: New York City and Laissez-Faire Planning in the Nineteenth Century," *Planning Perspectives* 2 (1987): 287–310.

5   "Broadway: New York, New York," *American Planning Association* (2014).

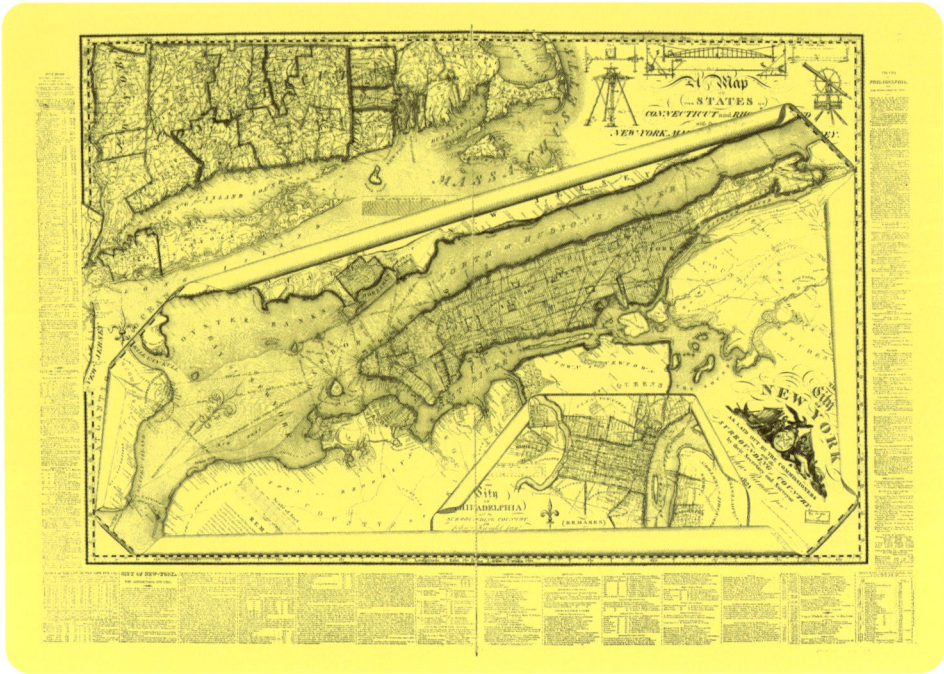

Fig. 1 **The Commissioners' Plan of 1811 Provisional Map, Released in 1807**

real estate developers, Broadway's diagonality also attracted strong opposition in 1811 from traffic planners and engineers, who saw its abrupt presence as confusing to traffic movement. However, a valuable legacy of this grid-diagonal tension is the production of major public open spaces designed as visual termination points at six-way "bowtie" intersections whenever Broadway crosses an avenue, resulting in some of the most treasured public spaces serving the public interest: Union Square, Madison Square, Herald Square, and Times Square, which set the stage for diverse and eventful communal life.[6] These irregular plots presented design challenges for architects to design for non-orthogonal footprints. Some of the most iconic buildings in New York that emerged from these challenges include the Flatiron Building designed by Daniel Burham (1902), Trinity Church by Richard Upjohn

---

6   B. Davis, "On Broadway, Tactical Urbanism." faslanyc, 2010; Stephen Carr et al., *Public Space* (Cambridge: Cambridge University Press, 1992).

(1864), and the Marine Midland Building by Gordon Bunshaft (1968).

In addition to the 1811 Commissioners' Plan, the Zoning Resolutions of 1916 and 1961 further induced dramatic changes to New York's skyline. The 1916 resolution marked the inception of city-wide regulations that, for the first time, imposed use restrictions, bulk restrictions, and administrative provisions. This landmark resolution was a multifaceted product shaped by various influences, including reform ideology, Fusion politics, the tumultuous state of the real estate market, and the agitation of local interests.[7] Striking a balance between aesthetics, economics, and health and safety considerations, the resolution aimed to accommodate a diversity of concerns and interests. The progressive era at the time prioritized public interest over market interest, placing the emphasis on addressing crises related to public health and population as the primary concern.[8] In this context, the protection of real estate value, while always significant, was relegated to a secondary consideration.[9] Fig. 2-3

The Zoning Resolution introduced the principle of the zoning envelope which determined the shape, size, and position of the building and prevented the construction of structures at the scale of the Equitable Building (1915), whose massive size blocked out natural sunlight for the street and its nearby neighbors.[10] The predefined zoning envelope effectively shaped the aesthetics of high-rise building design in New York and encouraged the wedding cake or ziggurat-shaped setback style—a terrace-like form toward the upper portion of a skyscraper—for owners who wished to exploit the maximum buildable volume allowed for the lot.[11] As a compromise between financial pursuits and comprehensive regulation, the setback style casted positive impacts such as increased privacy, exposure, light and air, and activated utilization of the tower's upper levels as commercial spaces or outdoor public spaces.[12] According to commercial architect Ely Jacques Kahn, "The New York zoning laws protecting property rights, light, and air

7   Stanislaw J. Makielski, *The Politics of Zoning: The New York Experience* (New York: Columbia University Press, 1966).
8   Elliott Sclar, "The Infinite Elasticity of Air: New York City's Financialization of Transferable Development Rights," *American Journal of Economics and Sociology* 80, no. 2 (2021): 353–380.
9   Mel Scott, *American City Planning Since 1890: A History Commemorating the Fiftieth Anniversary of the American Institute of Planners.* No. 3 (Berkeley: University of California Press, 1969).
10 NYC Department of Planning, *The Zoning Handbook* (New York: NYC Department of Planning, 2018).
11 Willis, *Form Follows Finance*, 19-23.
12 Hugh Ferriss, *The Metropolis of Tomorrow* (Mineola: Dover Publications, 2005).

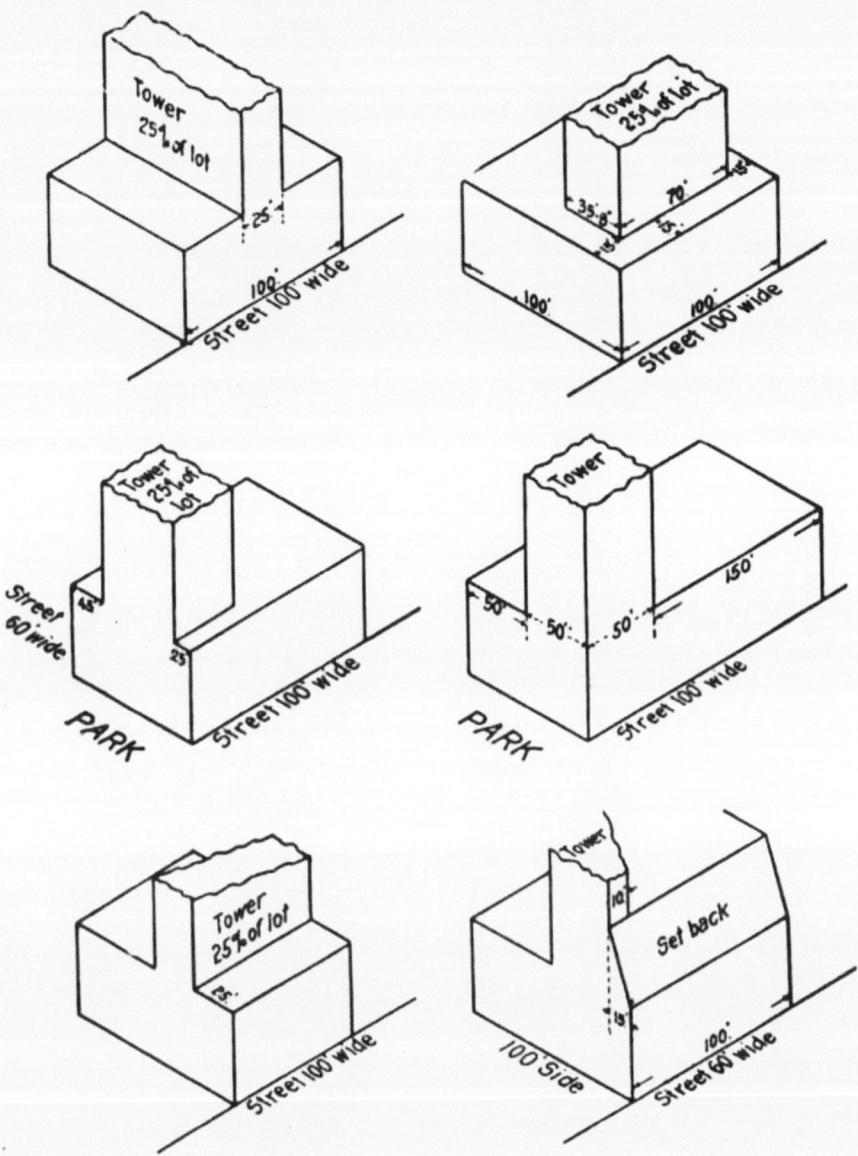

Setback Tower Options, 1916, Described in the 1916 Zoning Report

Fig. 2

Fig. 3   **The Equitable Building, Ernest R. Graham, 1915, New York**

have encouraged a new art by reason of the very restrictions they contain."[13]

The Zoning Resolution of 1961 improved upon certain limitations of the 1916 ordinance, such as minimum dimensions for inner lots and introduced floor area ratio (FAR), which limits the height of the building based on lot size.[14] The FAR allows for a number of variations to the ziggurat setback style, which gives developers and architects more design flexibility while still ensuring ample light and air.[15] An outcome of this change was the proliferation of the podium building defined by a thin tower without setback situated atop a large horizontal base less than six stories high, which conveniently incorporates commercial programs connected to the street. Fig. 4

While the city's zoning resolutions do not impose the specific design of buildings, the regulations increasingly define preset parameters for the basic forms of architecture and its relationship with the streetscape and surrounding neighborhoods, positioning design at the intersection of private and public interests that negotiate the needs of both sides while attempting to fulfill its own aesthetic, functional, performative, and qualitative aspirations.

In the transition to neoliberalism as the dominating political economy and cultural ideology in the United States near the end of the 20th century, the role of zoning evolved from a tool of municipal regulation to a set of fungible rights facilitating land rent financialization. This has aimed at attaining the highest achievable real estate values, leading to the rise of "zoning for sale" and intensified real estate development.[16] Such land rent speculation finds its deeper historical roots in capitalist America. In his examination of American metropolitanism in the late 19th century, scholar Richard Hofstadter observed that the society that emerged in America was agricultural in nature, but its true affinity lay more with the values of the land than with the land itself.[17] The freedom to speculate future gains on land value was closely linked to the pursuit of civil liberty and individual autonomy in a country teeming with new settlers.[18] Such emphasis on land value capture has

13 Ely Jacques Kahn, "Our skyscrapers take simple forms," *New York Times* 4 (1926): 22.
14 NYC Department of Planning, *The Zoning Handbook*, 2018.
15 Jerold S. Kayden, New York City Department of City Planning, and Municipal Art Society of New York, *Privately Owned Public Space: The New York City Experience* (New York: John Wiley & Sons, 2000).
16 Elliott Sclar et al., *Zoning: A Guide for 21st-Century Planning* (London: Routledge, 2019).
17 Richard Hofstadter, *The Age of Reform from Bryan to F.D.R.* (New York: Vintage Books, 1955).
18 Robert Fishman, *The American Planning Tradition: Culture and Policy* (Washington, D.C.: Woodrow Wilson Center Press, 2000).

Drawing, Study by Hugh Ferriss for Maximum Mass Permitted by the 1916 New York Zoning Law, Stage 4, 1922

Fig. 4

oscillated between being foreground and background under a succeeding shuffling of policy zeitgeists in recent history, but has always—and adamantly so—remained an important and embedded element in American urban history.

In recent times, the evolution of the transferable development rights (TDR) from a technical regulatory device to an exploitable value capture tool has created an artificial demand for air rights that has allowed developers to buy unused air space from neighboring buildings, in the absence of public review or community engagement, so they can construct even taller structures with more rentable floor area. The physical manifestation of such zoning fungibility is the emergence of an entirely new breed of architecture—"pencil towers" that are characterized as super-tall, super-skinny, super-expensive spires.[19] For instance, the 994-feet-tall One57 skyscraper, located on 57th Street on the southern edge of Central Park (now informally known as the "Billionaires' Row"), accurately exemplifies the extreme extent to which the expanding practice of development-rights trading through a Zoning Lot Merger has prompted the generation of such super-tall residential towers in New York sold at unprecedentedly high prices.[20] After spending 15 years assembling the property and air rights from nearby neighborhoods, the building's developer, Extell Development Corporation, reaped a worthy gain of $2 billion in sales value in 2014, setting records for the city's most expensive residences.[21]

The motivation to build tall is not only to build more, but to bring in hefty profits for developers in selling privatized and unobstructed views to the ultra-rich, who are, more often than not, non-local residents.[22] In another example, as the tallest residential tower in the world at the time of its completion, 432 Park Avenue reported an astounding sale of $7,592 per square foot of a condominium located on its 95th floor, comparing to the same unit halfway down the building that had been sold for $4,216 per square foot.[23] The concept of "the view"—the extent and range that an individual can see from a selected viewpoint—is a significant qualitative aspect of architectural

19 Oliver Wainwright, "Super-tall, super-skinny, super-expensive: The 'Pencil Towers' of New York's Super-Rich." *The Guardian* 5 (2019): 2019.
20 Oliver Wainwright, "Super-Tall, Super-Skinny, Super-Expensive."
21 Jason Barr, "Manhattan Profits (Part II): Return on Investment for a Superslim Skyscraper - Building the Skyline," *Building the Skyline - The Birth & Growth of Manhattan's Skyscrapers* (blog), July 17, 2020.
22 Matthew Haag, "How Luxury Developers Use a Loophole to Build Soaring Towers for the Ultrarich in N.Y.," *The New York Times*, September 23, 2021.
23 Haag, "How Luxury Developers Use a Loophole to Build Soaring Towers for the Ultrarich in N.Y."

design.[24] This feature has evolved into a marketable asset in the pursuit of private market value capture, exploiting the loopholes present in zoning laws.[25] As noted by planning scholar Elliot Sclar, the physical structure of cities exhibits a duality: it is locally unique, yet also highly generic, reflecting the Marxist and Keynesian macroeconomic dynamics of wealth creation and wealth holding.[26] Recent development in neoliberal policy practices and norms heavily reduces the agency of design to a mere "more is more" logic in service of short-term land value capture as opposed to long-term public concerns. This accelerating gear toward both functional and formal homogeneity sidelines design's more laudable abilities to create value through the production of high-quality public spaces, enhanced access, spatial flexibility, and connections to street life—all of the aspects that attend to issues of urban vitality, sustainability, and resiliency serving the greater public good.

2.2   Historic Overview of the Value of Design in Commercial Real Estate

The establishment of New York's city grid in 1811 ushered in a remarkable period of urban growth. The introduction of the Tariff Act in 1816, which imposed taxes on foreign imports in order to promote American-made goods, coupled with the groundbreaking completion of the Erie Canal in 1825, which connected the Great Lakes and the Atlantic Ocean through New York City, catalyzed the exponential growth of new industries. The surge in demand for manufactured products and capital, facilitated by expanding trade opportunities, set the stage for the flourishing of industrial enterprises. By 1840, the northeast region boasted an expansive network of canals and railroads, solidifying its prominence in the emerging national urban economy. With its strategic location, New York City emerged as the foremost beneficiary of the region's economic dominance, taking the central position in credit, marketing, industrial production, communications, and transportation, which led to a substantial influx

---

24   Yoshiki Yamagata et al., "Value of Urban Views in a Bay City: Hedonic Analysis with the Spatial Multilevel Additive Regression (SMAR) Model," *Landscape and Urban Planning* 151 (July 1, 2016): 89–102.
25   Chapter 4.4 presents a detailed analysis of the economic impacts of views and daylights in real estate pricing.
26   Sclar, "The Infinite Elasticity of Air," 353-380.

of immigrants from surrounding rural areas and Europe. Between 1800 and 1850, the city experienced a staggering 750% in population growth, marking one of the highest rates in world history.[27]

Strong trades with different regions played a crucial role in New York's next phase of urban economic growth. By 1850, the city's commercial banks had become significant sources of capital, greatly influencing commerce and industry. These banks became the largest and most diverse financial intermediaries, representing about four-fifths of all financial assets in the entire United States. In the second half of the 19th century, insurance companies, savings banks, and other non-bank intermediaries took on a greater role.[28] As New York's financial importance grew, it naturally became the ideal place to establish corporate offices. By the 1880s, the office building typology had emerged as a significant type of land use to accommodate the increasing number of staff overseeing regional and national operations. As the demand for space increased, real estate prices rose, creating momentum to build upward.

In 1885, Chicago-based civil engineer and architect William L. Jenney developed a steel skeleton that could support tall buildings, replacing the heavy masonry that had previously limited building heights to ten to twelve stories. This new design reduced the building's weight, allowing more light to enter and creating more interior space. At the same time, electric elevators matured, making skyscrapers convenient and practical. The first skyscraper, the Home Insurance Company in Chicago, set the prototype for the towers that followed in New York and Chicago between the late 1880s and 1920s. Fig. 5

Skyscrapers were practical, incorporating all the latest technologies and materials while saving corporations staggering land costs. The introduction of skyscrapers represented a shift in the city's economy. The era of individual merchants was replaced by corporations, relying more on mergers and capital movements than on international trade by ships.[29] As buildings grew in size, the associated costs increased, leading the finance sector to create new ways of arranging mortgages to fill the gap in the capital stack. With insurance companies and commercial banks becoming the primary

---

27 David R. Goldfield and Blaine A. Brownell, *Urban America: A History* (Boston: Houghton Mifflin, 1990).
28 Lois Severini, *The Architecture of Finance: Early Wall Street*, (Ann Arbor: UMI Research Press, 1983).
29 Severini, *The Architecture of Finance*, 23-26.

Home Insurance Building, William L. Jenney, 1885, Chicago

Fig. 5

patrons of the new building typology and single buildings achieving increased significance in terms of their physical and investment size, it opened new opportunities for real estate developers as well as architects to have greater impact in shaping the city.

The subsequent text offers an overview of Manhattan's real estate market, tracing its evolution from the inception of skyscraper construction in the late 20th century. It unfolds through narratives centered around the development of select prominent buildings. These structures played a significant role in shaping the operational landscape of real estate development and have also been instrumental in molding the evolving values attributed to the collaborative designs crafted by developers and architects.

The Equitable Life Assurance Building (1870)

Between 1870 and 1913, Manhattan's skyline drastically transformed from a city defined by four to five-story buildings to a metropolis of 50-story skyscrapers.[30] The burgeoning life insurance industry fueled the rapid growth of office towers. During the first half of the 19th century, insurance companies were often temporary and operated from simple storefronts.[31] It was only in the late 1800s that large, stable insurance companies emerged, and they embraced the new skyscraper typology, which could showcase their significance as well as convey reliability and safety to the public. Fig. 6

The Equitable Life Assurance Building is considered the catalyst of such a trend. The building was located at 120 Broadway, rising seven stories above ground, with a height of approximately 140 feet. It was an immediate financial success upon completion. Thousands of people visited daily to experience the world's first passenger elevator. The basement and first floor were occupied by banks. The 50 office units on the fourth, fifth, and sixth floor were exclusively occupied by lawyers. The top floor's rent was twice the amount of the other floors. Architect George B. Post, who consulted on the building's design, became the first tenant of the premium space, which had an unobstructed panoramic view of the city. The ingenious financial engineering of renting out the building allowed the Equitable Life Assurance Society, both the owner and developer, to occupy the entire second and third floor rent-free. In the

30   Sarah Bradford Landau and Carl W. Condit, *Rise of the New York Skyscraper, 1865-1913* (New Haven: Yale University Press, 1999).
31   Severini, *The Architecture of Finance*, 23-26.

The Equitable Life Assurance Building,
Arthur Gilman and Edward H. Kendall,
1870, New York

Fig. 6

first year of operation, $136,000 of rental revenue was generated, the equivalent of $3 million today.[32] A new type of financial machine was invented that made the land pay.[33]

It was reported by The Sun in 1868 that the Equitable Life Assurance Society's new business volume for the year was more than $6 million, which was the highest among all the businesses in the world.[34] The new headquarter building was considered instrumental in promoting the company's established wealth and an image of absolute sense of security to the public.[35] In addition to the two steam-powered elevators, the state-of-the-art office tower featured extensive iron framing, fireproof construction, and large window areas that brought natural light inside. The Second Empire mode, the popular style for government and institutional buildings since the Civil War, was the choice of architectural expression. The building featured high mansard roofs with dormers. Articulated walls emphasized the unprecedented number of floors, and the liberally applied gray granite represented stability, adding heaviness to the reading of the building.[36]

The architectural design was an essential means of conveying company status. However, the architect's contribution was considered superficial compared to the engineers in making the office tower. The complex technology and functional requirements involved in creating the new building type left a narrow scope for the architect, often limited to the design of exterior finishings.[37]

Most decisions that shaped the design of the building were made by a committee formed within the insurance company. In 1867, three years before the building's opening, the committee traveled to other American cities, such as Chicago, to gather information on building floor plans and associated costs. Subsequently, a design competition was organized. An extensive guideline was handed to the competing architects concerning the shape, size, number of stories, and preferred architectural style. The committee also specified the design for the area that their insurance company would occupy—a two-story galleried hall above a tall lobby. 11 architects submitted

---

32 Landau and Condit, *Rise of the New York Skyscraper*, 62-75.
33 Cass Gilbert was famously quoted as saying: "A skyscraper is a machine that makes the land pay."
34 "A Grand Commercial Edifice," *The Sun*, November 4, 1869, New York edition.
35 Shepard Bancroft Clough, *A Century of American Life Insurance: A History of the Mutual Life Insurance Company of New York, 1843–1943* (New York: Columbia University Press, 1946).
36 Landau and Condit, *Rise of the New York Skyscraper*, 62-75.
37 Landau and Condit, *Rise of the New York Skyscraper*, 62-75.

their plans, and eight firms were chosen to continue competing. Evident from the commonly found features represented in their design submissions, the competing architects blindly followed the design instructions.[38]

While it was demolished in 1912, the Equitable Life Assurance building was a financial success. Many insurance companies followed the same process hoping for similar financial yields. Their need to find outlets for their large capital reserves matched the risk profile of real estate development, which required a significant capital investment upfront.[39] In fact, until the mid-20th century, insurance companies were the most prominent builders of commercial towers.[40] This new standard of development continued to be followed by future builders of commercial skyscrapers, and similarities can still be found in current real estate development practices today.

Financialization and architecture

The 20th century witnessed a profound transformation in the real estate capital market. Following the Stock Market Crash of 1929 and the ensuing financial downturn, local mutual aid, building societies, and banks became reluctant to invest in real estate development. This void paved the way for a fresh wave of investors: life insurance companies. While most economic sectors shrank, the life insurance industry saw substantial asset growth, soaring from $15.3 billion in 1929 to $25.6 billion in 1938.[41] Legal limitations on insurance investments shielded the industry from much of the financial turmoil experienced elsewhere. In addition, to counter stock losses, many investors sought to bolster their life insurance value, presenting an unexpected revenue stream and a push to explore new investment avenues. Amid this economic slump, the life insurance sector faced an investment crisis.[42]

Life insurance companies have long been permitted to trade foreclosed real estate and to own their home office properties. It was only natural for state statutes to be adjusted to permit direct investment in income-generating real estate.[43]

38   Landau and Condit, *Rise of the New York Skyscraper*, 62-75.
39   Clough, *A Century of American Life Insurance*, 98-122.
40   Moses King, *New York: The American Cosmopolis, the Foremost City of the World* (Boston: M. King, 1894), 30.
41   Life Insurance Association of America, *Life Insurance Companies as Financial Institutions: A Monograph Prepared for the Commission on Money and Credit*, (Hoboken: Prentice-Hall, 1962).
42   Paula Kepos and Thomas Derdak, *International Directory of Company Histories* (Chicago: Saint James Press, 1995).
43   John W. McPherson, "Some Economic and Legal Aspects of the Purchase and Lease of Real Estate by Life Insurance Companies," *University of Pennsylvania Law Review* 97 (1948): 482.

The 1930s, marked by the New Deal's relaxed regulations, eased life insurers' access to the real estate market. In 1942, with Virginia becoming the first state to allow insurance companies to acquire rental real estate, the vast funds of life insurance companies started to channel into acquiring existing income-generating properties as well as new real estate development endeavors.[44] These insurers started to undertake ambitious projects in New York City, erecting tens of thousands of apartment units across the urban periphery and engaging in public-private redevelopment initiatives in the city center.[45] This era also witnessed a concurrent expansion of their ventures into commercial real estate with an eye to properties involving long-term rental contracts with tenants such as department stores, offices, and loft spaces.[46] By 1947, *The New York Times* highlighted a remarkable surge in life insurers' rental housing holdings, leaping from $40 million to $176 million within nine months. Concurrently, their investments in non-housing real estate doubled from $73 million to $150 million. This transformation left an indelible mark on the New York real estate landscape.[47]

As the influence of life insurance companies grew in large-scale urban projects, a significant transformation unfolded in the interplay between architecture and capital. This shift was characterized by two pivotal changes: a diminishing connection to local contexts and a pronounced increase in design standardization.

The importance of the geographic distance between capital sources and urban development weakened under the influence of life insurance companies. Operating from established financial hubs like New York and Newark, these companies gathered premiums from individual policyholders through local branches in various towns and cities. Subsequently, utilizing their real estate divisions, they channeled these funds from their headquarters to projects in different urban areas. This

44   In 1922, changes were made to the New York insurance code, permitting life insurance firms to invest in housing projects. This allowance ended in 1926 but was reinstated in 1938. Similarly, the New Jersey Code in 1929 allowed life insurance companies to invest in slum clearance housing. Additionally, the California code was altered in 1940, enabling insurance companies to build and own housing projects within the state. For more information, see: Robert E. Schultz and Raymond G. Schultz, "The Regulation of Life Insurance Company Investments," *The Journal of Insurance* 27, no. 4 (1960): 57–62.

45   Adam Tanaka, *Fiduciary landlords: Life insurers and large-scale housing in New York City,* (Cambridge: Harvard University, 2017).

46   "INVEST $87,000,000 in INCOME REALTY: Insurance Companies Taking Advantage of New Law as Outlet for Funds," *New York Times*, March 30, 1947.

47   "Insurance Companies Increase Investments in Income-Producing Realty to $144,000,000," *New York Times*, November 30, 1947.

decentralized approach often led to scenarios where an insurer from one city financed a project in another state, collaborating with a design team from yet another location. Consequently, the investor might have had no prior interaction with the developer or architect and little concern for the project's aesthetic or its impact on its surroundings. The separation of the developer, investor, and design team from the local context brought a shift in the familiar social dynamics within local development markets. This shift ushered in new selection criteria, emphasizing a merit-based system that strongly incentivized profit maximization over local familiarity or community impact.

When distance became less of an issue, a bureaucratic management system enabled the project team to enhance efficiency, ensuring financial stability significantly. By the mid-1900s, the burgeoning interest in income property mortgages led life insurance companies to nurture their cadre of real estate specialists. These experts, which involved construction managers, appraisers, and local real estate professionals, often with banking backgrounds, were responsible for selecting projects, overseeing their investments, and collaborating with developers and architects to safeguard their fiscal robustness. Operating from branch offices of life insurance firms and guided by a national real estate director, these specialists steered the flow of capital into architectural ventures nationwide. This structured management hierarchy facilitated market integration and the strategic redistribution of capital to regional markets, mitigating risks while assuring returns. Such a financialization trend increasingly dictated the collaboration among financiers, developers, and design teams, leading to the bureaucratization of design. Life insurance companies, founded on the idea of risk management, tailored their investment strategies tightly around financial security, narrowing the scope of land development processes. The evolving client demands, seeking a more financially oriented design approach, reshaped the dynamics within the design team. Developers, real estate advisors, contractors, and architects adapted to this shift, influencing and responding to the demand for integrating financial expertise into design projects.[48]

In many instances, the design parameters were largely predetermined before architects or planners entered the picture, as real estate and capital market requirements superseded architectural creativity. Striving for financial security, insurance

---

48 Sara Stevens, *Developing Expertise: Architecture and Real Estate in Metropolitan America* (New Haven: Yale University Press, 2016).

companies dictated the number of apartment or hotel units and office sizes and could veto elements like parking facilities and public spaces. They advocated heavily for standardized features and amenities they believed would resonate in the market. This norm was shaped by "comps," referencing comparable projects or their aspects in the vicinity and the experience of their professionals in the field. These meticulously tailored amenities aim to uphold the financial stability of life insurance companies while maintaining or enhancing their image as conscientious members of society.[49]

The Lever House (1952)

After World War II, new initiatives appeared in Manhattan's real estate development industry. International businesses heavily invested in building their corporate headquarters. The timing was right. The wartime residential rent restrictions imposed in 1943 prompted landlords of residential real estate to sell or convert their properties to commercial use for better returns.[50] Park Avenue was the top destination for global conglomerates.[51] Known for its unmatched urban character and social cachet, the address conveyed prestige among business leaders.[52] Post-war optimism and the prosperous business environment made companies seek out the finest quality buildings. Architectural design continued to be central to communicating company ethos. Radical architectural ideas were welcomed by business leaders who wanted to establish legitimacy through their future headquarters in the newly expanded American market. With an increasing number of skyscrapers dotting the skyline, confidence in building technology and engineering skills boosted the exploration of iconic architecture. Park Avenue was transformed into a street of icons representing the opportunities in the New World.[53]

In 1957, architecture critic Ada Louise Huxtable wrote in *The New York Times*, "The staples of our civilization—soap, whisky, and chemicals—have identified themselves with advanced architectural design and their monuments march up Park Avenue in a proud parade... New York's contribution to a dramatic revolution in architecture design."[54]

49   Stevens, *Developing Expertise*, 98-103.
50   Phyllis Lambert, *Building Seagram* (New Haven: Yale University Press, 2013).
51   James Trager, *Park Avenue: Street of Dreams*, vol. 73 (New York: Scribner, 1990).
52   Lambert, *Building Seagram*, 16-18.
53   Rem Koolhaas, *Delirious New York: A Retroactive Manifesto for Manhattan* (New York: Oxford University Press, 1978).
54   Ada Louise Huxtable, "Park Avenue School of Architecture: Business and Its New Sleek and Shiny Temples Have Transformed a Famous Residential Street," *New York Times*, December 15, 1957.

A new standard was born for the future office skyscrapers that valued architectural ideology over maximizing density.[55] The British soap company, Unilever, led the parade. New ideas were initiated by new leadership. In 1946, Charles Luckman was appointed as president for the Lever Brothers, the American arm of Unilever. It was considered the soap empire's most important market overseas.[56] In 1949, the company announced a wide-expansion plan in the United States, and building the new headquarters in Manhattan was a top priority.[57] Three years later, an approximately 300-foot-tall glass curtain wall tower was erected, interrupting Park Avenue's continuous row of masonry apartment buildings.

Charles Luckman was named the "New Prince" by *Time* magazine in June 1946, where his illustrative portrait made the cover. As a young successful businessman, Luckman daringly commissioned Skidmore Owings & Merrill (SOM) as the lead architect for the new headquarters. SOM was then a young firm without prior experience designing office towers. Their willingness to accept new ideas was the reason Luckman hired them: being an architect by training himself, he had his own vision for the tower's design. Maximizing the buildable area allowed by the zoning code was less of his concern. Since the entire 230,000 square foot space was to be exclusively used by the Lever Brothers, however, it was crucial that the building represented the company appropriately. From the start, openness was prioritized in the design. Luckman wanted pedestrians to freely walk through an open-air garden from the busy sidewalk of Park Avenue before entering the company's lobby. The materials used on the building were held to the highest standard, emphasizing the most modern American technology.[58] It was a radical departure from the safeguarded skyscraper development standards set by the insurance companies that continued to influence the industry.

The Lever House was articulated in largely two parts: the "tower" and the "podium." The podium was a three-story glass box sitting on the entire buildable area of the site. Inspired by Le Corbusier's pilotis, the first floor was open to

55 "Lever House," New York City Landmarks Preservation Commission, November 9, 1982.
56 Nicholas Adams, *Gordon Bunshaft and SOM: Building Corporate Modernism* (New Haven: Yale University Press, 2019).
57 "Lever Brothers Busy With Expansion Plans," *The Journal News*, October 5, 1949.
58 Charles Luckman, *Twice in a Lifetime: From Soap to Skyscrapers* (New York: W.W. Norton & Company, 1988).

Park Avenue exposing stainless steel cladded columns.[59] This made the two floors above look as if they were floating from the ground. Pedestrians freely walked underneath to the central garden that was open to the sky. The rectangular-shaped void of the podium above the garden brought in abundant day light to an otherwise dim space. The zoning regulation would have allowed the company to cover the full site with an eight-story building without setbacks. However, since maximizing the area was not the goal, SOM's clever interpretation of the zoning allowed to shape an elegant, slender "tower" instead. The Lever House was the first building to take advantage of the zoning provision that permitted buildings to rise without any height limits or setbacks if it covered only 25% of the lot.[60] The orientation of the tower was perpendicular to Park Avenue, breaking the existing pattern of building fronts that were parallel to the street. The unique tower orientation erased the block that would have been above the podium inviting additional light over the sidewalk. Openness was achieved. Fig. 7

The design did not follow the popular real estate notion of finding the highest and best use of the land, but Luckman persuaded the board by saying that the monumental design would be worth millions in advertising value for the company. The meticulously designed space also played a key role in hiring and retaining skilled employees through the assurance of the firm's status and prestige. In a speech entitled "Economic Value of Design," presented at the annual AIA convention in 1959, J.E. Drew, the public relations director of the Lever Brothers, stated that the straight lines of the glass curtain wall and the daring shape implied the cleanliness and progressiveness of the soap company. On the first day of opening there were 782 job applicants. The employee turnover rate was only about 37% of the average reported for other large companies in New York, making the Lever Brothers a "dream world" for management.[61]

The Seagram Building (1958)

Seagram was a Canadian distiller that made the best-selling whiskey in the North American market.[62] For their new headquarters, they selected the site at 375 Park Avenue, diagonally

59 Adams, *Gordon Bunshaft and SOM*, 50-57.
60 Leland M. Roth, *American Architecture: A History* (London: Routledge, 2018).
61 J.E.Drew, "The Economic Value of Design" American Institute of Architects Annual Convention, New Orleans, 25 June 1959; Thomas W. Ennis, "Company Edifices 'Sell' Products: Businesses Find That It Pays to Advertise With Good Architecture," *New York Times*, August 7, 1960.
62 Philip Siekman, "Bronfmans-Instinct for Dynasty," *Fortune*, 1966.

Fig. 7   **Lever House, Gordon Bunshaft and Natalie de Blois of SOM, 1952, New York**

across from the Lever House. Seagram invited several architects to advise on the design. Under the name "Project 'Skytop,'" research presented a range of massing options showing different design possibilities, paired with a comprehensive cost estimate. According to Seagram's building committee, financial performance was optimized at a 35-story building of about 500,000 square feet. Perreira & Luckman, the architecture firm founded by the former president of Unilever, Charles Luckman, was selected to complete the conceptual framework, concluding Seagram's extensive research. Their design was officially filed in 1954 and made public at a sales meeting showcasing a large-scale physical model.[63] Luckman's design was shaped like a "wedding cake," heavily influenced by the setback regulation of the 1916 zoning ordinance and the economic principles determined by the committee.

While the new design of the headquarters was being widely published, strong opposition formed from one of the closest members of Seagram's leadership: Phyllis Lambert, daughter of Seagram founder Samuel Bronfman, heavily criticized Luckman's scheme for its lack of "design." She wrote to her father in June 1954, "You must put up a building which expresses the best of the society in which you live, and at the same time your hopes for the betterment of this society."[64]

An artist in Paris, Lambert was the creative voice in the owner's family. To her, architecture had value in society: it influenced the way of living for the company's people as well as for those in New York and the rest of the world. The opportunity seemed lost in the business-as-usual procedures Seagram's executives and building professionals were applying to the project.[65] Real estate development companies considered architecture little more than a commercial product and continued working with architects to emulate the buildings they saw elsewhere in the city. A fresh new approach was in dire need, and Lambert's proposal to start the design from scratch was granted by her father.

As the newly appointed planning director, Lambert conducted thorough research to determine the best architect to match the ambitions set both by herself and the company. An architect who already had experience building a large-scale office tower was preferred, but more importantly, these past

63   "Park Ave. To Get New Skyscraper: Seagrams Plans a Gleaming 34-story Headquarters – Voisin to Lose Home," *New York Times*, July 13, 1954.
64   Lambert, *Building Seagram*, 32.
65   Lambert, *Building Seagram*, 8-9.

projects had to be inspiring. Rather than inviting architects to another round of a design competition, she took a more hands-on approach by seeking advice from various professionals that placed architectural design at the center of their practice. She conducted a series of interviews with influential architects, the heads of architecture schools, historians, critics, writers, editors, and curators. A year and a half later, contracts were signed to appoint Ludwig Mies van der Rohe as lead architect, with Philip Johnson to support the design work, and Kahn and Jacobs to provide local knowledge related to permitting and construction.[66]

Mies van der Rohe's design was rooted in practical considerations. He started the design by gathering professional advice on the real estate market, New York City building code regulations, and spatial requirements related to the tower's engineering. Once the "facts" were defined, numerous preliminary studies concerning the form, siting, structure, enclosure, and public plaza were conducted promptly. Fig. 8

In 1955, the conclusion of Mies van der Rohe's extensive design analysis was presented to Seagram's building committee and the CEO. A 38-story tower with a five-story and a 10-story wing building on the back. The tower stood 90 feet away from Park Avenue on a calm public plaza raised three steps from the busy streets. Using bronze skin was a radical idea that was never used in buildings before.[67] The bronze I-beam mullions composed a regular rhythm throughout the surface of the building creating shadows on the same-colored tinted glass that filled in between. The scheme was approved by Seagram within a week. The overall design was completed in 18 months, and the same amount of time was spent on construction. In December 1957, the members of Seagram started to move in. The company occupied six floors using 25% of the building's office space. It took two more years to finish the interior for the rest of the tenants to move in. The building was fully completed inside and out when the last tenant, the Four Seasons Restaurant, opened its doors in July 1959.

Upon completion, the Seagram building was the most expensive office building ever built in Manhattan or anywhere else in the world. They spent $45 per square foot for construction, with a $48 million total cost for the development.[68] This is

---

66   Lambert, *Building Seagram*, 32-37.
67   Lambert, *Building Seagram*, 38-71.
68   $5 million to acquire the land and $43 million for the construction and other related expenses.

The Seagram Building, Ludwig Mies van der Rohe, 1958, New York

Fig. 8

equal to roughly $450 per square foot and $430 million today. The entire building was financed by Seagram's own funds without involving mortgages. It was a bold investment decision that entailed high risk; however, the project was financially profitable from the first year. The building's operating expenses were easily covered by the rent that Seagram was paying for the space they occupied. The rent from other tenants was all profit. The rentable space was already 90% occupied in the opening year. Tenants were willing to pay $7 to $8.30 per square foot, higher than the average of $5.25 per square foot for similarly large, newly constructed buildings in the same neighborhood. The high rents yielded a net income of $400,000 the first year, equal to $4 million today.[69]

Design Premium

By 1960, *The New York Times* noted the trend: "The idea that good architecture is good business is becoming axiomatic in corporate management circles."[70]

The unique investment strategy of both the Lever Brothers and Seagram—investing in new architectural ideas, looking at long-term return in public goodwill, and institutional advertising while generating competitive return from rents—proved to be a viable business model for others to follow.

The norm of filling every square foot of the legally allowed volume was finally being challenged. When the banks—institutions known for taking a conservative position in making investments—started hiring outstanding architects to design their headquarters soon after the Seagram Building, New York's urban form was no longer a byproduct of the zoning regulation. In fact, the appreciation of Seagram Building's public plaza spurred the revolution of New York's zoning ordinance to incentivize developers to provide more open public space by offering an additional density bonus.

Developers, investors, and architects reconfigured architectural modernism to support business-oriented agendas.[71] Clients recognized the architects' creativity in integrating financial goals and zoning regulations into their rational forms. In addition, the glass curtain walls representing modern architecture were conceived as cutting-edge American technology that added significant value in increasing marketability and securing tenants.

69   "Seagram's Bronze Tower," *Architectural Forum*, July 1958.
70   Ennis, "Company Edifices 'Sell' Products."
71   Stevens, *Developing Expertise*, 13.

As Lever House and the Seagram Building proved to pay their way after completion, many architects and builders shared the benefits. The two projects were often cited by clients who had corporate ambitions. They inspired the construction of iconic structures with increased budgets, allowing building professionals to explore better spatial quality. Buildings with unique designs were increasingly considered to have a higher value than the generic buildings on the market.

In 1984, architecture critic Ada Louise Huxtable wrote, "In New York, rental response related directly to a building's recognition factor on the skyline. Identity and novelty make the building a different product that adds a competitive edge."[72]

From Owning
to Renting

A recession in the 1970s put an end to the post-war economic expansion. The national economic stagnation, which continued until the early 1980s, was clearly reflected in New York's real estate market. As a result, the commercial logic of developing and owning company headquarters was actively rethought. With the increased uncertainty of the market, companies favored capital liquidity. Headquarter buildings that required high maintenance became a growing liability. Rather than concentrating corporate funds on the head offices, companies sought to diversify the risk by selling their prized buildings and renting the space back or moving out of the city to lower the management costs.[73] The sale proceeds of these trophy buildings provided ample cash to the companies. In addition, renting the same space from the buyer long term created a win-win situation for both parties. The seller could continue operating from its prestige location while significantly reducing expenses associated with operating the building as an owner. From the buyer's side, this presented an opportunity to purchase a building with an anchor tenant and a stabilized revenue stream which increased the security of the investment. Insurance companies that valued stable cash flows were among the most active buyers of bespoke office towers along Park Avenue. While the Metropolitan Life Insurance Company was the owner of the Lever House long before the trend, the Seagram building was sold to the Teachers Insurance and Annuity Association (TIAA) in 1978, and the Dai-Ichi Mutual Life Insurance Company bought

72   Ada Louise Huxtable, *The Tall Building Artistically Reconsidered: The Search for a Skyscraper Style* (Berkeley: University of California Press, 1992).
73   Philip O'Neill, "Financial Narratives of the Modern Corporation," *Journal of Economic Geography* 1, no. 2 (2001): 181–99.

two-thirds of ownership of the Citigroup Center on 399 Park Avenue in 1987.[74]

The financial premiums of the headquarters towers seemed to have survived the test of time. When the Lever House building first became available in the rental market in 1999, a 20-year lease was signed for a rent of $70 per square foot, approximately 80% higher than Manhattan's average office rent of $39 per square foot.[75] Having a Seagram Building address continued to represent prestige among the finance elites that occupied the space. In 2007, at a time when office rents were at a record high, the building's vacancy rate was as low as 2% with rents starting at $165 per square foot, more than 2.6 times higher than the $63 per square foot average office rent in Manhattan.[76]

The Real Estate Royals

While insurance companies took a passive role as an investor of real estate and the international corporations turned from owner developers to primary tenants, privately owned real estate development companies became the leaders that actively shaped Manhattan's urban form. As companies often owned and managed within one family, they accumulated fortunes by successfully surviving the economic downturn of the 1970s and the influx of well-capitalized foreign investment companies in the 1980s.[77] Through generations, they exercised influence in the real estate market by establishing a network of high-profile contacts through industry coalitions such as the Real Estate Board of New York (REBNY). Increasingly, real estate development projects became a vehicle for a complex financial structure involving various investors of equity and debt.

Unlike the ambitious corporate headquarters, buildings simply meant business for the real estate families.[78] Properties were rigorously examined as an investment asset, prioritizing the stakeholders' financial objectives. They assessed the value of the potential real estate project, compared it with the cost of production, and evaluated the net income with other alternative uses of the asset. The project only proceeded if the outcome was seen to be the most profitable. In addition, due to the competitive nature of securing land and sourcing capital, private development companies were incentivized to extract the highest economic return in every opportunity. Projects became

74   Eric N. Berg, "Citicorp Selling Part Offers Headquarter," *New York Times*, October 3, 1987.
75   "Metro Business; Alcoa Will Renew New York Presence," *New York Times*, November 26, 1999.
76   Adam Piore, "Finance elite toasts Seagram Building," *The Real Deal*, October 23, 2007.
77   David Samuels, "The Real-Estate Royals: End of the Line," *New York Times*, August 10, 1997.
78   Lambert, *Building Seagram*, 233.

increasingly transaction focused.[79] The building was sold once the rental income was stabilized soon after the construction completion. The prompt return of capital and profit realization encouraged developers to expedite the building process. In the interest of time and control, speculative developments were preferred rather than customizing for the end-users to comprehend their spatial needs. The long-term building quality, sustainability, and energy performance became less of a concern. It diminished the need for architectural innovation and social objectives once prevalent in the post-war Manhattan development industry.

With a few additions and subtractions in the list, private real estate companies continued to dominate New York's development landscape. In 2020, nine out of the 10 most active developers in New York were privately owned. In a single year, they developed 54 properties with an accumulated area of approximately 23 million square feet.[80]

Building Boom and the "Starchitects"

In 2019, New York experienced the most significant building boom. A staggering $60.6 billion was spent on construction alone, marking the highest record for New York's history.[81] Among the new ground-up projects, buildings designed by internationally renowned architects made numerous headlines in the media. In 2018, *Curbed New York* reported that there were 36 ongoing projects in Manhattan alone designed by "starchitects"— architects credited as visionary designers who achieved celebrity status.[82] While the international work by these designers was primarily in the cultural sector, in New York, 72% of the buildings were for commercial use, all privately-owned and managed by real estate development companies.[83] Fig. 9

At a glance, the monumental structures designed by these starchitects seem distant from the typical workings of commercial real estate, where efficiency is valued most. The higher-than-standard service fees only account for a small portion of the added budget that real estate developers need to consider when commissioning a starchitect. In many cases, more than

79   Patrice Derrington, *Built Up: An Historical Perspective on the Contemporary Principles and Practices of Real Estate Development* (London: Routledge, 2021).
80   Kathryn Brenzel, "NYC's 10 Most Active Developers of 2020," *The Real Deal*, December 28, 2020.
81   Office of the State Comptroller, "The Construction Industry in New York City Recent Trends and Impact of COVID-19," *Office of the New York State Comptroller* (June 2021).
82   Zoe Rosenberg and Tanay Warerkar, "The Star Architect-led Projects That Will Transform NYC's Skyline, Mapped," *Curbed NY*, July 26, 2018.
83   In this writing, commercial real estate is defined as land and buildings that generate profit through capital gain and/or rental income with emphasis toward office and mixed-use building types.

Fig. 9   Yearly Construction Spending in New York City

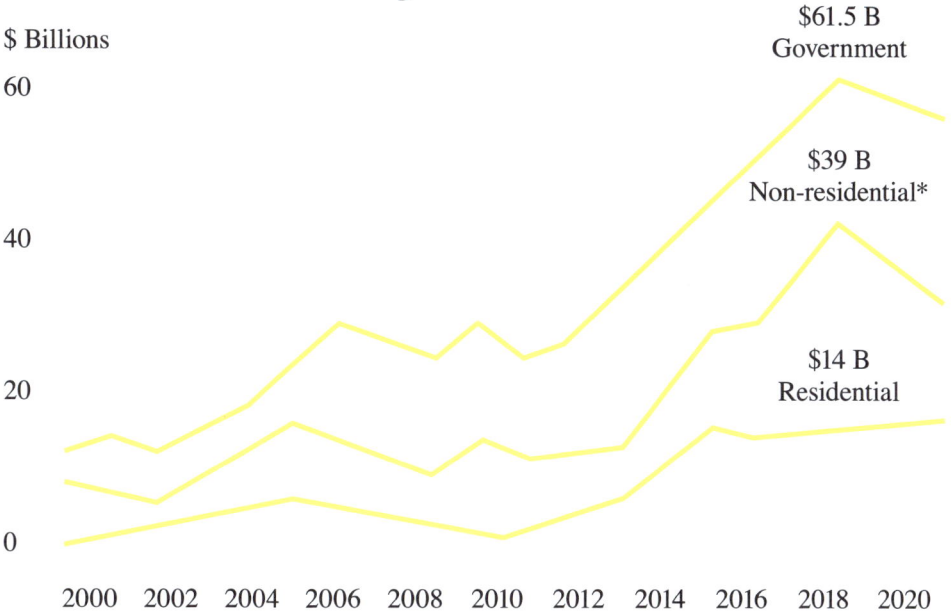

$ Billions

$61.5 B
Government

$39 B
Non-residential*

$14 B
Residential

60

40

20

0

2000 2002 2004 2006 2008 2010 2012 2014 2016 2018 2020

Note: The graph shows the highest construction spending in 2018.
Source: Dodge Data & Analytics, NYS Department of Labor, public sector capital budgets. U.S. Census Bureau, Urbanomics. * E.g. office, retail, hospitality, and institutional buildings

one architecture firm needs to be hired to provide local knowledge and technical support. Also, frequently, their design requires special structural treatment that results in a significant increase in the construction cost.

However, in the past two decades, private developers, who typically favored highly dependable firms to prevent such risks, have begun hiring renowned architects for office and multi-family residential buildings under the assumption that higher design fees corresponded to greater returns.[84] The complication in the process and the higher fees of such architects are generally accepted with a notion of an exchange for media attention, getting favorable business conditions by catalyzing political consensus and providing a legitimate brand image for both the building and the developer.[85]

84   Davide Ponzini, "The values of starchitecture: Commodification of architectural design in contemporary cities," *Organizational Aesthetics* 3, no. 1 (2006): 10–18.
85   Leslie Sklair, "Iconic Architecture and the Culture-ideology of Consumerism," *Theory, Culture & Society* 27, no. 5 (2010): 135–59.

425 Park Avenue

Almost 50 years after the opening of the Seagram Building, another ambitious office tower was being planned on Park Avenue. The developer, L&L Holdings, declared the project a "once-in-a-lifetime development opportunity to build a full city block in the global center of commerce."[86] In 2006, L&L holdings won the ground lease of 425 Park Avenue for 84 years. The previous ground lease was to expire in 2015, giving the developer nine years to plan for the new building.

The location presented a substantial value-add opportunity. The high demand and the above-average rents of Park Avenue were enough to justify building a new state-of-the-art office tower. From the start, achieving an iconic design was considered an essential amenity to attract high-rent-paying tenants to the area. However, unlike the Seagram Building, the security of the investments that enabled the project had to be prioritized. Finding the balance of creativity and profitability was an added challenge to an otherwise risk-averse development strategy that resembled how insurance companies built in the past.

Design was managed within strict boundaries. The design competition kicked off in May 2012. L&L holdings invited 10 of the most distinguished international architecture practices that could represent the vast possibilities within the contemporary design language. In addition to the area requirements, a new set of evaluation criteria were handed to the selected companies. It encompassed a design to exemplify advancement with contemporary expression worthy of its address, a conducive space for creativity and cultural interaction, flexible floor plans to maximize functionality, sustainability goals of achieving LEED Gold, and lastly, to meaningfully address the budget and to maximize the building's value.[87] The submitted proposals were vetted by several reviews with an internal committee that consisted of academics, architects, engineers, and investors. The overall competition process took six months until appointing the winning architect.

Design As
An Amenity

Since signature design was the primary tool to attract tenants in the speculative development of 425 Park Avenue, the architect was the focal point of the building's marketing strategy. A new website was created to broadcast the various design

---

86 David Levinson, "425 Park Avenue," 2012.
87 The four finalists of the design competition were Foster and Partners, Office for Metropolitan Architecture (OMA), Rogers Stirk Harbour and Partners, and Zaha Hadid Architects.

presentations given during the competition. The physical models and visual material submitted by the four starchitects were exhibited on several occasions: from meetings with the city municipalities and communities in order to garner support for the project to cultural events to boost public awareness. The marketing effort continued during the construction as well. From the moment of breaking ground, live footage of the construction site was screened online 24 hours a day. The same website outlined the amenities exclusive to tenants—a fine dining restaurant operated by a Michelin star chef, a sculpture garden on the 12th floor created by a renowned Japanese artist and a year-round entertainment program curated by an Academy award-winning film director.[88]

The construction of 425 Park Avenue started in 2016, the structure topped out two years later, and completed in October 2022. The extensive marketing effort seemed to have come to fruition even before completing construction. A lease taking half of the rentable area was signed in 2016 with an agreed rent of $300 per square foot, well above the current average rent of $75.90 in Manhattan, setting the highest office rent record in New York's real estate history.[89] The pre-let tenant added certainty to the future revenue of the building, significantly lowering the developer's financial risk. Once again, iconicity achieved a premium in the market.

The Rise of Luxury Residential Towers

The skyscraper construction in Manhattan moved in waves. The city underwent a prolonged downturn from 1990 to 1997, attributed to the early 1990s economic recession. Recovery took place between 1998 and 2012, with the peak in 2010. Since 2010, over 30 buildings, each surpassing 650 feet in height, have been slated for construction in Manhattan, sustaining the upward trend. Rising office rents, however, were not the drivers of the resurgence of the island's skyscraper construction. The increase in the value of apartment prices far outpaced the appreciation of office buildings, fueling the boom in high-rise residential development.[90]

According to a report from the New York Building Congress, between 2013 and 2014 residential construction spending rose by 60%, but the number of constructed units was expected to increase by a mere 22%. The disparity between

88 425 Park Avenue, https://www.425parkave.com/
89 Ryan Boysen, "The Priciest Lease in NYC History May Have Just Been Signed," *BISNOW*, February 17, 2016.
90 Jason Barr, "The Economics of Skyscraper Construction in Manhattan: Past, Present, and Future," *International Journal of High-Rise Buildings* 5, no. 2 (2016): 137–44.

construction spending and the actual number of units was partly due to the surge in larger, luxury condominiums, with fewer units going up around Central Park and in other exclusive pockets of Manhattan.

The development strategies for those luxury condominiums were similar to those for 425 Park Avenue: in many cases, architects with international recognition were invited to a design competition held by private real estate development companies. In fact, out of the 26 commercial development projects that were designed by "starchitects," 21 (80%) of projects were for residential use. An exclusive amenity package that came with a renowned architect's signature design was provided to the condo buyers who were ready to pay a large premium compared to other types of residential buildings.

International investors were the critical demographic creating demand for the luxury residential market. By late 2013, Extell Development stated that more than half of the buyers of One57, a skinny pencil tower condominium in Billionaire's Row near Central Park, were foreigners, with 15% coming from China. They were the type of investors that looked for hard assets like real estate, searching for higher returns after the 2008 recession. It has been argued in some reports that residential real estate functions as a "safe deposit box," and that New York is perceived to provide a sense of security through the socio-cultural character of the city combined with high liquidity.[91]

However, around 2015, a confluence of global economic headwinds and unfavorable changes to the property and transfer taxes cooled interest among international investors. Leaving a glut of newly built luxury condominiums unoccupied. Nearly half of the new condo units in Manhattan that came to market after 2015 remain unsold.[92] Fig. 10

Post-Building Boom

"The new luxury condominium market is burdened with a tremendous amount of supply. In 2020, we had 8.7 years of sellout, meaning it would take 8.7 years to sell all unsold Manhattan new development condos," Jonathan Miller, president of Miller Samuel appraisers, stated.[93]

While the after-effects of the over-supplied luxury housing with inflated price points lurked over the real estate market

91 Fernandez et al., "London and New York as a Safe Deposit Box for the Transnational Wealth Elite," *Environment and Planning A: Economy and Space* 48, no. 12 (2016): 2443–61.
92 Of 7,727 apartments, a total of 3,695 units remain unsold. "December 2019, Market Report," *Nancy Packes Data Services*, 2020.
93 James Tarmy, "New York Luxury Real Estate Could Be a Bargain in 2021," *Bloomberg*, December 27, 2020.

Fig. 10 The Rise and Fall of Starchitect Condo Prices

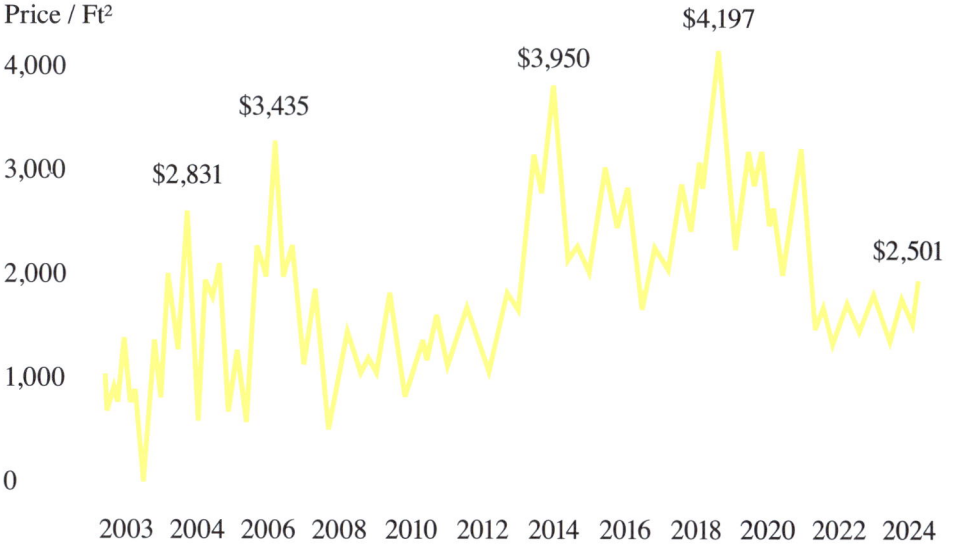

Price / Ft²

$2,831

$3,435

$3,950

$4,197

$2,501

4,000

3,000

2,000

1,000

0

2003 2004 2006 2008 2010 2012 2014 2016 2018 2020 2022 2024

Note: The median price of condominiums designed by international "starchitects" in New York City marks the highest price per square foot in 2019. Source: CityRealty Starchitect Condo Index.

in 2020, a global pandemic turned everything upside down. In just nine months, the Coronavirus reversed a decade-long growth in New York real estate. The number of condo transactions plummeted close to 50% of the previous year. The rising vacancies inspired landlords to come up with deep price cuts and provide concessions that were rarely seen. They offered 13–20% discounts for luxury condo sales, multiple months of free rents, and gave complimentary fee waivers to renters at the owner's expense.[94]

Active development projects faced worsened circumstances with stalled supply chains, escalating material costs, and months-long construction site shutdowns. Projected 4,000 condo units for 2020 dwindled to merely 1,000 delivered to the Manhattan residential market.

On top of the vulnerable market condition, many articles were published on lawsuits around construction flaws, loan

---

94 A year-end survey by CityRealty, projected they would reach 7,452, totaling $13.9 billion in 2020. In 2019, there were 11,673 transactions and $23.7billion in sales.

defaults, and bankruptcy related to high-end residential towers. One of the private development companies specializing in luxury residential condominiums went through multiple lawsuits that involved forged documents and sham financials, resulting in overleveraged projects that failed to perform. The condo board of one of the pencil towers on Billionaire Row sued the developer over 1,500 building defects, pointing out design flaws that caused flooding, stuck elevators, and intrusive noise and vibration in units. Many contracts were broken, lenders were skittish, and foreclosures were looming.

Three years into the pandemic, office landlords face challenges with an emerging remote work culture and a significant rise in interest rates since 2022. The reduced demand for office space appears to be permanent.[95] Floors of office buildings have been emptied, with tenants taking smaller spaces as an increased number of employees work from home. With falling office property values due to lower occupancy rates and higher borrowing costs, real estate companies actively seek new revenue streams to avoid bankruptcy. New tax incentives have been introduced to promote the conversion of underutilized office buildings into residential uses. Nonetheless, landlords have been hesitant to take action due to the structural obstacles and unpredictability of construction costs. It is reported that nearly two-thirds of New York City's 400 million square feet of office space is facing obsolescence.[96] In such a dim future projection of the market, design's influence on building value becomes questionable.

Developers respond to supply and demand for space when planning for a new project. As suggested by the contrasting examples, at the right timing, the iconic design can be reflected in the higher sale prices and rents paid by tenants, who, in turn, have value added to their operations. But as construction and planning permission take time, buildings may be ready just when the market is falling apart. Developers are constantly faced with the decision of whether investing in a premium design product is worth the risk. It may provide a critical edge in a saturated market, but rents or sale prices may fall to such levels as to threaten the yield when set against the higher than standard costs. When making this pivotal decision, many risk-averse developers remain skeptical of design's value to their projects. The debate continues when it comes to design and real estate.

95   Gupta et al., "Work From Home and the Office Real Estate Apocalypse," *National Bureau of Economic Research*, 2022.
96   Matthew Haag, "A Bleak Outlook for Manhattan's Office Space May Signal a Bigger Problem," *New York Times*, April 25, 2023.

2.3 Manhattan Real Estate Market Since 2001

To study real estate value, we introduce a data-driven approach and explore the tools wielded to quantitatively break down and assess different metrics that contribute to value. Our approach centers on harnessing advanced data analytics to make sense of this vast pool of information. The aim is to craft a new framework that quantifies design value, moving beyond traditional methods that often relies on qualitative evaluations. This is paired with a comprehensive research methodology that remains agile, adapting to the intricate nature of design value. Through the combined power of data analysis and a flexible research methodology, we seek to provide a nuanced understanding of design value grounded in empirical evidence.

The urban landscape of New York City, with its myriad architectural styles and real estate trends, is an optimal setting to test and refine this approach. The city is a dynamic environment where significant real estate stories have unfolded over the past 200 years. New York City's active real estate market, especially in the commercial sector, provides us with a rich collection of data from the past two decades, essentially a living record, which enables us to examine the interconnectedness of architectural design, location, time, and market trends.

The early 2000s began with a boom in luxury real estate, driven by technological advancements, globalization, and economic growth. High-end condos sprang up throughout the city, with a focus on amenities and lifestyle offerings. Simultaneously, architectural practices started incorporating more sustainable design principles, following increased global awareness of climate change. This period also witnessed a resurgence of interest in urban living, which sparked significant development in the city's core and previously industrial neighborhoods. Further, the advent of digital technology started to reshape the design and real estate industries, with data-driven decisions becoming an essential part of the business. The use of advanced modeling and simulation software enabled architects to create more efficient, innovative, and visually striking designs.

Fig. 11 The last two decades have also been marked by some of the most significant challenges the city has faced: the September 11 terrorist attacks in 2001, the subprime mortgage crisis in 2008, and the COVID-19 pandemic in 2020. These occurrences have profoundly shaped both the office and residential real estate markets, leaving an indelible imprint not

Fig. 11

New York City Real Estate Market Milestone

Total Sales Volume ($ billions)

$12.5

$10

$7.5

$5

$2.5

$0

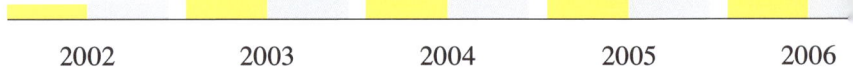

2002	2003	2004	2005	2006
World Trade Center site cleanup ends.

LMDC announces new, international, open-design study of World Trade Center site and surrounding areas. | 300 Madison Ave. construction complete, design to withstand catastrophic damage.

General Motors Building record sale for an office building.

Time Warner Center's penthouse record sale for residential building. | Average price for Manhattan apartment tops $1 million for first time in history. | First private sector LEED Gold building, The Helena, 580 unit, residential apartment completed.

Hudson Yards site available for development due to failure in plan for NY Jets Westside stadium and 2012 Olympics. | High Line elev greenway grou breaking.

Construction c One World Tra Center begins. A month later, 7 World Trade Center comple

StreetEasy firs technology company to di NYC real esta |

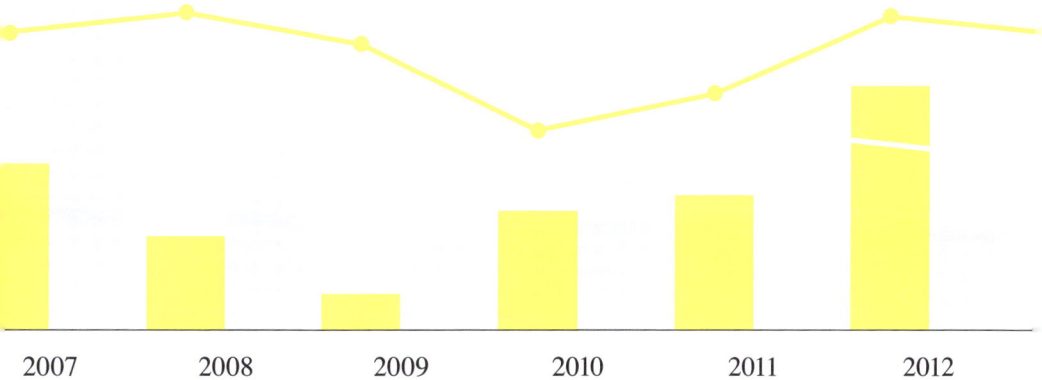

2007	2008	2009	2010	2011	2012
r Stearns loses two ge funds, sing on ritized rime tgages, have rred almost l losses, king onset of tgage crisis.

hner npanies pays rd $1.8 billion 66 Fifth Ave. | Lehman Brothers collapses as financial crisis accelerates.

Bear Stearns collapses after operating for 85 years, signaling widespread panic on Wall Street.

Due to the economic downturn, real estate developer Macklowe fails to secure refinancing and defaults on approx. $7 billion worth of debt. | High Line opens, spurring a slew of residential projects on the West Side.

General Growth Properties files for bankruptcy, described by Reuters as "the biggest real estate failure in U.S. history."

Residential sales plummet as buyers hastily withdraw from their purchase agreements. | Google's purchase of 111 Eighth Ave. for $1.8 billion revitalizes the Manhattan commercial scene, sparking a surge in the Midtown South tech industry frenzy.

WeWork's first space opens in Soho. | Sales at One57 start before completing construction. Building's units collectively marketed for $2 billion.

Conde Nast agrees to take 1 million square feet at One World Trade Center, positive impact for Lower Manhattan's commercial market. | Related Companies and Oxford Property Group break ground on 28-acre Hudson Yards project.

Hurricane Sandy submerges much of Lower Manhattan, estimated $8.5 billion in property damage on private landlords.

One World Trade Center tops out, becomes the tallest building in Manhattan. |

2013	2014	2015	2016	2017

Four World Trade Center opens to tenants and the public.

Zillow buys NYC listing portal StreetEasy for $50 million.

Chinese development company pays $1.4 billion for a 40 Fifth Avenue, making it the most valuable office tower in the country at $3.4 billion.

One57, hailed as Manhattan's inaugural "Pencil Tower," finishes construction, boasting 1,004 ft, 75 floors, claiming title of tallest mixed-use skyscraper in Manhattan.

WeWork attains unicorn status with a $1.5 billion valuation, soaring to $47 billion by Jan 2019, then plummeting to $8 billion within a few months.

432 Park Avenue complete, 1,397 ft, 85 floors, pencil tower with a width to height ratio of 1:15.

Median Manhattan home price hits $1 million for the first time.

One57 sets a record with the sale of a penthouse for $100.5 million.

After a six year run, commercial rents peak and the retail market starts to decline.

The $4 billion Oculus transit hub opens at the World Trade Center, $2 billion over budget and seven years late.

Chinese buyers pour a record $14.3 billion into New York real estate before Beijing's capital controls and corruption crackdown start to close the tap.

The City Council rezones Midtown East – four years after the initial proposal.

Chinese insurance group's CEO is detained in Beijing, prompting other Chinese real estate investors to start dumping assets.

USD/Ft²

$2,000

$1,500

$1,000

$500

$0

2018	2019	2020	2021	2022

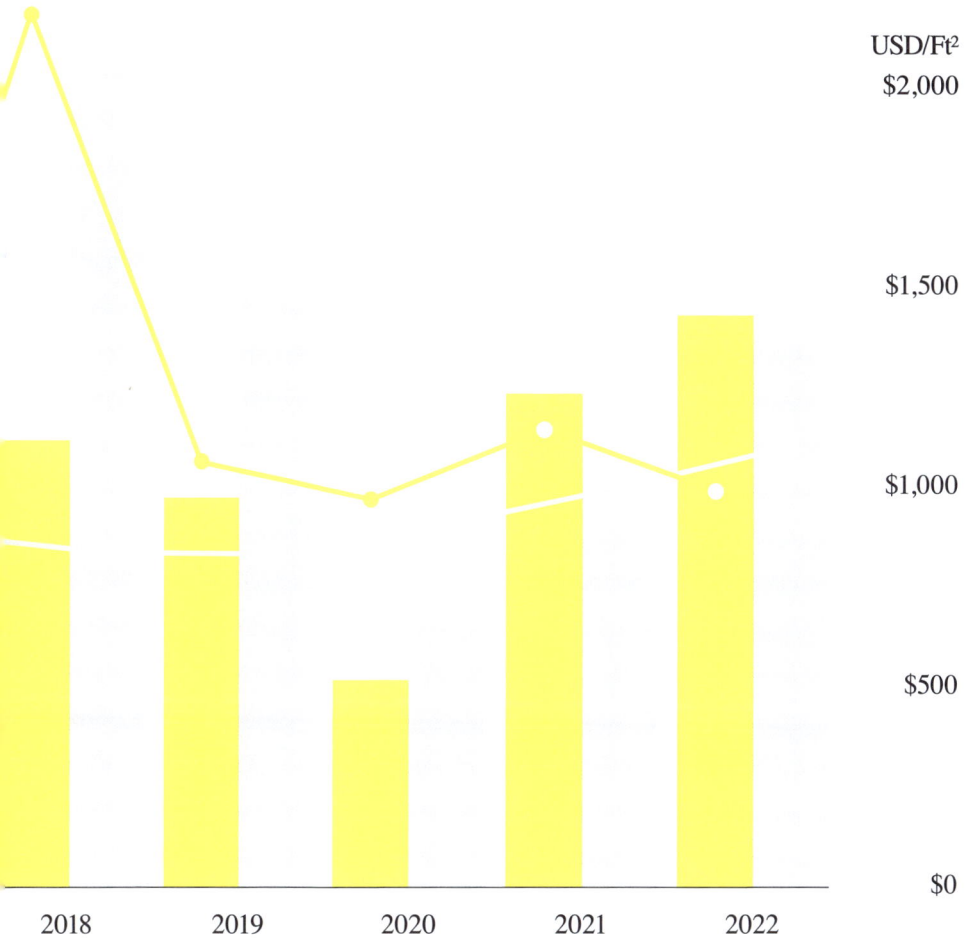

he median
Manhattan home
rice dips below
1 million for
e first time
a three years.

ederal tax
form takes
fect, capping
eductibility of
ate and local
come taxes
nd depressing
ome sales in
e tri-state area.

WeWork
cancels its IPO.
SoftBank's CEO
later publicly
apologizes for
investing in co-
working company.

Hudson Yards
opens, largest
private develop-
ment in U.S.

Amazon cancels
plans for a Long
Island City
campus after
opposition by
activists and the
start of Senate.

NYC identifies
first COVID-19
case in March
2020. Within one
month, over
70,000 infected
cases, over 2,500
deaths related to
COVID-19.

Rent and sale
prices decreased
significantly
mostly in the
Manhattan area,
accompanied by
strong rent and
sale price growths
in the suburb.

111 West 57th
St, aka Steinway
Tower completed.
1,428 ft, 84 floors,
pencil tower with
width to height
ratio of 1:24
becomes most
slender skyscraper
in world.

According to
Mondragon and
Wieland, trend of
people moving
to New York
City continues in
2022. This results
in an increased
demand for
rental properties
and decrease in
available rental
inventory, leading
to higher rental
prices than 2018.

merely on Manhattan but throughout the city. While distinct in their nature, these events have collectively shaped New York City's real estate market, causing shifts in demand, influencing prices, and changing the landscape of the city. They have highlighted the resilience of Manhattan's real estate market, which, despite facing considerable adversity, continues to adapt and evolve in response to these challenging circumstances.

9/11: Manhattan and the Financial District (2001–2007)

Toward the conclusion of the 1990s, the significant expansion in finance, insurance, and real estate, along with the influence of the dot-com bubble, contributed to Manhattan's office market reaching an unprecedentedly low vacancy rate of 7.5%. However, as the new century unfolded, signs of a potential slowdown became evident, leading to a gradual softening of Manhattan's real estate market until September 11, 2001.[97]

The 9/11 terrorist attack significantly impacted the market, affecting approximately 31 million square feet of office space, equal to 10% of the total stock of Manhattan's office market. The destruction in Lower Manhattan contributed to large-scale job losses and a severe office market recession around the area. Wall Street was particularly impacted, losing approximately 18,500 jobs in the aftermath of the attacks, marking the most substantial wave of job cuts since 1987. In October 2001, New York's office space vacancy rate reached its highest point at 9.9% since 1998. Additionally, by 2002, the typical rental rate for prime buildings had fallen by 10% to an average of $67.55 per square foot compared to the pre-9/11 rate of $75.48 per square foot.[98]

At large, the Manhattan real estate market experienced a rapid recovery, with the availability of properties returning to pre-crisis levels in about three years and rental prices increasing within a five-year period. Lower Manhattan saw a slower rebound, however. It took until 2007 for the area's average office rent and leasing activity to fully recover to their pre-9/11 levels.

Nevertheless, during this time, New York's office building sale prices experienced an unexpected surge, breaking records even with decreasing rents, higher vacancy rates, and market conditions worsened. One example is the General Motors Building, located at Fifth Avenue and 59th

---

97 "Office Vacancy Rate Climbs in New York," *New York Times*, November 10, 2001.
98 John Holusha, "Office Vacancies Rise, as Do Building Prices," *New York Times*, September 15, 2002.

Street, which was sold for an unprecedented $1.4 billion ($764 per square foot) in August 2003. This record was surpassed four years later when 666 Fifth Avenue was sold. These transactions signified a substantial display of the market's confidence in the long-term value of prestigious buildings, the revival of the Midtown office market, and the influence of lower interest rates.[99]

Simultaneously, the housing market rebounded swiftly after 9/11, spurred by significant interest rate reductions by the Federal Reserve. The interest rate consistently declined from 3.5% in 2001 to below 1% in 2004, eventually recovering to and exceeding 3.5% in 2005.[100] Mortgage rates also sharply dropped, going from 8% in 2000 to as low as 5.2% in 2003, and never fully returned to pre-9/11 levels, contributing to an unprecedented housing boom.[101] By 2003, the housing market had returned to pre-9/11 levels and continued to flourish. The average sale price for a Manhattan apartment surged from $778,575 in 2001, surpassing the $1 million mark for the first time in 2004.[102] Despite the earlier wave of job cuts, Wall Street enjoyed record compensation, reaching $34 billion in 2006 and $33 billion in 2007, thanks to the thriving regional economy and a robust housing market until the onset of the subprime mortgage crisis in 2008.[103]

During this period, several factors contributed to the resilience of New York City's commercial real estate market. Key among these was the city's commitment to revitalize Lower Manhattan through concerted recovery efforts involving government initiatives, private investments, and public-private partnerships. Monetary policy decisions by the Federal Reserve, such as significantly lowering interest rates, made borrowing cheaper and stimulated both individual and institutional real estate investments.

The recovery of the regional economy, spearheaded by record Wall Street compensations, also bolstered the commercial real estate market. Growing businesses increased the demand for commercial office space, while the emergence of technology companies like StreetEasy in 2006 invigorated

99   Charles Bagli, "G.M. Building Sells For $1.4 Billion, A Record," *New York Times*, August 30, 2003.
100   "Federal Funds Rate - 62 Year Historical Chart," *Macrotrends*, 2022.
101   Erika Giovanetti, "Review of Historical Mortgage Rates: See Averages and Trends by Decade," *US News*, November 22, 2023.
102   "The Douglas Elliman Report, 2001-2010," *Miller Samuel*, 2011.
103   Jena McGregor, "The Key Comparison to Make With This Year's Wall Street Bonuses," *Washington Post*, December 5, 2021.

the sector by driving up demand. Large-scale developments like the Hudson Yards project and the construction of the new World Trade Center, along with record-breaking luxury real estate sales, further instilled optimism about the market's future. However, the 2008 financial crisis reminded us that the commercial real estate market, despite its resilience, is not immune to broader economic trends and crises.

Subprime Mortgage Crisis (2008–2013)

In 2007, commercial real estate market indicators returned to their pre-9/11 levels and reached their peak in 2008, with office rents reaching $71.26 per square foot. However, the subprime mortgage crisis struck in the same year. In the subsequent year, commercial real estate rents had plummeted by more than 31%, and it took seven years for them to fully recover. Office vacancy rates in Manhattan surged to 11.9% in 2008, representing an alarming 46% increase in just one year. In 2009, rents dropped to approximately $50 per square foot. Despite these challenges, Manhattan's commercial real estate market exhibited remarkable resilience in the face of adversity. Rents eventually rebounded to pre-crisis levels in 2013 and continued to rise until 2019.[104]

The diversified nature of New York's economy contributed significantly to this resilience. Even with Wall Street's struggles during the crisis, other sectors such as technology, media, and healthcare remained relatively stable and continued to require commercial space. Despite the city's financial hardships, the city's attractiveness as a global commercial hub remained undiminished. Google's purchase of 111 Eighth Avenue in Manhattan marked the start of the rush of tech companies in Midtown.[105]

In addition to the robust economic diversity, the strategic responses of both commercial property owners and tenants helped to buffer the market. Instead of defaulting, many commercial property owners focused on retaining tenants by offering lower rents, while tenants looked for stability and took advantage of these incentives. As a result, lease renewals spiked, totaling 29.2 million square feet in the five years following the crash. This was 12.6 million square feet more than the renewals between 2003 and 2007, which amounted to

---

104 Patrick McGregor, "Real Estate's Recovery in New York City," *PropertyShark*, April 27, 2020; Timea-Erika Papp, "New York City's Recovery: Can History Help Estimate the Timeline?" *Commercial Property Executive*, April 13, 2020.
105 Alan Rosinsky, "Market Report: A Look at NYC Office Sales Activity From 2010 to 2020," *Metro Manhattan*, February 4, 2020.

16.6 million square feet. In this climate of renegotiated leases, WeWork opened its first coworking service in Soho in April 2010, representing a new trend in commercial space utilization and giving a fresh lease of life to the market.[106]

The office market was indeed affected by the crisis, but it didn't experience the same level of collapse as the residential market. The housing market faced a substantial economic downturn triggered by the collapse of Lehman Brothers and the federal government's takeover of mortgage buyers Fannie Mae and Freddie Mac in September 2008. This led to a sharp drop in home prices, widespread foreclosures, and a notable increase in unemployment rates. Within just four months, the number of residential sales in Manhattan nearly halved, and sales prices declined by 10%.

It took nearly two years for the Manhattan housing market to return to pre-crisis levels. The recovery was once again primarily driven by government incentives, such as a reduction of the federal interest rate to below 1% and the expansion of first-time homebuyer credits. As a result, the number of residential sales increased by 21% at the beginning of 2010, and median prices began to rebound, leading to a 1% uptick in the number of sales and an 8% rise in the median sales prices compared to 2008.[107]

In the midst of the recovery of the housing market, One57 started construction in 2009. This building represented a significant milestone as the first supertall structure erected on 57th Street. Designed by French architect and Pritzker Prize laureate Christian de Portzamparc, One57 is credited with inaugurating the era of supertall skyscrapers and the ultra-luxury residential market in Manhattan. Sales for the building began in December 2011, well in advance of its completion in 2014. Despite facing criticism from the architectural community for its imposing size and design, One57 swiftly established records for the city's most expensive and second-most expensive residences, with sales prices of $100.5 million and $91.5 million, respectively.

The emergence of these "supertalls" that have increasingly become a part of New York's unique skyline over the past two decades is a result of certain real estate practices and zoning regulations, specifically the utilization of a Zoning Lot

106 Kevin Sun, "How Manhattan's Office Market Responded in Previous Recessions: TRD Insights," *The Real Deal*, April 20, 2020
107 Matthew Strozier, "Comparing Manhattan's Housing Market After 9/11, Lehman," *The Wall Street Journal*, September 8, 2011.

Merger (ZLM). A ZLM is a form of transferable development right (TDR) that allows unused Floor Area Ratio (FAR) to be transferred from one zoning lot to another, usually an adjacent lot. This legal mechanism allows the creation of one large zoning lot from several smaller ones without altering their tax status. The transferred building rights, or "air rights," permit a developer to construct a building that's substantially larger than what could have been built on the original lot. This has encouraged the development of supertalls, as developers could effectively pool development rights from several smaller lots onto a single lot, allowing them to build higher. This not only maximizes the value of expensive real estate but also provides unique, panoramic views that command premium prices. Moreover, the economic climate and changing market dynamics have further catalyzed this trend, as evident from the fact that ZLMs and supertall developments have largely followed the peaks and troughs of the broader economy.

Record Breaking Years (2014–2019)

Manhattan remained attractive to office investors even after the financial crisis, and the six years following the recession witnessed a growing interest in the market.

From 2015 to 2018, office rents in Manhattan saw only a modest 2% growth. However, in 2019, rents experienced a significant 10% surge, reaching a new high of $80.43 per square foot. This increase was driven by the introduction of premium-priced office spaces and landlords raising rent due to increased demand.

A substantial portion of Manhattan's rent growth in 2019 can be attributed to the construction of several large blocks of premium office space, each exceeding 100,000 square feet. Eight of these sizable blocks were priced at or above $100 per square foot and became available in 2019, collectively adding 2.2 million square feet of premium office space at the top end of the price range.

Notably, newer buildings constructed since 2000 and those that underwent significant renovations secured more than 50% of leases for spaces exceeding 5,000 square feet in the same year. This trend was driven by tenants' consistent preference for high-quality office spaces, encouraging property owners and investors to upgrade their assets to better cater to the rising demand for well-lit, spacious buildings with enhanced efficiency and additional amenities.[108]

---

108 "2019 H2 Manhattan Office Market Review," *CBRE*, January 1, 2020.

Similarly, starting in 2014, there was a significant increase in new construction fueled by ultra high-end residential buildings. Residential construction spending saw a remarkable 73% increase from 2013 to 2014, reaching a total of $11.9 billion. This achievement was not only a record, even when accounting for inflation, but it also marked the first time in New York's history that annual residential spending surpassed $7 billion.[109]

However, despite the substantial increase in spending, the number of new housing units constructed in 2014 only grew by 11% compared to the previous year, resulting in an addition of just 20,329 units. This was significantly lower than the annual average of 30,000 new housing units created between 2005 and 2008. This disparity between spending and actual construction can be attributed to the surge in the development of larger luxury condominiums in affluent neighborhoods such as Midtown and areas near the High Line.[110]

A key factor driving this trend was the influx of wealthy overseas investors, who possessed substantial purchase power and had high expectations for their investments. Developers and architects were encouraged by this trend and continued to construct iconic towers filled with luxury amenities to cater to this high-end market. The effects of this shift are still evident in the evolving city skyline and the continually rising bar for luxury living.[111]

COVID-19 Pandemic and Its Aftermath (2020-Present)

New York City was arguably among the most dramatically impacted locations by the sweeping effects of the pandemic on the real estate market. As a major node of the international travel network, the city was one of the earliest to confront COVID-19 in the United States. Multiple waves of the virus rapidly spread in 2020, forcing the city's residents to reevaluate the stakes of staying in the dense urban center. The rapid decline of real estate transactions occurred as soon as residents moved outbound to suburbs and other cities. However, New York's reopening after three months paved the way for a steady and eventually accelerating renewed boom of the real estate market in 2022. Since the city's first identified COVID-19 case in March 2020, New York's hyper-dense urban environment exacerbated the

---

109 NYC Construction Spending Reached $36 Billion in 2014; a 26 Percent Increase From 2013," *New York Building Congress*, April 2015.
110 Janet Babin, "Luxury Condos Help Fuel NYC Construction Boom," *WNYC*, October 23, 2014.
111 Stefanos Chen, "The Decade Dominated by the Ultraluxury Condo," *New York Times*, January 10, 2020.

spread of the virus.[112] Concerns about public health and mandatory restrictions began to demonstrate their effects on the city's commercial real estate, leading to the closure or departure of numerous service businesses in the city. Consequently, many commercial real estate tenants were unable to meet their rent obligations, while also contemplating the vacating of their premises to mitigate financial losses. According to a report from *The New York Times*, Vornado Realty Trust, one of the biggest commercial landlords in New York, collected just around 20% of its total rent payment on time at the beginning of April and May.[113] This drastic fall in revenue for landlords highlighted the significant financial strains brought about by the pandemic, which not only impacted individual businesses but also the broader real estate landscape of the city.

The residential real estate market also quickly felt the effects of the outbreak. A Bloomberg report estimated over 160,000 households moved out of the city between March 2020 and February 2021.[114] The rapidly declining demand caused an unbalanced market where rent and sales prices dropped significantly during the first and second waves of the pandemic. A study of infection data and real estate transaction data documented a negative and significant relationship between the number of infection cases and house prices in New York City. According to the data, every 1,000 additional COVID-19 cases among 100,000 residents in given areas led to an average value drop of $60,000 for one- or two-family homes, suggesting that concerns about health and safety directly influenced real estate market dynamics.[115]

Roughly three months after the "stay-at-home" order, the city initiated a phased reopening plan for the latter half of 2020.[116] Even as some local restaurants and retailers began to revive their operations, the real estate market still grappled with challenges. Notably, a migration pattern emerged, with residents relocating from the city center to the suburbs. By analyzing transaction data from the fourth quarter of 2020 and comparing it to the same period in the preceding five years

---

112 Joseph Goldstein and Jesse McKinley, "Coronavirus in N.Y.: Manhattan Woman Is First Confirmed Case in State," *New York Times*, March 2, 2020.
113 Matthew Haag, "New Threat to New York City: Commercial Rent Payments Plummet," *New York Times*, May 21, 2020.
114 Marie Patino, "More People Are Moving to Manhattan Than Before the Pandemic," Bloomberg, June 8, 2022.
115 The authors controlled studied areas using Modified Zip Code Tabulation Areas (MODZCTAs)
116 J. David Goodman, "After 3 Months of Outbreak and Hardship, N.Y.C. Is Set to Reopen," *New York Times*, June 7, 2020, sec. New York.

(2014 to 2019), researchers observed significant decreases in rent and sale prices in the urban core, predominantly the Manhattan area, and robust growth in rent and sale prices in the suburbs.[117] Toward the end of 2020, the median rental price in New York City dropped significantly compared to that during the same time in 2019, with 21.7% less in November and 17.3% less in December.[118] However, boroughs outside of Manhattan usually faced less significant price reductions. For instance, the median rental price in Queens and Brooklyn were 18% and 11% lower, respectively, than those in the previous year.[119] This suggests a pandemic-induced shift in resident preferences toward less densely populated areas, potentially reshaping the city's real estate market dynamics.

The same phenomenon also applied to real estate sales. The pandemic might have triggered a permanent shift of interest from Manhattan to adjacent boroughs, especially Queens and Brooklyn. Lower living expenses, a hybrid work mode, and the historically low interest rate in late 2020 were motivational drivers for home buyers to move outside of Manhattan.

However, during the first half of 2021, gradually relieved restrictions and increased vaccinations prepared the momentum for a rebounding real estate market. In the second quarter, the median price for resale apartments in Manhattan hit a record-high price at $999,000. With over 3,500 sales in the second quarter, the market experienced a 150% increase from the second quarter of 2020.[120] The revived market also witnessed some purchasing interest that was previously unseen. Buyers were particularly interested in luxurious apartments with features such as outdoor patios, spacious balconies, and rooftop spaces.[121] Multiple reports and blog articles argued that the values of outdoor spaces have raised significantly since the pandemic.[122] Despite the inconsistent valuation of the pricing premiums created by outdoor spaces, the inclusion of outdoor spaces, such as balconies, shared patios, setback terraces,

117 Arpit Gupta et al., "Flattening the Curve: Pandemic-Induced Revaluation of Urban Real Estate," *Journal of Financial Economics* 146, no. 2 (November 1, 2022): 594–636.
118 Stefanos Chen and Sydney Franklin, "New York Rents Continue to Slide, While Sales Rebound in Brooklyn," *New York Times*, January 14, 2021.
119 Stefanos Chen and Sydney Franklin, "New York Rents Continue to Slide, While Sales Rebound in Brooklyn," *New York Times*, January 14, 2021.
120 Robert Frank, "Manhattan Real Estate Prices Reach Record as Buying 'frenzy' Takes Hold," *CNBC*, July 2, 2021.
121 Frank, "Manhattan Real Estate Prices Reach Record as Buying 'frenzy' Takes Hold."
122 Tim McKeough, "Today's Must-Have Amenity? A Little Green Space," *New York Times*, October 15, 2021, sec. Real Estate; Natalie Wong, John Gittelsohn, and Noah Buhayar, "New York's Empty-Office Problem Is Coming to Big Cities Everywhere," Bloomberg, September 25, 2022.

and rooftops, became undoubtedly an important measure of quality apartments and commercial spaces. In the meantime, reports also indicate that the rental market reached a new peak in terms of new signings since the start of the pandemic. Not only was there an over 60% increase of new lease signings compared to those in August 2020, but also an over 5% increase of median rental price.[123] The robust growth of both prices and transactions in the second half of 2021 marked a successful comeback of the real estate market.

In 2022, the continuous growth of demand and decline of rental inventory since the previous year led to New York City's rental prices reaching above the price level in 2018.[124] Meanwhile, remote working also encouraged tenants to increase their housing budgets in order to find spacious, comfortable apartments for both living and working.[125] These factors have all contributed to the uprising trend of real estate pricing in the last few years.

Bearing witness to the twists and turns of New York City's real estate market in times of both economic turmoil and health crises offers a compelling insight into the city's resilience and its urban dynamism. The drama of this vast cityscape and its architectural and urban design elements characterized by inviting daylight, captivating views, serene green spaces, and the commanding presence of its buildings have evolved from luxurious adornments to fundamental necessities. This change in perspective and the significant transformations occurring within the real estate market, including shifts in geographic preference and new value attributed to design features, highlight the critical role design plays in shaping our built environment, its economic worth, and our overall well-being. As we navigate into a future that is inevitably shaped by changing lifestyle preferences, technological advancements, and crises, it becomes more essential to understand and communicate the value of design tangibly and quantitatively.

123 Natalie Campisi and Rachel Witkowski, "New York After Covid-19: How Are Rent And Real Estate Prices Doing? – Forbes Advisor," *Forbes*, September 23, 2021.

124 Marie Patino, "More People Are Moving to Manhattan Than Before the Pandemic," Bloomberg, June 8, 2022.

125 John A. Mondragon and Johannes Wieland, "Housing Demand and Remote Work," *Working Paper*, Working Paper Series (Cambridge: National Bureau of Economic Research, 2020).

3 City and Data

Constructing a design dataset enhances design agency and illuminates the previously obscure processes of asset valuation in buildings.

3.1 New Digital Avenues

Finance experts once operated as the cartographers of value, probing the murky depths of market dynamics and charting the course of value exchange. Now, the boardrooms and the trading floors teem with algorithmic augurs and numerical necromancers, divining patterns in the cryptic oracles of spreadsheets and databases. Today, data serves as a powerful tool that guides financial practitioners through the complex maze of the financial realm. It helps them parse complex market trends and translate them into stories that can be understood. In the skilled hands of data scientists, rows and numbers unfold into riveting tales of boom and bust, of profit and loss, spinning a web of stories that spans the expansive epochs of economic cycles and histories. Finance and data find their roles intertwined—to excavate and relay the stories concealed in our shared experiences. Through the prism of analysis and interpretation, these experiences metamorphose into invaluable insights, shedding light on the complex workings of our economic machinery.

A Real Estate
Perspective:
Data Science for the
Built Environment

For over 30 years, there has been a push within the built environment to gather financial data in order to enable the sector to compete with other financial assets such as equities, bonds, commodities, and even forex (FX) trading. As the 21st century neared, an increasing cohort of core data companies began to collect information about real estate transactions and rents, but this notion of a systemic approach to understanding patterns of risk and return in real estate was quite new. After the 2008 financial crisis, however, there was a strong interest in developing information that could help explain the patterns of events that systemically impact society and in what ways we can avoid poor governance in real estate. What we understand from this period now is that we were in the infancy of data collection for the built environment and developing an acumen for studying the longterm impacts and effects of what a building was and who it was for.

If we skip ahead in time to 2018 and beyond, we see a data science movement in real estate. There is a shift from just a few to well over 500 data science providers in the marketplace today. This rapid expansion and growth in the real estate sector has created a transformation in how business transpires and the role of data scientists, statisticians, econometricians, and machine learning specialists in helping decision-makers answer questions. Data science is increasingly becoming core to the decision-making process in the design, construction, development, and operation of buildings and cities.

During the process of design and construction of a building, many varying skills come together. Currently, knowledge domains from geographers, planners, architects, contractors, bankers, and developers must coordinate across a mélange of documents and spreadsheets to reinvent the making of a building each time, relying on the tacit knowledge of a few individuals. However, data science is working to expand the margins of knowledge to help coordinate and organize the industry to unlock better buildings for sustainability, equitability, and health. In this way, data science is the key to disseminating the story and experience of what a building or urban design is envisioned to be in the coming period.

The Modeling Process

Over the last 50 years, asset valuation models have been the main tools developed and refined to understand real estate value drivers, particularly the value impacts of location and building characteristics. Sherwin Rosen's hedonic asset pricing model is a widely used approach to assess real estate property values based on a hybrid or repeat sales approach that measures users' willingness to pay for certain utilities using a regression framework and historical transaction data.[1] The multivariate model intends to statistically break down potential value drivers into componentry and assess their isolated impacts on the value of a property when holding other independent factors constant. Expectedly, drivers such as location and proximity to the Central Business District, building age, size, height, and status of renovation have yielded robust statistical significance in value impacts over the past decades of empirical research.[2] Fig. 12

However, these building and neighborhood characteristics describe just the crudest building elements and their contexts; they do not consider features or impacts produced as part of the design work. The limit to understanding design value drivers could be a result of both a lack of attention to the subject in general and difficulties in systematically gathering building data. In addition, there is hardly any consensus on categorizing design features among practitioners and researchers

1 Sherwin Rosen, "Hedonic Prices and Implicit Markets: Product Differentiation in Pure Competition," *Journal of Political Economy* 82, no. 1 (January 1974): 34–55.
2 Andrea M. Chegut, Piet M. A. Eichholtz, and Paulo J. M. Rodrigues, "Spatial Dependence in International Office Markets," *The Journal of Real Estate Finance and Economics* 51, no. 2 (August 1, 2015): 317–50.

Fig. 12   **Hedonic Regression Model**

$$\log P_i = \alpha + \beta X_i + \delta G_i + \varepsilon_i$$

Building Value = External Factors + Internal Characteristics

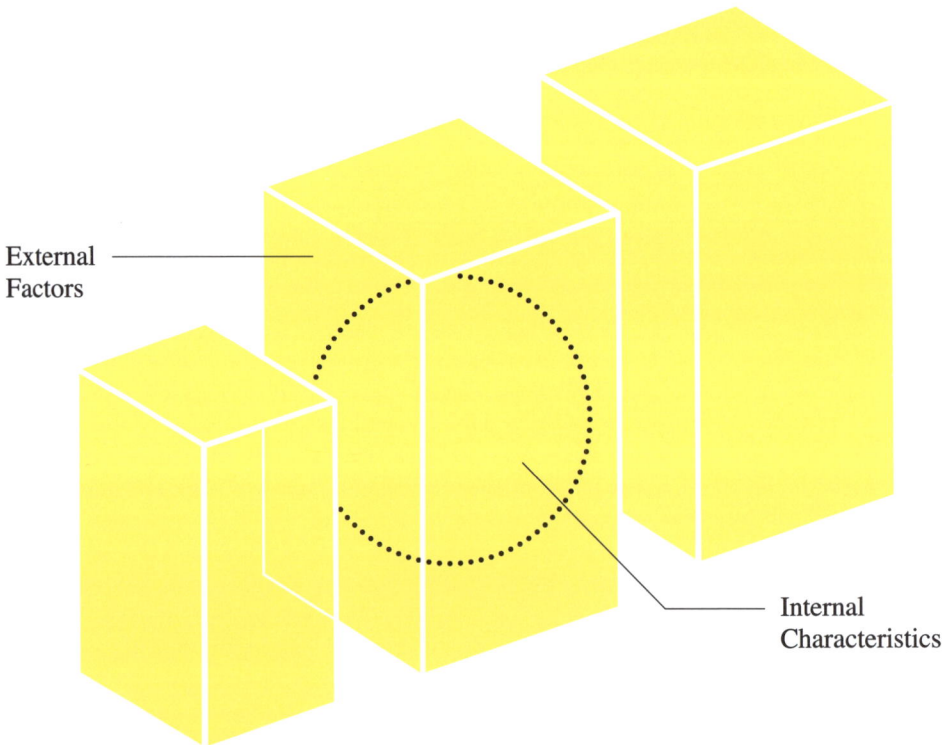

External Factors

Internal Characteristics

Note: We estimated a semi-log linear regression model where we explain the transaction price per square feet for a given building (i) as a cross-section, where (Xi), building features, time and location fixed effects (sub-market), buyer, seller and lender types and (Gi) is the vector of design feature variables, ε_i is the error term. α is a constant, β and δ are estimated coefficients. The Hedonic Pricing Method is an asset pricing method that starts from the premise that the transaction price of a property is affected both by internal characteristics and external factors.

External Factors: Location, Transaction Time, Building Age, Size, Parcel Area, LEED Status, etc.

Internal Characteristics: Building Amenities, Mechanical, Electrical, and Plumbing (MEP) Quality, Building Occupants Use, etc.

in the community of architects, urban designers, and planners, exacerbating the difficulties of generating quantitative data to describe design, a critical endeavor this book strives to commence.

What Is Data?

When we use the term "data," we define it as individual facts, statistics, or items of information, often numeric. In a more technical sense, data is a set of values of qualitative or quantitative variables about one or more persons or objects, while a datum is a single value of a single variable.[3] Data is commonly referred to in scientific domains as instructions for computation, but it is often also a representation of the human experience. Moreover, it is a systematic collection of experiences that can be organized for analysis to help inform creation and decision-making.

Data has an unfortunate reputation for being something intangible and abstract. It is a representative set of information that we use to signal that an event has occurred. The existence of events or information, in rudimentary terms, can be recorded in a database as one, and the absence of information or events is recorded as zero. Mathematically, the weight of the one then carries a greater significance and signals in a model that this event literally counts, and very simply, when there is a zero, it does not count. When we start to aggregate the ones and zeros, we can then calculate the relative occurrence of people, places, and things happening. However, statisticians, economists, and data scientists are always working to get at something deeper. The data-generating process produces data that is able to capture events and experiences temporally, spatially, individually, and without bias. In this way, data represents our human, emotional, mental, physical, connected, and disconnected experiences. It is our collective story—what is common and what is quirky and unique about all of us—and data scientists spend a lot of time listening and observing what the data has to tell us.

In this endeavor toward understanding the true data-generating process, data can minimize and expose bias. When we use models and statistics, we uncover facets of the data that can display our bias or hide it from relevant stakeholders. As data scientists, we have an ethical and technical responsibility to remove bias from models to improve the understanding of results and their impact on stakeholders.

3   "OECD glossary of statistical terms," OECD (2008): 119.

Capturing Data for Building and Urban Design	One critical aspect of any data science strategy for capturing the relationship between design, development, and real estate is the level of usage of internal and external data sources in each phase of the process. Many architectural firms, urban design firms, and landscape architecture firms do not capture their own data. We generally have no collective record of the decision-making process that occurred in curating and executing the vision of buildings. In this way, data science for design is all about gathering data about our own design experiences to be able to listen and learn from our own portfolio. Furthermore, it asks whether there are external experiences of design events outside of one's own firm.

An understanding of internal and external data can significantly help designers decide where and when to deploy resources for data science, i.e., purchase external data for market analysis or focus on internal data using data management solutions. For example, a designer needs more external data than internal data during the initial planning stage because they need to analyze the experience of potential users of the building. However, when in the feasibility stage, there is a great need to work at the intersection of internal and external data with prior experiences and meet other planning and developer expectations.

The first step in any design strategy for data science is using the data a firm already has based on its prior experiences. Rather than allowing design proposals, regardless of their success or failure, and operational details to languish on a hard drive, it is crucial for firms to begin establishing a cloud-based data architecture. This can help to build data science acumen within the firm of what has occurred.

Datasets for Design and Development

As part of the workflow of design, there are limited approaches to systematically collecting prior design experiences. Post-occupancy analysis is limited for various reasons. Principally, data ownership and code compliance inhibit post-occupancy data collection to return to the design firm to assess what elements of the design are working for occupants and what features are not. In fact, the historical record and experience should not strangle the present or future's ability to meet current needs. In this way, historical data about design outcomes can be counterproductive to the design process. However, understanding the current landscape of available data providers can help prepare real estate stakeholders to make better decisions on a data science strategy.

Sun Jung Park made the distinction between data providers—those who collect, aggregate, and disseminate data—and solution providers—those who provide systems to organize a firm's data across the real estate development process.[4] They collected information on over 500 data providers. Within the analysis, they included the architectural design process. They surveyed both relevant data providers and solution providers and analyzed their pertinent characteristics for decision-makers for helping to create a data science strategy. Some of the variables captured included interactive platform availability, application programming interface (API) availability, real estate product type coverage, regional coverage, data volume and frequency, and underlying data collection and verification methods. Among these factors, API is a relatively new characteristic for real estate data companies. It acts as an intermediary function that allows users to connect source data or software directly onto their own platform.

Among the organizations that provide external data, data platforms were the most popular style of data delivery. Almost a quarter of companies relied on crowdsourcing for data collection. This style of data gathering is growing, and its reliability could potentially increase as databases evolve. Notably, one-tenth of the companies provided hardware to enable internal data collection, a crucial resource for companies that have yet to initiate their data science strategies. More than half of the data companies provided API, indicating the industry's direction toward a more fluid and connected use of data from various sources. This observation can be attributed to the continual nature of tasks such as conducting market analysis or feasibility analysis and updating project underwriting throughout the real estate development process. Concurrently, tasks associated with design and construction implementation are gaining increased significance across the development process. What this means for real estate development is that there is a need for internal data solution providers to help design internal data architectures for efficient real estate development processes.

Image capturing is the most commonly utilized solution type that aids developers in managing internal data during the construction phase, allowing them to meticulously document construction progress and ensure a comprehensive record of the project's evolution. Doxel.AI deploys a robot surveyor with cameras, while Openspace uses smartphone cameras— or cameras attached to construction hard hats—to capture

---

4   Sun Jung Park, "Data Science Strategies for Real Estate Development" (Thesis, Massachusetts Institute of Technology, 2020).

construction site images and inspect construction progress. Through computer vision, these solutions can analyze and process images into actionable data that site managers can easily implement into their daily operations. Similarly, Aspec Scire utilizes drone-attached cameras to capture site images for various construction and development-related tasks, such as land surveys, construction progress tracking, and project completion assessment. Moving from the construction stage to stabilization, developers need to listen to internal data more than ever. The most frequently used solution type is sensor and tracking technology that detects and captures built-environment data such as temperature, water leakage, energy consumption, machine productivity, and space usage. These solutions are often provided as part of an integrated building operations and property management platform that allows property managers to act upon insights as a preventive or reactive maintenance measure.

For design, critical data collection occurs for project delivery with Revit. This software is increasingly used to not only capture design decisions but also input them into an implementation pathway for construction. Further, the advancement of digital twins for design and construction has significantly enhanced the ability to map out the pathways of a building's design and development process, providing value not only prior to building construction but also continuing to offer insightful data even after the building is complete.

Real Estate Data and Design: Collecting New Datasets

Data science is a relatively new discipline (although the concepts it incorporates, such as statistics, data analysis, and machine learning, have been around for much longer). Its versatility has allowed it to intertwine with a wide array of STEM disciplines, including science, computer science, engineering, economics, and manufacturing. However, over time, the way that we listened to experiences in those disciplines has found application in other domains. In the context of the built environment, which traditionally leaned toward more manual processes, the adoption of digital systems and data collection has been a somewhat delayed evolution. Nonetheless, the built environment sector is now catching up rapidly. For nearly two decades, data science has been progressively advancing in real estate. The initial developments were around financial and engineering processes, where building scientists and practitioners strived to revolutionize building design, architectural practices, and financial modeling to develop performance benchmarks for transactions involving homes and buildings.

As progress was made in both of these disciplines, digitization processes increasingly converged, creating a more integrated and efficient approach to real estate development.

Data providers compile comprehensive data of both commercial and residential real estate investments and transactions and provide analytics services using the organized data. For residential real estate, public agencies may also provide reliable access to historical data. For instance, the National Association of Realtors, as well as the realtors associations at the state level, organizes the latest data related to home sales and provides market outlook reports.[5] The Federal Housing Finance Agency (FHFA) documents data of single-family home values from over 400 cities in the United States that extend back to the mid-1970s. Research institutes, such as the National Bureau of Economic Research (NBER) and Harvard's Joint Center for Housing Studies, also provide critical housing-related data for real estate studies.[6]

From the perspective of real estate, data was first collected in the late 1800s to increase realtors' sales. Under an agreement to compensate each other for helping sell the properties, real estate market information previously kept private started to be shared among their peers. Listing agents accumulated data on properties for sale, and brokers connected with the buyers actively utilized the information to sell. Currently, two databases are commonly used in the United States: Multiple Listing Services (MLS) for residential market data and Commercial Information Exchange (CIE), for other types of properties.

As technology evolved, the property information listed on paper transitioned to a digital form and moved to the Internet. Real estate data became available to the broader network of professionals outside of brokerages. From the 1980s, new businesses appeared that provided real estate market analysis using the database. In recent years, there is also an additional type of data provider: real estate listing websites such as Zillow and Trulia. These listing websites reshaped real estate marketing and transactions by 1) connecting directly market participants, such as landlords, tenants, and realtors,

---

5   National Association of Realtors: https://www.nar.realtor/research-and-statistics.
6   NBER's Historical Housing Price Data: https://www.nber.org/programs-projects/projects-and-centers/7703-historical-housing-price-data?page=1&perPage=50; Joint Center for Housing Studies: https://www.jchs.harvard.edu/research-areas/housing-markets-conditions; It is important to mention that individual economists' research project, such as Prof. Robert Shiller's well-known book *Irrational Exuberance* (2000), which documents home price data from the late 19th century to the 2000s, is another source of extracting residential real estate data.

with listing information; 2) offering data analytics services to decision-makers in the market such as investors and asset managers, and at the same time; and 3) crowdsourcing the latest transaction data and information about changes made to the real assets, such as maintenance, renovation, and reconstruction.[7] These listing websites, therefore, became frontline data compilers who constantly update their database by recording the latest market information.

Data has become an important asset for developers seeking a competitive edge. Real estate companies searched for digital tools to inform their decisions for buying, selling, and managing their properties more efficiently. The term "proptech" started to circle around the commercial real estate industry in 2009 and became a buzzword a decade later. New York is considered the global hub of proptech for its explosive growth. In 2019, proptech start-up companies in New York raised more than $2 billion from venture capitalists, which was a 133% increase from the year before.

The value of real estate is increasingly being assessed based on market data. However, what is missing from the existing data providers is one who focuses on buildings' data, even the simplest data of the architect. Indeed, almost all real estate transaction databases incorporate several columns of information to describe building characteristics, but this kind of information usually reduces the description of buildings into oversimplified features such as number of floors, years since built, gross floor area, and building footprint. None of them pays attention to the buildings' design merits. In 2002, the Real Estate Standard Organization (RESO) created a data dictionary to fulfill the need to facilitate the exchange of data through a uniform structure. Under the extensive categories established by RESO, information on design is limited to the architecture style, construction material, type of flooring, and window features, diminishing the agency of design in real estate trades.

There are likely two primary reasons behind the conundrum as to why building design data is not systematically collected. First, the industry lacks integrated databases and standards for design and construction management professionals to submit digital building information, such as CAD drawings, 3D digital models, and Building Information Modeling

---

7   For an in-depth discussion about listing websites' impacts on practices in the real estate market, see: Joe Shaw, "Platform real estate: Theory and practice of new urban real estate markets," *Urban Geography* 41, no. 8 (2020): 1037-1064.

(BIM) data. The building construction and design industry remains unconvinced of the commercial viability of collecting such data. Second, a consensus on standardized methods to categorize building design features is still absent among researchers and professionals. Architectural works often boast unique aesthetics, incorporating elements of astonishing geometry, innovative structural systems, novel materials, and advanced technological equipment. These "elements" are interwoven and collectively impact the overall appearance and functionality of a building. However, a universally accepted approach to conceptually dissecting a designed building project is still not established, creating a hurdle for systematic analysis and classification.

Design serves as an integral component throughout different phases of real estate development. From the project's inception, design supports the conceptualization of the project's vision, offering analytical leadership by identifying both the potential utilization and physical limitations of the site. As the development progresses, through iterative processes, design further refines and enhances the project to meet the client's economic requirements and improve the overall user experience. Design also becomes a potent means of communication, effectively bridging the various disciplines involved in the building construction process. Design is multifaceted, highly specialized, and interdisciplinary. In current practice, a socially diverse group of experts develops design. Architectural work is increasingly distributed and dispersed, collaborative and entrepreneurial, knowledge-based, and open-sourced. A new type of design service continues to be added as the technology and methodology used in analyzing buildings advance.

However, such robust efforts are not being communicated to other disciplines engaged in the built environment. Compared to design's significant contribution in creating urban form, design often gets bypassed when making critical decisions in commercial real estate. Data empowers design agencies by bringing transparency to a murky area. To gain agency for design, a valid measuring system that could capture the sensitivity and complexity of the discipline is in dire need.

The rising use of BIM during design and construction management in the past decades might create a shift to the collection of building data through a much more standardized and scalable approach. Beyond just a 3D representation of the physical entity, BIM is a system that integrates extensive information related to a building, such as building geometry with quantified measurements, equipment performance (such as the HVAC system), and environmental information (such as room temperature, utility usage, and building code access). In that sense, BIM provides a possible solution to disintegrate building design into small- and medium-scale components, which correspond to various design and functional attributes. Currently, there are private actors and public agencies participating in building and maintaining BIM libraries.[8] However, most of these online libraries focus on providing subscription services to businesses from the architecture, engineering, and construction (AEC) industries. Real estate analysts and researchers rarely pay attention to incorporating BIM data into modeling or prediction. However, adopting such data into real estate practice and analysis could mark a pivotal moment in how we understand our buildings through data. By encouraging analysts and researchers to leverage BIM data, we could unlock new depths of understanding, enhancing modeling, prediction, and overall decision-making in the real estate industry.

Digital Twinning

The expanded use of BIM and the extensive process of data accumulation over time resonate with the rising popularity of the digital twin concept in recent years, which essentially entails a detailed digital replica of the physical environment. The notion of a digital twin has gained considerable traction within fields such as architecture, urban planning, real estate development, construction, and property management—even policymaking.

The concept of a digital twin is relatively recent, with its origins dating back to 2003 when Michael Grieves, in collaboration with John Vickers of NASA, introduced it during a product management course at the University of Michigan.[9] Initially, the concept represented a basic understanding of creating a virtual duplicate of a physical product, primarily focusing on using digital tools to replicate real-world objects. Over the subsequent two decades, advancements in computational and sensing technologies in manufacturing and complex system design offered

---

8   Private actors include NBS National BIM Library (https://www.nationalbimlibrary.com/en/what-is-nbs-national-bim-library/), an online library of BIM objects. Public agencies include the U.S. General Service Administration, which has a BIM documentation for government properties and has published a BIM guideline document. For more information, see: https://www.gsa.gov/real-estate/design-and-construction/3d4d-building-information-modeling/bim-guides.
9   Michael W. Grieves and John Vickers, "Digital Twin: Mitigating Unpredictable, Undesirable Emergent Behavior in Complex Systems," *Springer eBooks* (2016): 85-113.

new opportunities for the digital twin concept. Researchers formally defined this concept in various journal articles during the early 2010s, with a focus on the practical applications in engineering and manufacturing.[10] Subsequently, academic and industrial interest in digital twins began to grow significantly.[11]

A notable outcome of the rising popularity of digital twins is the emergence of diverse applications tailored to different fields. There is an expanding body of literature that delves into nuanced aspects of digital twins, encompassing topics such as physical-physical interaction, virtual-virtual interaction, twinning/modeling techniques, data synchronization, and more.[12] Nevertheless, the fundamental elements of digital twins remain rooted in Michael Grieves' original descriptions, which consist of three key components: physical entities, their corresponding full-scale virtual counterparts, and the interconnectedness facilitating data exchange.[13] Every piece of information generated by either the physical or virtual aspects is captured and processed within the integrated digital twin system.

The core of implementing a digital twin solution in practice lies in modeling and fusing data generated from both the physical and virtual sides. Here, modeling encompasses not only the creation of virtual representations from physical entities and vice versa but also simulation, which may provide some predictive insights.[14] Data fusion, on the other hand, pertains to data preprocessing, mining, and optimization. Every component of a digital twin system generates data. The ability to seamlessly integrate diverse types and volumes of data serves as the foundation for digital twins to realize their potential beyond mere 3D representation, such as validating changes, simulating potential outcomes, and optimizing production processes of the target of twinning. It is not difficult to realize, therefore, that the digital twin concept seems to be widely applicable to a variety

---

10   Eric J. Tuegel et al., "Reengineering Aircraft Structural Life Prediction Using a Digital Twin," *International Journal of Aerospace Engineering* 2011 (January 1, 2011): 1–14; Mike Shafto, Conroy Mike, Doyle Rich, Glaessgen Ed, Kemp Chris, LeMoigne Jacqueline, and Wang Lui, "Modeling, simulation, information technology & processing roadmap," *National Aeronautics and Space Administration* 32 (2012): 1-38; Edward Glaessgen, and David Stargel. "The Digital Twin Paradigm for Future NASA and U.S. Air Force Vehicles," in *53rd AIAA/ASME/ASCE/AHS/ASC Structures, Structural Dynamics and Materials Conference - Special Session on the Digital Twin*, (Honolulu: AIAA/ASME/ASCE/AHS/ASC, 2012), 1818.
11   Fei Tao et al., "Digital Twin in Industry: State-of-the-Art," *IEEE Transactions on Industrial Informatics* 15, no. 4 (April 1, 2019): 2405–15.
12   David Jones et al., "Characterising the Digital Twin: A Systematic Literature Review," *CIRP Journal of Manufacturing Science and Technology* 29 (May 1, 2020): 36–52.
13   Michael Grieves, "Digital twin: manufacturing excellence through virtual factory replication," *White paper* 1, no. 2014 (2014): 1-7.
14   Tao et al., "Digital Twin in Industry," 2405-15.

---

of activities that may benefit from data-driven supervision. Consequently, the influence of the concept extends not only to manufacturing industries but also to consumer product design. While digital twins serve as optimization tools for streamlining factory production processes, they also find applicability in the development of expensive and intricate industrial products such as cutting-edge electric vehicles, high-end robotic cleaners, or personal devices.

Digital Twin at City-level

The City Digital Twin (CDT) is seen as a progression from the digital twin model while also holding unique historical ties to urban studies. Urban cybernetics is arguably an antecedent to CDT. Here, cybernetics, defined in Norbert Wiener's seminal work *Cybernetics: Or Control and Communication in the Animal and the Machine* (1948) refers to a practice and study of managing organized systems through a control loop made up of sensors, actuators, and advanced controllers. Such setups self-regulate to ensure the seamless operation of intricate systems, like production lines. This principle was extended to cities via Jay Forrester's renowned yet debated work, *Urban Dynamics* (1969). This concept proposed an expansive city framework to tackle urban issues, such as joblessness and housing. The book was harshly criticized by scholars in the 1970s for its unrealistic tech-centric solutions that failed to capture urban nuances and ignored complex societal impacts.[15] However, the core idea continued to influence academic discussions on urban modeling till the end of the 20th century. The blossoming of Information and Communication Technology (ICT) since the late 1980s led to the birth of the "smart city" notion. While smart city is a broad concept that is often defined differently in various countries and cities, a significant portion of "smartness" focuses on real-time monitoring, governance, and improvement of civic services, driven by sensors and data-driven loops.[16]

More explicitly, there are two technological applications that significantly contributed to the growth of City Digital Twin (CDT) in the past decades. First is the ubiquitous presence of Geographic Information Systems (GIS) and Global Positioning Systems (GPS). These tools can depict anything

---

15 Douglass B. Lee, "Requiem for Large-Scale Models," *Journal of the American Institute of Planners* 39, no. 3 (May 1, 1973): 163–78; Horst W.J. Rittel and Melvin M. Webber, "Dilemmas in a General Theory of Planning," *Policy Sciences* 4, no. 2 (June 1, 1973): 155–69: E. S. Savas, "Cybernetics in City Hall," *Science* 168, no. 3935 (May 29, 1970): 1066–71.

16 Lily Kong and Orlando Woods, "The Ideological Alignment of Smart Urbanism in Singapore: Critical Reflections on a Political Paradox," *Urban Studies* 55, no. 4 (January 16, 2018): 679–701.

from structures to individuals and can amalgamate diverse data layers, such as power consumption or traffic dynamics. To specify, while GPS-oriented apps like Google Maps and Waze cater to real-time urban transit, GIS zeroes in on cataloging and portraying organized data sets, including population metrics and architectural layouts. The second catalyst has been the advancement of BIM within the realms of architecture, engineering, construction, and real estate management (as discussed in the previous section). BIM, transcending mere 3D visualization, offers a holistic data suite linked to buildings from infrastructural details to safety aspects. Due to its encompassing nature, BIM has become indispensable for multifaceted construction tasks. From a professional standpoint, BIM epitomizes the digital twin, merging 3D design with functionalities like operational surveillance and data logging. This successful model made experts ponder its scalability—could it expand from single edifices to whole cities? Essentially, CDT is visualized as a system of interlinked digital twins, with every BIM-rendered structure acting as a segment of this grand digital blueprint.

On the practical side, Zurich and Singapore stand out as forerunners in city-wide digital twinning efforts. Both initiatives embarked on drafting an intricate 3D city diagram, with aspirations to augment it with supplemental data strata. For instance, in Zurich, the design incorporated aspects like terrain, urban segments, and rooftops, drawn from an array of tech sources, targeting the elevation of city management and urban planning processes. Singapore's endeavor was equally comprehensive, embracing elements like flora, infrastructural components, and BIM data from developers. Nevertheless, both projects leaned more toward data integration and visualization than actual modeling and simulation, likely due to the elevated tech requisites of the latter. Given the intricate nature of cities, crafting a digital twin at the city-level presents unique challenges, unlike the more straightforward product-level twins. To navigate this, one perspective recommends fragmenting a city digital twin into more focused sub-twins, such as those for buildings or roads.[17] The underlying assumption is that narrowing the focus could possibly enable more efficient modeling and simulation, reminiscent of age-old manufacturing systems.

17 Sergey Ivanov et al., "Digital Twin of City: Concept Overview," 2020 Global Smart Industry Conference (GloSIC), November 17, 2020; Qiuchen Lu et al., "Developing a Digital Twin at Building and City Levels: Case Study of West Cambridge Campus," *Journal of Management in Engineering* 36, no. 3 (May 1, 2020); Chris Andrews, "ArcGIS: The Foundation for Digital Twins," Esri Industries, January 11, 2021.

| A Practical Focus on Data | A practical approach to building digital twins should pivot from primarily focusing on 3D modeling and interface design toward structuring a robust hardware and software infrastructure as the backbone of digital twinning.[18] The core objective is to amplify the range of urban data by optimizing sensing and surveying infrastructure. This viewpoint underscores enhancing urban sensing devices and public cloud servers, which aggregate diverse data from population statistics and mobility patterns to energy usage and land development. In doing so, this approach inherently builds upon the wide data infrastructure of the city, ensuring that quantifying design is deeply integrated and informed by the extensive urban data landscape.
We posit that the true potential of digital twins hinges on a cross-disciplinary data integration strategy. Consolidating wide data from varied sources is imperative to dissect and explore the nuances that animate cities. Integration can span various scales: urban-wide models combining spatial dimensions with economic indices, subterranean systems, or building-specific data incorporating transaction records and occupancy details. This cross-disciplinary approach naturally establishes a feedback loop between building-level digital twin development, real estate analytics, and the overarching city-level digital twin. This feedback loop allows for the continuous update and refinement of models based on real-world analytics and outcomes. Furthermore, human-centric "invisible" data, such as census info, mobile usage, social interactions, and health metrics, plays a role. Consequently, digital twins, when merged with this expansive data spectrum, can illuminate unseen aspects and clarify ambiguous ones. |
| Incentivizing Digital Twin Development through Visualized Data | Our foundational endeavors to value building design uses New York City's vast data landscape—covering such aspects as real estate transactions, urban greenery, building structures, and user experiences—as a template. The visualization of this real estate data does not only support analytics but also actively incentivizes the development of both building-level and city-level digital twins. Many of the studies in this book employ a data-intensive approach and have indeed forged preliminary yet foundational elements of a city-scale digital twin, driven by their interdisciplinary insight needs. The results highlight |

---

18   Martin Tomko and Stephan Winter, "Beyond Digital Twins – a Commentary," *Environment and Planning B: Urban Analytics and City Science* 46, no. 2 (December 11, 2018): 395–99; Li Wan, Timea Nochta, and Jennifer Schooling, "Developing a City-Level Digital Twin –Propositions and a Case Study," International Conference on Smart Infrastructure and Construction 2019, January 1, 2019.

how quantifiable design metrics influence commercial buildings' financial valuation in urban contexts. This understanding transcends physical urban landscapes, echoing even in digital realms where spatial attributes carry monetary value, as evidenced by the rising value of properties. This interplay of city-level wide data integration and analytics creates a virtuous cycle, where the benefits and applications of digital twins reinforce further understanding of the built environment.[19]

3.2 Research Methods

Over the past several years, the MIT Real Estate Innovation Lab has been developing computational frameworks, known as the Wide Data Experiment, that integrate architectural and urban design into financial econometric methods in order to automatically calculate real estate pricing and development valuation. The Wide Data Experiment is essentially a combination of publicly available data from New York government entities and private data providers such as Real Capital Analytics (RCA) and Compstak. The integrated database provides fundamental hedonic variables for asset pricing analysis. Using the Wide Data Experiment's geometric, geospatial, and relational databases, we have begun to test valuation forecasts at the urban scale. `Fig. 13`

Each of our studies endeavors to provide empirical evidence demonstrating the financial value of design within commercial real estate in the context of Manhattan, using transaction and rental data spanning nearly two decades, from 2000 to 2017. For each study, we begin with a basic asset pricing model that includes data provided by transaction and rental data providers Real Capital Analytics and Compstak.

Real Capital Analytics (RCA) is a private data provider specializing in property transaction data based in New York City. The database collects data from a network of independent sources, with particular emphasis on the building transaction data that includes financing details, prior transaction history, and true owner identification to complete profiles. From this database, we use variables including the transaction price for

---

19 To push forward this endeavor requires an inclusive group of actors—not only architects, urban planners and designers, policymakers who are more traditional urban-related fields, but also emerging tech industry players. One leading actor is Epic Games, who developed the widely adopted Unreal Engine, which is promising for realizing digital twin applications. For more information, see: https://www.unrealengine.com/en-US/digital-twins.

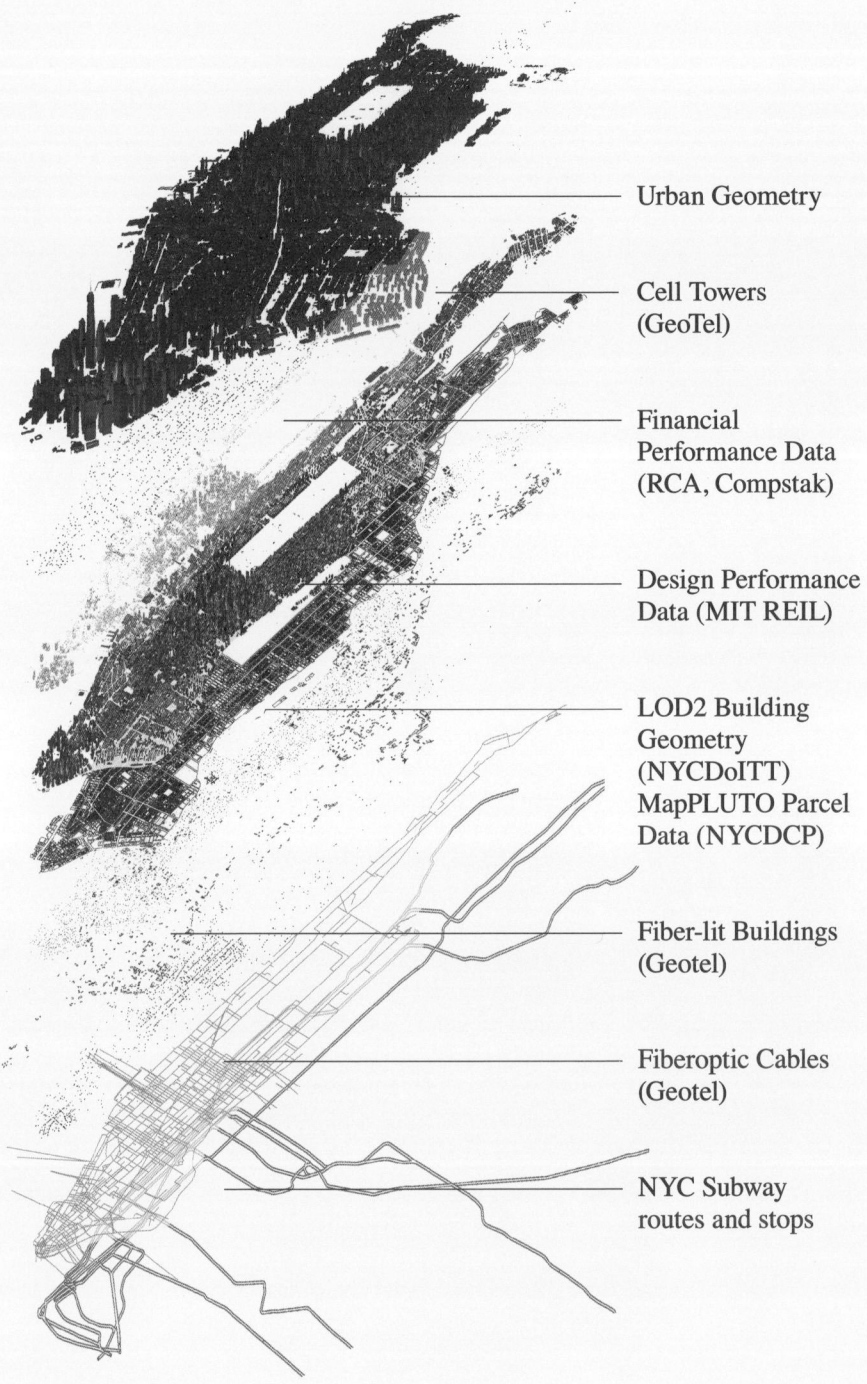

Fig. 13   **The Wide Data Experiment**

Urban Geometry

Cell Towers
(GeoTel)

Financial
Performance Data
(RCA, Compstak)

Design Performance
Data (MIT REIL)

LOD2 Building
Geometry
(NYCDoITT)
MapPLUTO Parcel
Data (NYCDCP)

Fiber-lit Buildings
(Geotel)

Fiberoptic Cables
(Geotel)

NYC Subway
routes and stops

each contract signed, which becomes the dependent variable. We extract location and transaction time data for individual property transactions to control for both time and location. In studying Manhattan's commercial real estate dynamics, we also employ the submarket designation provided by RCA to control for relative location quality, specifying seven areas in Manhattan: Downtown, Midtown East, Midtown South, Midtown West, Upper East Side, Upper Manhattan, and Upper West Side. To control for different types of real estate buyers and sellers, we also control for buyer type, seller type, and lender type provided by RCA. These range from corporations, funds, governments, institutional, offshore, private, and Real Estate Investment Trusts (REITs). Other variables from this database we use include the building's transaction year, built year, number of floors, building area, land parcel area, and renovation year.

On the other hand, we also extract the building class feature for each building that is transacted from the Compstak dataset to control for the overall quality of the buildings in the sample dataset and match the observations from the RCA dataset. A building identification number (BIN) was assigned for each transaction observed in the RCA database and matched with the Compstak data set to improve accuracy.

Compstak is a private commercial real estate data platform with offices in New York and Los Angeles. The data is crowdsourcing from verified and active professionals at commercial brokerages and appraisal firms and provides lease and sales comparable data. The Compstak database contains variables that include lease contract characteristics, tenant profile, and market variables, to name a few. In our research, we have included the "Building Class" variable in our regression analysis. In commercial real estate, the absence of an industry-wide standard or certification for building quality leaves the task of assessing commercial buildings to tenants, owners, and brokers themselves. Among the few existing frameworks, the Building Owners and Managers Association (BOMA) is the sole organization with a functional definition for building class. Class A buildings, which cater to premier office users, boast top-tier rents, high-quality finishes, cutting-edge systems, excellent accessibility, and a strong market presence. Class B buildings, on the other hand, compete for a broader range of users, with rents falling within the average range, featuring fair to good finishes and adequate systems but lacking the same level of competitiveness as Class A properties. Class C buildings target tenants seeking functional space with rents below the area's average. Given the potential influence of architectural style on building class, we incorporate building class as a controlled factor in our model.

In summary, our dataset includes 3,318 transaction observations for 1,540 unique commercial real estate properties in Manhattan over the 2000–2017 period. Buildings in the sample have an average transaction price of $143 million, with the most expensive property priced at $3.4 billion. The average age of buildings in our sample is 90 years, with the oldest one constructed in 1799. 31.1% of the observations belong to building Class A, 48.7% in Class B, and 20.1% in Class C. Location-wise, 18.1% of the observations are found in the Downtown submarket, 73.3% in Midtown, and 8.6% in the Uptown submarket. All building samples have similar Walk Scores, with an average score of 99.2, due to the highly connective urban tissue of Manhattan. Our sample also indicates that most buyers in the market (41.0%) are real estate private companies, amongst other corporations, funds, institutional investors, REITs, government entities, and offshore investors. As for sellers, our sample shows that private companies remain the largest seller type (28.8%). Lastly, commercial mortgage-backed securities (CMBS) make up the largest lender type category (22.3%), followed by other lenders such as regional or local banks (13.4%), national banks (12.5%) and international banks (10.1%). `Fig. 14-18`

Our rental transaction dataset, focusing on commercial real estate leases in Manhattan, records 22,201 leasing agreements for 1,655 unique properties from 2003 to 2016. The yearly distribution of leases demonstrates a noticeable trend: between 2012 and 2014, the number of rental transactions experienced a significant increase (ranging from 2,123 to 2,181), approximately doubling in volume compared to the year 2003, which marked the lowest point in transaction numbers (1,001). The properties in this dataset show an average effective rent of $60 per square foot annually, peaking at $576.5. The dataset reveals a mean lease duration of 92.6 months, including an average of 3.7 months of rent-free periods. The size of the leased spaces varies widely, with the largest recorded lease covering 16,800 square feet, while the smallest is a modest 400 square feet. The buildings, averaging 78 years in age, with the most historic dating back to 1853, are predominantly Class A (56.1%), followed by Class B (37.3%) and Class C (4.7%). Geographically, 16.9% of leases are in Downtown, 75.3% in Midtown, and a smaller 3.9% in Uptown Manhattan. These buildings vary significantly in size, ranging from 6,956 to 2,749,931 square feet, with an average

Fig. 14 **The Wide Data Experiment Summary: Building Sales Data From 2000–2017**

Total of 3,318 Transactions for 1,540 Buildings

Building Class:

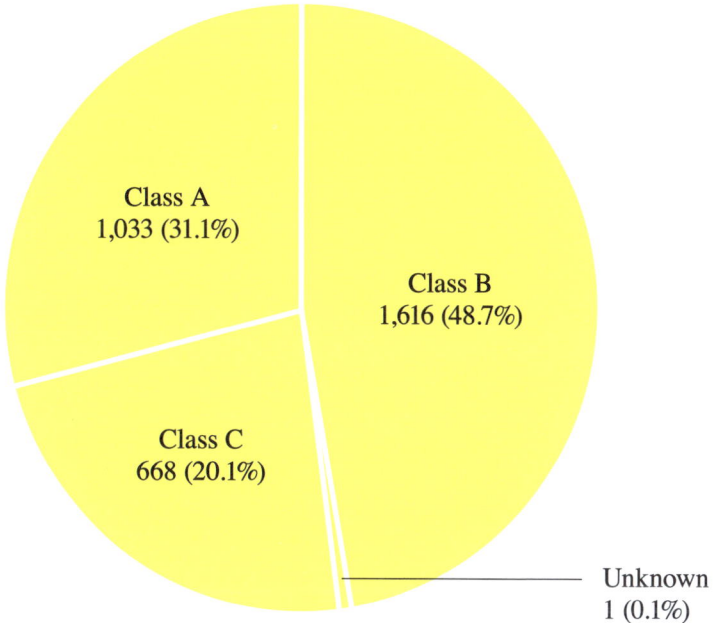

Class A
1,033 (31.1%)

Class B
1,616 (48.7%)

Class C
668 (20.1%)

Unknown
1 (0.1%)

Construction Type:

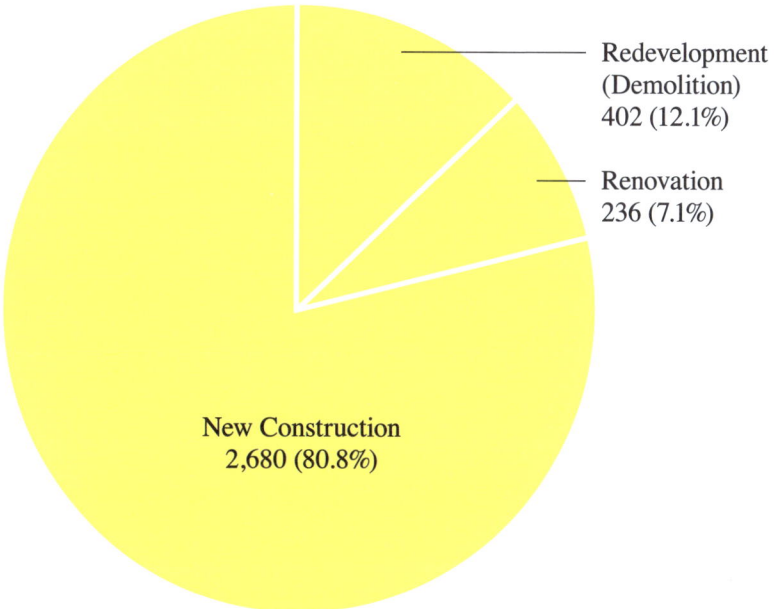

Redevelopment
(Demolition)
402 (12.1%)

Renovation
236 (7.1%)

New Construction
2,680 (80.8%)

Fig. 15

The Wide Data Experiment Summary: Building Sales Data From 2000–2017

Transaction Characteristics

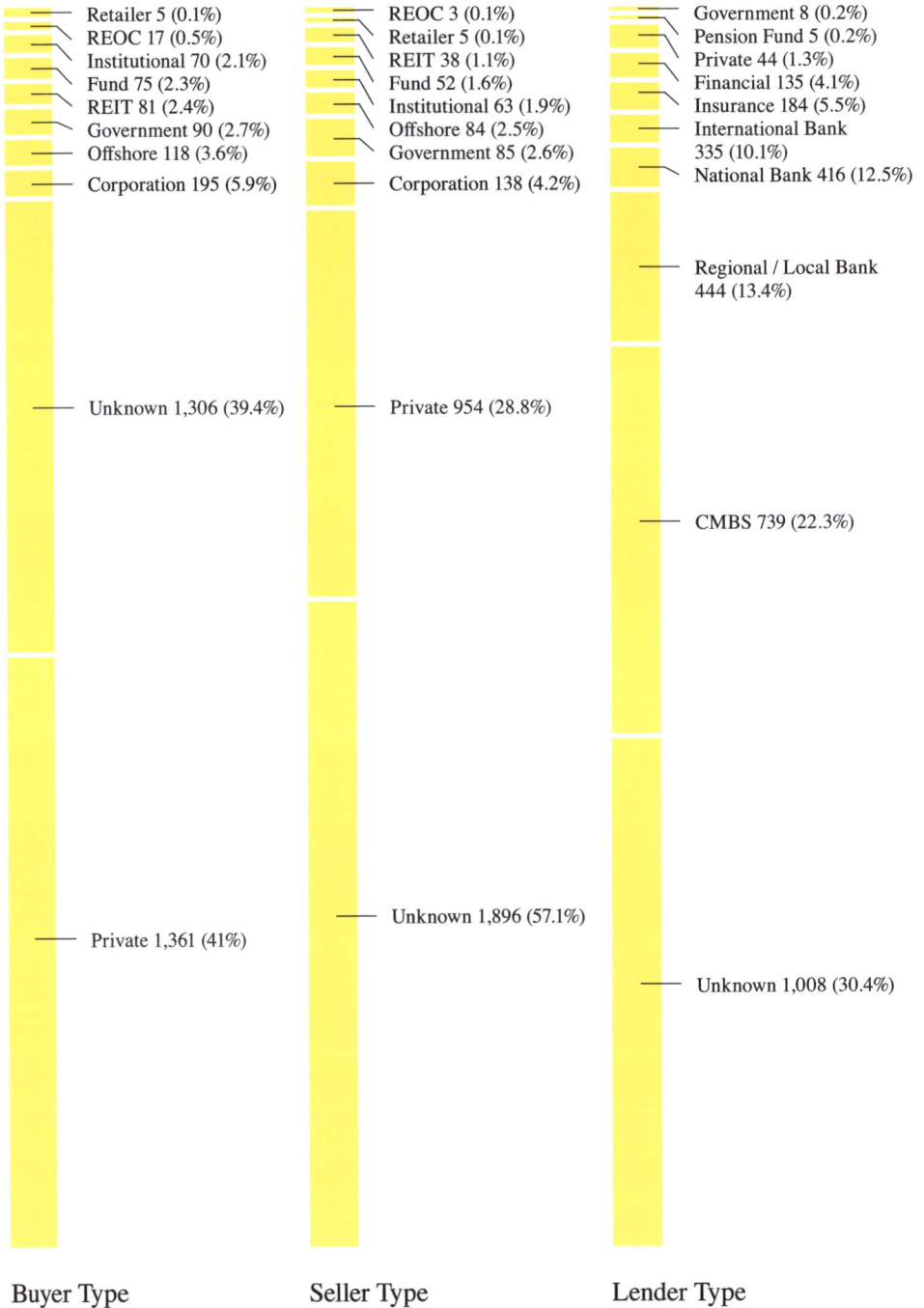

Buyer Type

Retailer 5 (0.1%)
REOC 17 (0.5%)
Institutional 70 (2.1%)
Fund 75 (2.3%)
REIT 81 (2.4%)
Government 90 (2.7%)
Offshore 118 (3.6%)
Corporation 195 (5.9%)
Unknown 1,306 (39.4%)
Private 1,361 (41%)

Seller Type

REOC 3 (0.1%)
Retailer 5 (0.1%)
REIT 38 (1.1%)
Fund 52 (1.6%)
Institutional 63 (1.9%)
Offshore 84 (2.5%)
Government 85 (2.6%)
Corporation 138 (4.2%)
Private 954 (28.8%)
Unknown 1,896 (57.1%)

Lender Type

Government 8 (0.2%)
Pension Fund 5 (0.2%)
Private 44 (1.3%)
Financial 135 (4.1%)
Insurance 184 (5.5%)
International Bank 335 (10.1%)
National Bank 416 (12.5%)
Regional / Local Bank 444 (13.4%)
CMBS 739 (22.3%)
Unknown 1,008 (30.4%)

Fig. 16 **The Wide Data Experiment Summary:
Building Sales Data From 2000–2017**

● Building Transaction Price

	N	Min	Max	Mean	Std Dev
Transaction Price	3,318	$178.6K	$3.4B	$143.2M	$296.9M
Price per Ft^2	3,318	$19.2	$6.8K	$633.3	$532.3

● Building Characteristics

	N	Min	Max	Mean	Std Dev
Building Age	3,318	3	224	90.3	30.5
Number of Floors	3,318	1	102	16.9	13.3
Area (Ft^2)	3,318	902	3M	270K	428.5K
Land Area (Ft^2)	3,318	200	686M	573.8K	19.6M
Walk Score	3,318	86	100	99.2	1.2

Fig. 17 **The Wide Data Experiment Summary:
Building Sales Data From 2000–2017**

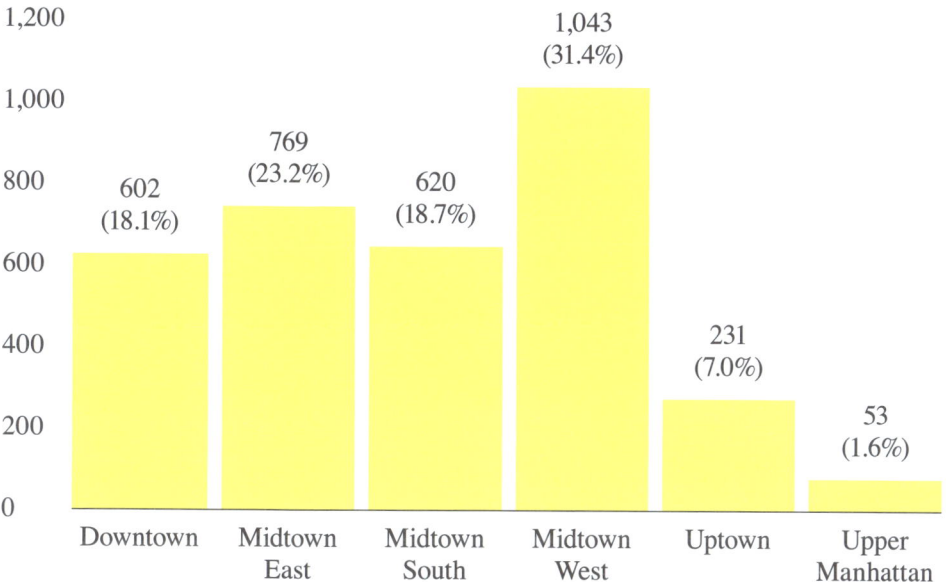

No. of Buildings

Downtown: 602 (18.1%)
Midtown East: 769 (23.2%)
Midtown South: 620 (18.7%)
Midtown West: 1,043 (31.4%)
Uptown: 231 (7.0%)
Upper Manhattan: 53 (1.6%)

Fig. 18

The Wide Data Experiment Summary: Building Sales Data From 2000–2017

Sales Transactions per Year

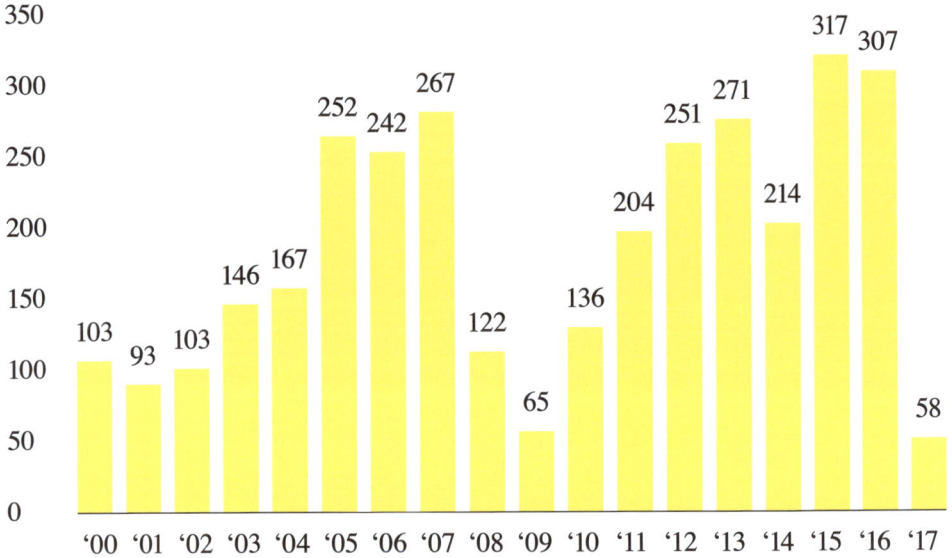

floor count of 30 and the tallest building reaching 102 floors. Despite this variety, the Walk Score remains consistently high, averaging 97, a testament to Manhattan's interconnected urban environment. Fig. 19-22

In addition to these foundational variables, we also measure and create new variables that represent building design features for each study, be it building design award status, external geometric features, daylight, views, the presence of urban greenery, green building innovation, and more.

In each study, we employ the hedonic regression model to analyze and understand commercial real estate pricing dynamics. The hedonic model serves to capture the impact on asset pricing (either transaction price or rental price) of both internal and external characteristics of a property, allowing an analysis of a cross-sectional dataset and measurement of design features in the real estate marketplace. For each analysis, the dependent variable is either the transaction price data variable provided by RCA or the net effective rent drawn from the Compstak dataset, both of which indicate the financial value of a building. The independent variables include those other variables from RCA and Compstak

Fig. 19 **The Wide Data Experiment Summary: Building Rental Data From 2003–2016**

Total of 22,201 Rental Observations for 1,655 Buildings

Building Class:

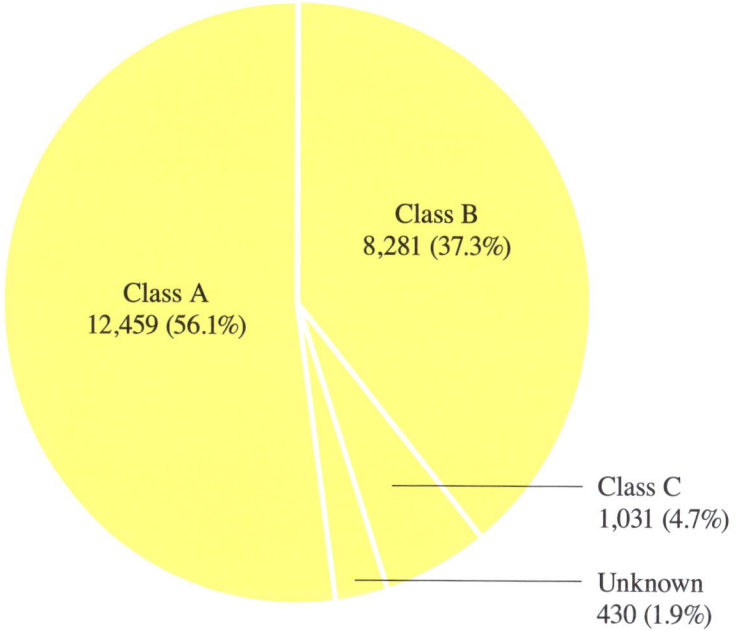

Class B
8,281 (37.3%)

Class A
12,459 (56.1%)

Class C
1,031 (4.7%)

Unknown
430 (1.9%)

Construction Type:

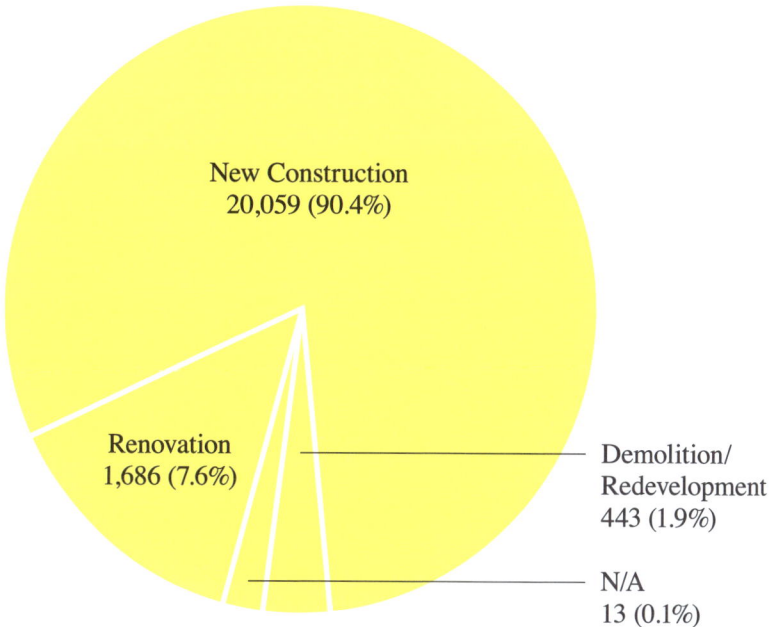

New Construction
20,059 (90.4%)

Renovation
1,686 (7.6%)

Demolition/
Redevelopment
443 (1.9%)

N/A
13 (0.1%)

Fig. 20

The Wide Data Experiment Summary: Building Rental Data From 2003–2016

- Rental Market Characteristics

	N	Min	Max	Mean	Std Dev
Lease Term (months)	22,201	12	2,256	92.6	52.9
Free Rent (months)	22,201	0	50	3.7	3.6
Effective Rent ($ / Ft² / Year)	22,201	17.5	576.5	60	53.6

- Building Characteristics

	N	Min	Max	Mean	Std Dev
Building Age	22,201	6	181	77.8	29.8
Number of Floors	22,201	1	102	29.8	15.5
Building Size (Ft²)	22,201	6,956	2,7M	607K	558K
Transaction Size (Ft²)	22,201	400	168K	14K	20K
Walk Score	22,201	0	100	97.1	14.7

Fig. 21

The Wide Data Experiment Summary: Building Rental Data From 2003–2016

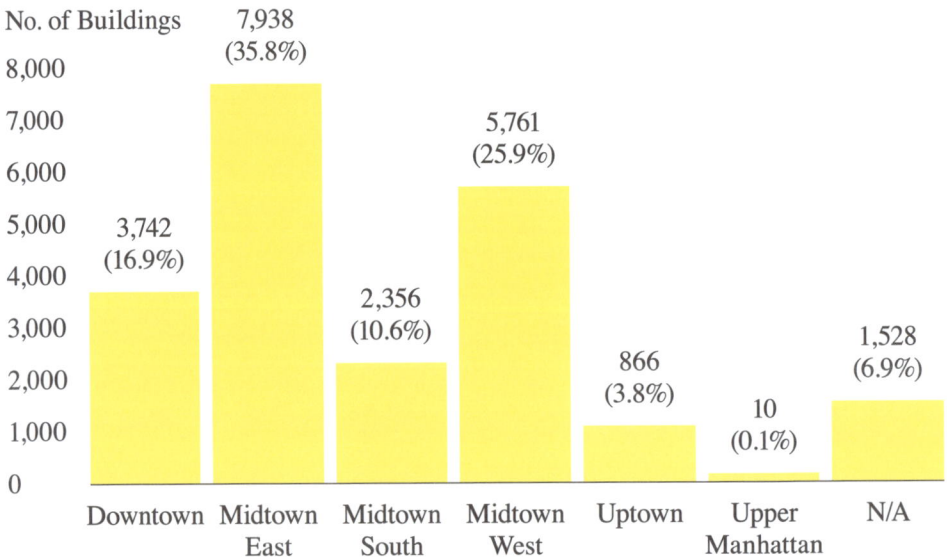

No. of Buildings

- Downtown: 3,742 (16.9%)
- Midtown East: 7,938 (35.8%)
- Midtown South: 2,356 (10.6%)
- Midtown West: 5,761 (25.9%)
- Uptown: 866 (3.8%)
- Upper Manhattan: 10 (0.1%)
- N/A: 1,528 (6.9%)

Fig. 22

The Wide Data Experiment Summary: Building Rental Data From 2003–2016

Rental Transactions per Year

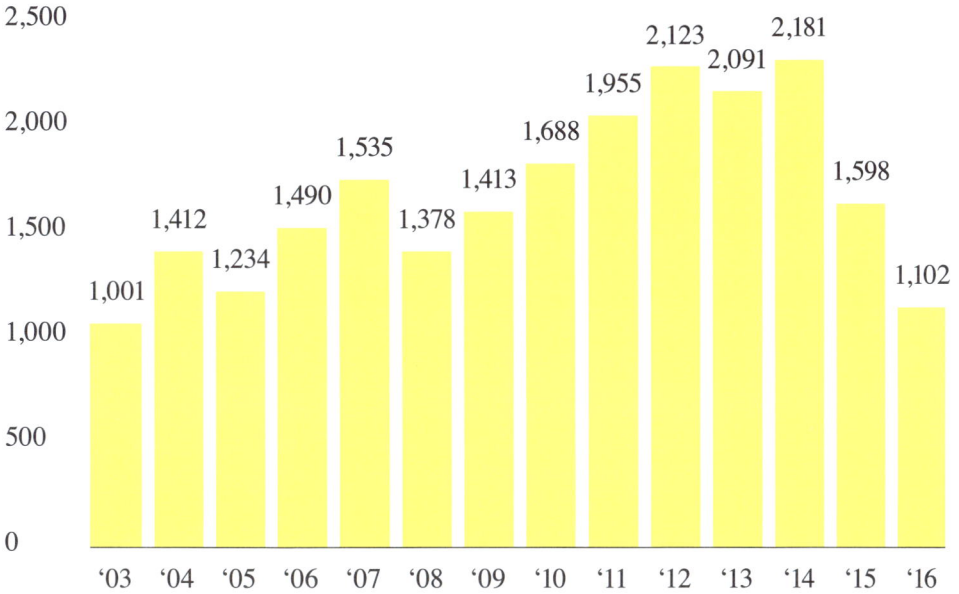

we have just introduced above. To consider the walkability of the neighborhood, the Walk Score variable was implemented using the data provided by Walkscore.com. The Walk Score ranges from 0 to 100, where neighborhoods with access to public transit, better commutes, and proximity to the people and places achieve higher scores. The addresses of individual buildings observed in the building transaction sample dataset was matched with the Walk Score provided on the website. In addition to these variables, we also add a "design feature" variable which would allow us to understand the effect of design on the financial value of the underlying asset. For each study, we compare the average characteristics of buildings with design features with those of control samples—buildings without design features.

For those not steeped in the nuances of statistical analysis, understanding how to interpret the results of a hedonic regression can seem daunting. At its core, this method dissects the price or rental value of a property into its constituent attributes to assess how each factor—such as design, location, age, or size—individually impacts the overall value, holding other factors constant. Imagine a property as a puzzle made up of various pieces; hedonic regression helps to pinpoint the value added by each of those pieces.

When interpreting a regression result table from a hedonic analysis, it is helpful to start with the big picture before zooming into the details. The Adjusted R-square (or R-square in simpler models) offers a snapshot of how well the model explains the variation in property prices based on the variables chosen, such as architectural style or location. A higher Adjusted R-square signifies a strong correlation between the property's features and its value, suggesting that our selected factors do a satisfying job of accounting for differences in price.

With this overarching understanding, we then delve into the specifics provided by the coefficients. These figures quantify the impact of individual variables on the property's price, effectively translating abstract features into concrete value adjustments. For example, a positive coefficient for "Green Spaces Nearby" indicates an increase in value for properties closer to parks, with the coefficient itself telling us how much that proximity is worth in monetary terms.

Next, the p-values associated with each coefficient assess the statistical significance of these impacts, helping us discern whether the observed effects are reliable or possibly due to random chance. A p-value below 0.05 typically confirms the variable's significant influence on property values, allowing us to proceed with confidence in the validity of our findings. Here, asterisks play a pivotal role, acting as indicators of statistical significance. Typically, one asterisk (*) next to a coefficient or p-value signals a significant impact, with a p-value below 0.05, implying confidence in the feature's effect on property prices. Two asterisks (**), used for a p-value below 0.01, and three asterisks (***), used for a p-value below 0.001, denote even higher levels of confidence, highlighting the most reliable findings in the model.[20]

These key components structure a comprehensive framework for interpreting hedonic regression results, which seek to bridge the gap between design and real estate analytics, demonstrating how various property characteristics, from

---

20 In addition, we may also consider more advanced components from the result table, such as the standard errors and confidence intervals. The former provides insight into the precision of the coefficient estimates; lower standard errors indicate a higher level of confidence in the estimated impacts, suggesting that our predictions are likely close to real-word values. The latter, confidence intervals, providing a range for the true impact of a feature, bolster our understanding of each variable's significance. If this range consistently excludes zero, it underscores the feature's definitive role in influencing property prices.

architectural design to environmental features, contribute to its economic valuation. In a world that once mapped the contours of value through human expertise and intuition, the terrain of real estate analytics is now being reshaped by the seismic waves of data science. As we stand on the precipice of a new era of digital innovation, one in which design and data merge in unprecedented ways, our work seeks to forge this uncharted path, illuminating the new frontiers of real estate innovation.

Our approach centers on harnessing data analytics to make sense of this vast information pool. The aim is to craft a new framework that quantifies design value, moving beyond traditional—often subjective—qualitative evaluations. This is paired with a comprehensive research methodology that remains agile, adapting to the intricate nature of design value. Through the combined power of data analysis and a flexible research methodology, we seek to provide a nuanced understanding of design value grounded in empirical evidence. The urban landscape of New York City, with its myriad architectural styles and real estate trends, is an optimal setting to test and refine this approach.

4   The Value of Design

A comprehensive collection of evidence, conducted between 2018 and 2023 at the Real Estate Innovation Lab at MIT, aims at expanding the discussion on the value of design.

Past attempts at systematically linking design with finance have generally been scarce. Due to the lack of data that assesses design, only a handful of academic research papers have been published documenting the relationship between building design and real estate value. In most cases, the evaluation of design is hindered by the absence of clear operational definitions. Consequently, assessments often rely on whether a design has achieved award-winning or landmark status. In other words, the assumption is that if a building is designed by an award-winning architect, it must inherently possess distinctive design qualities. Most of the research demonstrates that design may create a premium and yield positive externality for nearby building valuations.[1] Such studies have suggested a tangible financial premium associated with well-designed buildings, often using traditional methods like regression analysis and qualitative data gathering to deduce economic benefits.[2] However, such approaches alone were insufficient for fully capturing the nuanced economic contributions of architectural design.

In this context of limited exploration, Hough and Kratz cracked open the discussion with a groundbreaking study in 1982. The researchers meticulously examined the economic repercussions of distinguished architectural design within Chicago's CBD area. Their findings revealed that buildings recognized for their design excellence through awards were able to command rent prices up to 23% higher than their counterparts that did not receive similar accolades. Yet, their analysis extended beyond mere awards. The research also delved into tangible factors such as proximity to the city center, the age and size of the buildings, their height, and the availability of dining facilities, offering a comprehensive view of how architectural design influences economic value.[3]

Building upon the methodology of Hough and Kratz, subsequent research efforts have ventured into exploring the correlation between architects' awards and the perceived quality and market performance of their buildings. These studies aimed to determine whether buildings designed by architects distinguished with prestigious awards commanded a

---

1   Gabriel M. Ahlfeldt and Alexandra Mastro, "Valuing Iconic Design: Frank Lloyd Wright Architecture in Oak Park, Illinois," *Housing Studies* 27, no. 8 (November 1, 2012): 1079–99.
2   Some of the most common data collection approaches include survey responses, interviews, and expert-led grading.
3   Douglas E. Hough and Charles G. Kratz, "Can "good" architecture meet the market test?" *Journal of Urban Economics* 14, no. 1 (1983): 40–54.

premium over their counterparts within the same locale. Researchers such as Cheshire and Derick, as well as Fuerst, McAllister, and Murray, focused on the economic valuation of architectural works in both the U.K. and the U.S., specifically those credited to architects honored with significant awards.[4] Notably, Fuerst, McAllister, and Murray expanded their analysis to a national scope, examining U.S. office buildings conceived by architects who had received either the Pritzker Prize or AIA Gold Medal. Their analysis revealed that such buildings could secure a 5 - 7% increase in rental rates and an impressive 17% surge in sales prices compared to similar buildings in the same market.[5] This line of inquiry underscored the economic benefits of engaging renowned architects for projects. Yet, these studies did not fully address the influence of distinct design features on a building's economic value, often attributing the increased value primarily to the architects' renown.

Shifting gears, another group of studies aimed to peel back the layers on how various building traits play a role in determining value. One of the focuses examines the overarching theme of architectural style. For instance, in 1989, Asabere, Hachey, and Grubaugh dug into how different architectural styles might sway the value of residential properties, sorting homes into categories such as townhouses and condos. In addition, Lindenthal chimed in with a noteworthy point: a neighborhood's stylistic uniformity can actually give property values a lift, spotting a 3.5% value bump in places where houses matched up nicely, whereas the more eclectic or mismatched designs didn't fare as well.[6] Meanwhile, Plaut and Uzulena undertook a similar investigation in Riga, Latvia, peeling through the layers of time to understand how design from different periods weighed in economically.[7] The other focus looks at more measurable aspects like age, size, height, and how close they are to local hotspots. For instance, while Buitelaar and Schilder delved into the impact of architectural styles as well, they incorporated detailed variables into their hedonic pricing model, including lot size, year of

4   Paul Cheshire and Gerard Dericks, "'Iconic Design' as Deadweight Loss: Rent Acquisition by Design in the Constrained London Office Market," *RePEc: Research Papers in Economics*, January 23, 2014; Franz Fuerst, Patrick McAllister, and Claudia Murray, "Designer Buildings," 166–84.
5   Fuerst, McAllister, and Murray, "Designer Buildings," 166–84.
6   Thies Lindenthal, "Beauty in the eye of the home-owner: Aesthetic zoning and residential property values," *Real Estate Economics* 48, no. 2 (2020): 530-555.
7   Steven Plaut and Egita Uzulena, "Architectural design and the value of housing in Riga, Latvia," *International Real Estate Review* 9, no. 1 (2006): 112–131.

construction, type of dwelling, parking facilities, and terms of land lease to provide a more nuanced understanding of design's economic significance.[8]

However, the way people perceive design is often influenced by the intended messages within those designs.[9] The mix and match of various design elements, like the pattern of windows, the materials used, and the general shape and bulk of the building, play a big part in how we see and feel about a building's style and look.[10] To gain a deeper understanding of design's value, it is essential to look at the possibility of turning these design features into something we can measure and analyze in detail. One of the early studies by Vandell and Lane in 1989 attempted to look into the detailed design elements beyond architectural styles. To address the lack of "design" data, the study enlisted a group of architects to evaluate the appearances of 102 premier office buildings in Boston and Cambridge, Massachusetts. The architects disentangled multiple design elements of a building into specific categories: façade decorativeness, color and texture of the surface material, and the overall form of the building. The results confirmed a strong positive correlation between the design scores and rents. Buildings rated in the top 20% for design quality were predicted to extract over 20% higher rents than those in the bottom 20%. However, while the high-quality design of a building usually entailed more expensive for construction, it did not show a strong impact on reducing the building's vacancy rate.[11] A more recent study by Nase, Berry, and Adair in 2016 also evaluated design elements such as façade fenestration, building material, and the building's overall massing composition based on expert scores. The overall design score of the building was derived by averaging the scores of each design component. Buildings that achieved higher scores were further studied to understand whether they were also highly valued by the real estate market.[12]

8 Edwin Buitelaar and Frans Schilder, "The economics of style: measuring the price effect of neo-Traditional architecture in housing," *Real Estate Economics* 45, no. 1 (2017): 7–27.
9 Nathan Crilly et al., "Design as communication: exploring the validity and utility of relating intention to interpretation," *Design Studies* 29, no. 5 (2008): 425–457.
10 Chiu-Shui Chan, "Can style be measured?" *Design Studies* 21, no. 3 (2000): 277–291; Carlie Ranscombe et al., "Visually decomposing vehicle images: Exploring the influence of different aesthetic features on consumer perception of brand," *Design Studies* 33, no. 4 (2012): 319–341.
11 Kerry D. Vandell and Jonathan Lane, "The Economics of Architecture and Urban Design: Some Preliminary Findings," *Real Estate Economics* 17, no. 2 (June 1, 1989): 235–60.
12 Ilir Nase, Jim Berry, and Alastair Adair, "Impact of quality-led design on real estate value: a spatiotemporal analysis of city centre apartments," *Journal of Property Research* 33, no. 4 (2016): 309–331.

In short, these studies almost unequivocally reported value premium on well-designed buildings, signaling a positive correlation between design quality and real estate value. Yet, researchers often underscore the challenge of interpreting their findings. The essence of design, a blend of both tangible and elusive elements, complicates efforts to quantify its economic impact. An inherent conflict of assessing those qualitative features with quantitative analysis seems inevitable. But more importantly, there has been a dearth of design-related data to advance the study and start uncovering its complex effects on the economic value of real estate.[13] In this light, leveraging the abundance of urban data in New York City and the enhanced computational capacity of reality-capturing technologies, our lab conducted a series of research to take a closer look at the building's design features and assess their impacts on property economics.

The rest of this chapter unfolds through a series of research efforts, each zeroing in on different aspects of design. Section 4.1 examines the influences of spatial experiences and a detailed category of design awards on property prices in Manhattan, challenging the notion that any award alone is a marker of design's economic value. Section 4.2 broadens the discussion on design value by introducing a catalog of new design metrics that can potentially be measured using emerging technologies. The following sections showcase a selection of several important design features from this catalog and evaluate their effects on real estate transactions. These features encompass external design features that influence the appearance of buildings (Section 4.3), access to views and natural light within office spaces (Section 4.4), high-quality interior layout design (Section 4.5), the presence of street-level greenery around office buildings (Section 4.6), and the inclusion of sustainability-related features in building design and construction (Section 4.7).

With these studies, our goal is to foster a nuanced understanding of design value based on empirical evidence, thereby encouraging further exploration of generating novel data to quantitatively describe design features. It is an ongoing and long-term endeavor, through which we aspire to push the boundaries of how we think about design's role in the real estate market, moving beyond the simple equation of an architect's fame equals more value and toward a more comprehensive appreciation of design's multifaceted contribution to our built environment.

---

13 Jean Baudrillard, *For a Critique of the Political Economy of the Sign* (London: Verso Books, 2019).

4.1 City Couture: On Awarded Architects

The field of American architecture as we know it today was founded in the late 19th century.[14] Starting in 1865, organized educational programs began to shape a rational design theory and a standardized work model for the profession. From 1897, the right to use the title "architect" was allowed only through state registration giving official recognition to the profession. At this time, an architect's office was most commonly a place of collaboration, where both the "master architect" and the rest of the office staff were engaged in every stage of the work. Architecture offices also functioned as an extension of architecture schools. Prospective architects acquired the rudimentary skills and understanding of the operation by working at the offices of those already in practice. A staff of 10 was generally considered a large office.

By the turn of the 20th century, architecture offices had to respond to the demand generated by the increasing size of buildings and the complexity of construction, which increased economic pressure to sustain the office as a business. Architecture offices with a staff of more than 100 had become a staple in the field in North America.[15] The shift from generalization to specialization was palpable in the discipline. For more efficient management, many tasks and stages of architecture formerly under the control of the master architect were distributed among the members of the business. Positions for principals with different professional areas of expertise—centered on design, management, and business development for example—commonly arose in offices with more than ten employees.[16]

As a result, the decision-making process was also segmented by delegating responsibilities to groups that only performed a designated task under their supervising principals. The work was organized by a new type of employee whose primary responsibility was supervising the work process as a liaison between the principals and the other workers. The general competence to participate in the various types of work

---

14 The first architecture program started at MIT in 1865. The registration of architects by states began in 1897, in Illinois. See: Spiro Kostof, *The Architect: Chapters in the History of the Profession* (New York: Oxford University Press, 1986).
15 Kostof, *The Architect*, 309-344.
16 "1950 Survey of the Architectural Profession: Progress Report," *The Survey of Education and Registration* (Washington D.C.: American Institute of Architects, 1951).

needed in a small office setting was no longer required of individual employees. In large offices, employees were expected to become specialists in a specific area, spending the majority of their careers focusing on those activities. Consequently, the design outcome was frequently a replica of previous work, intentionally standardized and anonymous.

By the late 20th century, architecture practices diversified in scale and the types of specialized services they provided to cater to the demands of the complex building process. The architect's contribution to real estate also evolved beyond the traditional concept of design: solely defining the shape and material of a building. In 1986, writer Weld Coxe introduced a new matrix to identify the organizational strategies of architecture firms in an article published in *Architectural Technology*.[17] He defined three types of architectural design firms: those with strong ideas, those with strong delivery, and those with strong services.

The strong idea firms offer unique competencies for cutting-edge and creative projects. They are built on the charisma and reputation of an individual designer, usually the firm's founder. The founder's name frequently becomes the brand of the office, such as Foster and Partners, Gehry Partners, Zaha Hadid Architects, and so on. The principal's recognition and reputation directly influence the firm's prosperity. Because of their high degree specialization, renowned firms frequently work without borders in the type of building programs as well as their geographical locations.[18]

Firms with strong delivery tend to produce more routine projects and services, where economic efficiency and the repetition of tried-and-true architectural solutions are the main focus. Projects are processed in accordance with standard details and specifications developed through experience, offering quick outcomes at low costs. They tend to specialize in a single type of program, such as hospitals, power plants, laboratories, hotels, and so on. Clients appreciate the practice's ability to save time and money, as evidenced by repeated results.

Lastly, firms with strong service provide dependability through extensive experience building complex projects. The pillars of this category are large-scale corporate offices with

17   Coxe et al., "Charting Your Course," *Architectural Technology* 5 (1982): 52–58.
18   Davide Ponzini, "The Values of Starchitecture: Commodification of Architectural Design in Contemporary Cities," *Organizational Aesthetics* 3, no. 1 (January 3, 2010): 10–18.

a long-standing history. These companies prioritize organizational efficiency and deliver consistent quality. The names of such firms are frequently the initials of the founders, such as SOM, KPF, and HOK. The founders are no longer engaged, but the firm's legacy lives on through professional business management organized as partnerships with a hierarchical structure. Under management, groups with specialized functions deliver a one-stop-shop solution to the clients. The list of services provided by such architecture offices is constantly expanding. As the foundation of the business, firms provide services in architectural and interior design for various building types. Graphic design is offered for branding needs to better represent the client's building in the market. City planning and community planning work are provided to governments and private real estate developers as consulting services. Recently, energy performance design has been in increasing demand to help clients' buildings meet the sustainability goals of cities and stakeholders. Furthermore, engineering services typically outside the scope of the architecture, such as structural, mechanical, electrical, and plumbing design are added through mergers with specialty companies.

Today, Coxe's matrix still holds true, and is particularly visible in New York, where the architecture industry has increased at a significantly faster pace than in the rest of the country. In New York, architecture jobs grew by 23% from 2006 to 2016, compared to a 3% increase in the United States overall.[19] Between 2016 and 2022, New York added 2,708 registered architects, ranking second after Wisconsin. In terms of total architects, New York holds the second position with 21,043, following California, as per the 2022 NCARB survey.[20] In New York, 526 architecture companies are registered according to the AIA architecture firm inventory published in 2021. With no shortage of architects to serve a client's needs, the question is who the client should choose to work with.

Awards

The Grand Prix de Rome, created in 1729, is generally considered the first architectural prize. Since then, the number of awarding bodies for architecture and the built environment has continually increased. Prior to 1960, there were no

19 Naomi Sharp, "New York by Design," Center for an Urban Future, May 2018, https://nycfuture.org/research/new-york-by-design.
20 "NBTN 2023 Jurisdictions," National Council of Architectural Registration Boards Blog, August 7, 2023, accessed December 30, 2023, https://www.ncarb.org/nbtn2023/jurisdictions.

more than 10 organizations across the globe, but by 1980, the number had reached 20. This was followed by an exponential growth, with more than 150 prominent organizations honoring architectural design excellence on an annual basis today.[21] Fig. 27

The consequences of this increase in awards are challenging to assess. Between 2007 and 2009, the number of awards given annually to both individuals and organizations in the United States increased fourfold, from roughly 100 to almost 400 per year. It then quadrupled again in 2016, reaching 900 awards in 2020 alone. This exponential increase is related to the emergence of private businesses with the sole purpose of presenting prizes for architecture and the built environment. In extreme cases, these organizations grant hundreds of awards each year.[22]

We can assume that awards offer reasonable indications of what is valued as architectural design quality. However, the recent surge in the number of awards and awarding organizations raises questions about their credibility, undermining the value they once represented. The opaque nomination process and brief announcements made to the public, often through a selection of photos of built works, limit the award's ability to convey the critical implications of the laureate's accomplishments in architecture.

Nonetheless, prestigious awards such as the Pritzker Prize continue to captivate the public. The announcement of the yearly recipient of the prize generates international headlines. When the news breaks, the winner experiences a torrent of demands for lectures, media appearances, and interviews. While an architect's award status does not ensure the success of a future project, it can often serve as a deciding factor when choosing between architects with comparable competence and size. Requests to compete for exclusive projects come next, followed by commissions for new projects. For example, only Pritzker Prize Laureates were invited to compete in the United Nations' 1998 design for a second skyscraper in New York.

---

21 Jean-Pierre Chupin, Carmela Cucuzzella, and Georges Adamczyk, *The Rise of Awards in Architecture*, (Wilmington: Vernon Press, 2022)
22 The Farmani Group, the Chicago Athenaeum, and the International Awards Associate (IAA) are notable North American entities that award more than 100 prizes in a single year.

Fig. 27

An Exponential Growth in the Number of Architecture Awards

Number of Awards

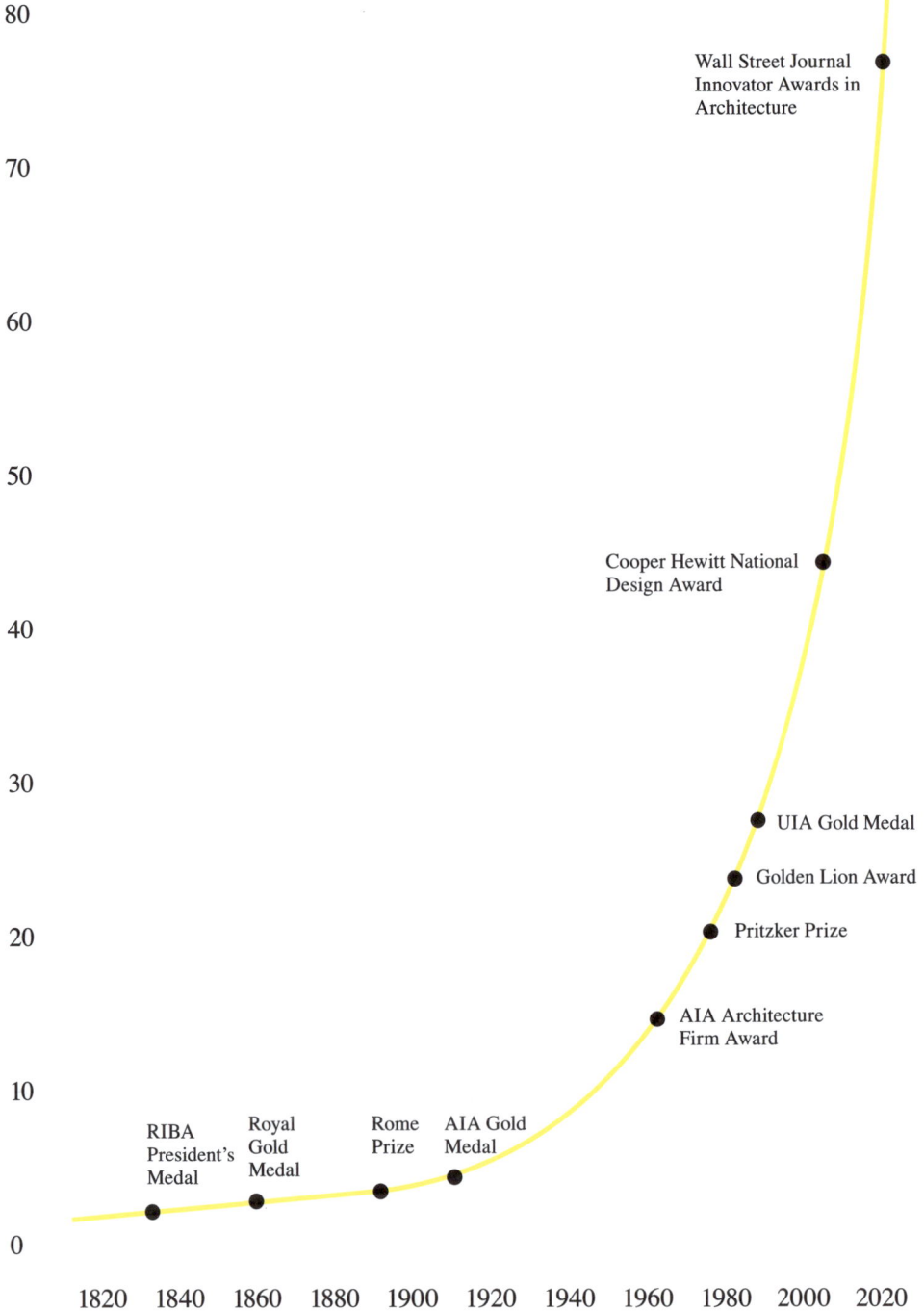

80 — Wall Street Journal Innovator Awards in Architecture

70

60

50 — Cooper Hewitt National Design Award

40

30 — UIA Gold Medal

Golden Lion Award

20 — Pritzker Prize

AIA Architecture Firm Award

10

RIBA President's Medal

Royal Gold Medal

Rome Prize

AIA Gold Medal

0

1820 1840 1860 1880 1900 1920 1940 1960 1980 2000 2020

| Building an Awarded Design Database | To analyze the awarded architect's contribution to real estate value, we have chosen eight awards under three categories. The first group, the lifetime achievement awards, recognizes the architect's accumulated body of work as the most crucial criterion. These awards are typically given to architects with more than 30 years of experience based on their career contribution to expanding the knowledge of the industry. Through realized projects that advance the understanding of the spatial experience or broaden the theory, the laureates are considered to have the highest recognition in the field of architecture. The RIBA Royal Gold Medal, AIA Gold Medal, Pritzker Prize, UIA Gold Medal, and Venice Architecture Biennale's Golden Lion for Lifetime Achievement Award are considered for this study. Fig. 28 |

The second set of awards, comprising the architecture category of the Cooper Hewitt National Design Award and the Wall Street Journal Innovator Awards in Architecture, specifically recognized the groundbreaking achievements of emerging and younger architectural firms. Candidates for the awards do not need an extensive portfolio. They are recognized for completing notable projects that received attention during the year of the award. These awards can be subjective, focusing on a single building's accomplishments or the advancement of new technologies.

While the previous two groups acknowledge an individual, the third category honors the company. The AIA Architecture Firm Award recognizes that architecture is a collective effort. The award is given to firms that have demonstrated expertise through consistent, high-quality work while emphasizing the importance of maintaining an equitable and collaborative office environment. Importantly, it considers not only a project's impact but the management of the company and the employees' well-being.

For this research, we tracked the award winners of these eight awards across the three categories from 1940 to the present. Out of the 234 awarded architects, 18 of them designed office buildings that still stand in Manhattan today. Fig. 29

In addition to the variables in the hedonic regression introduced in Chapter 3, the architect information for each Manhattan office building in the database was searched and matched manually. The information was gathered using multiple sources that include the architect's web portfolio, architecture magazines, articles from various publications, and websites.

The data was further treated to control for the location factor. Using the Geographic Information System (GIS) and based on the latitude and longitude, a 0.25-mile radius zone was created for each building by an award-winning architect to flag all other office buildings around the area. Four clusters of office building groups were created, containing at least one building designed by an awarded architect and one building designed by a non-awarded architect. Fig. 30-31

Out of the 489 Manhattan office buildings identified in the integrated database, 52 buildings were designed by award-winning architects, and 89 transactions were observed in those buildings between 2000 and 2019.

The Value of Awarded Design

The regression analysis result shows, with all other conditions remaining the same, that buildings designed by award-winning architects are sold with a 23.1% premium compared to buildings by non-award-winning architects with positive and significant coefficients. Fig. 32

The transaction premiums were also recognized when further specifying the award categories. The buildings designed by the laureates of the Lifetime Achievement Award and emerging architect categories were sold with a 17.7% premium. The designs by AIA firm award winners recorded a

Fig. 28 **Architecture Award Categories Considered in the Research**

Awards	Organization	Frequency	First awarded	Since 1950
● Royal Gold Medal	RIBA	Annual	1848	69 awarded
● Gold Medal	AIA	Annual	1907	59 awarded
● Gold Medal	UIA	Triennial	1984	26 awarded
● Golden Lion	Venice Biennale	Biennial	2000	12 awarded
● Pritzker Prize	Pritzker Foundation	Annual	1978	41 awarded
● Innovator Awards	WSJ	Annual	2010	7 awarded
● National Design Award	Cooper Hewitt	Annual	2000	26 awarded
● Architecture Firm Award	AIA	Annual	1962	55 awarded

Fig. 29 **Filtering Data**

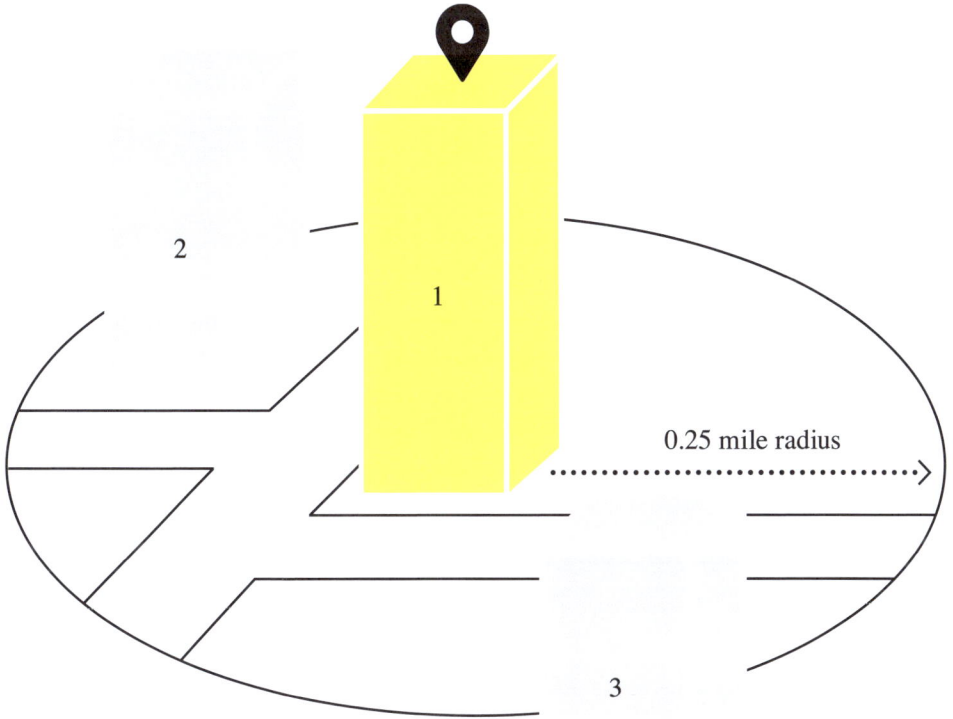

1 Office Buildings Designed by Awarded Architects
2 Office Buildings Within Radius
3 Office Buildings Outside Radius are Removed from the Data Set

Note: Illustration of data filtering to construct the control group data set. In a scientific experiment, a control group refers to a subset that is distinct from the main experiment, ensuring that the independent variable under examination does not affect the outcomes. This segregation enables the examination of the sole impact of the independent variable on the experiment and eliminates other potential interpretations of the results.

Fig. 29 **Filtering Data**

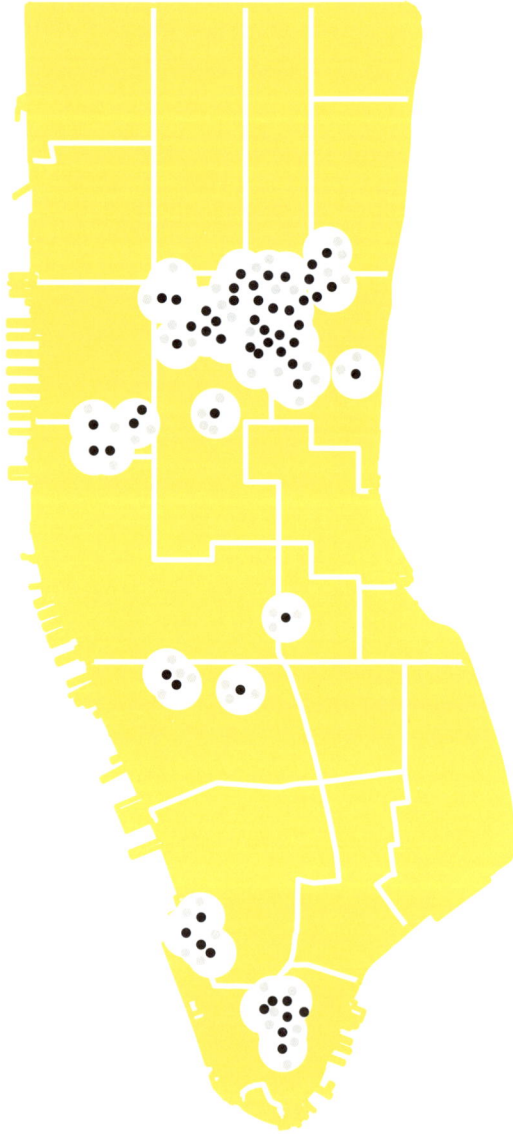

Result:

52 Awarded Design Buildings
89 Awarded Building Transactions
489 Office Buildings
846 Total Transaction Observations

Note: Illustration of data filtering to construct the control group data set. In a scientific experiment, a control group refers to a subset that is distinct from the main experiment, ensuring that the independent variable under examination does not affect the outcomes. This segregation enables the examination of the sole impact of the independent variable on the experiment and eliminates other potential interpretations of the results.

Fig. 30

Total Transaction Observations

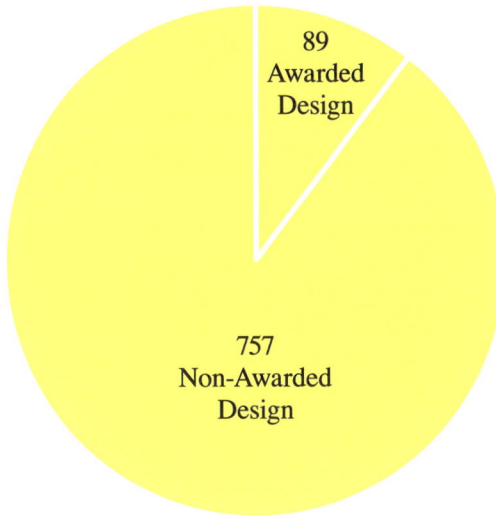

89
Awarded
Design

757
Non-Awarded
Design

Fig. 31

Interest Variables

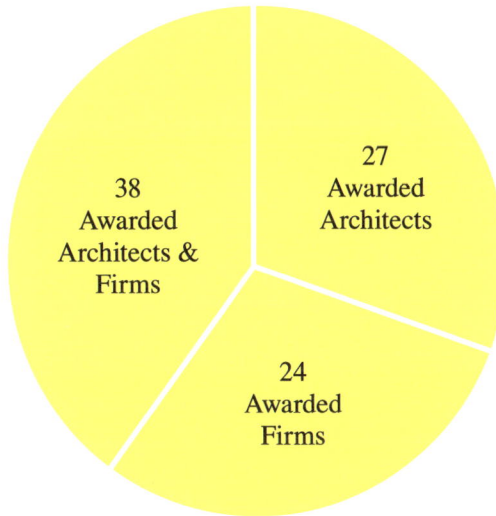

27
Awarded
Architects

38
Awarded
Architects &
Firms

24
Awarded
Firms

The transaction sample data set contains 489 commercial office buildings with 846 transaction observations. In this set, 52 buildings were designed by awarded architects/firms (treated group) and 437 buildings were designed by non-awarded architects (control group). Information on the architects and firms are assigned to each building in the data set. Out of 318 architects and firms in total, 194 were non-awarded architects, 20 were awarded architects and 104 architects were unidentifiable.

Awarded Architects	Buildings designed by winners of the Lifetime Achievement Awards, Innovation Award, and/or National Design Award.
Awarded Firms	Buildings designed by AIA Architecture Firm Award winners.
Awarded Architects and Firms	Buildings designed by winners of both a Lifetime Achievement Award and an AIA Architecture Firm Award.

higher premium at 32.1%, and the buildings designed by firms included in all categories showed a transaction premium of 20.9%.

The buildings designed by award-winning architects consistently show a positive relationship with their real estate value. While we accounted for other factors that influence real estate value—location, time of sale, age of the building, class, size, and number of floors—construction costs were not included in the dataset. One could argue that the higher construction costs required to realize the awarded architect's ambitious design drive the building value; thus, the observed premium can simply mean that the building was more expensive. Where this may be a valid concern, our research considers that the building's construction cost is already reflected in the building's transaction value. This is because real estate valuation typically considers projected cash flow, which considers construction costs and the depreciation of the structure.

While the study's findings indicate a link between an architect's recognition and the value of real estate, it is still unclear what qualities of these architects contributed to the value increase. Although it needs to be taken with a cautionary

Fig. 32 **Award Winning Architect Design**

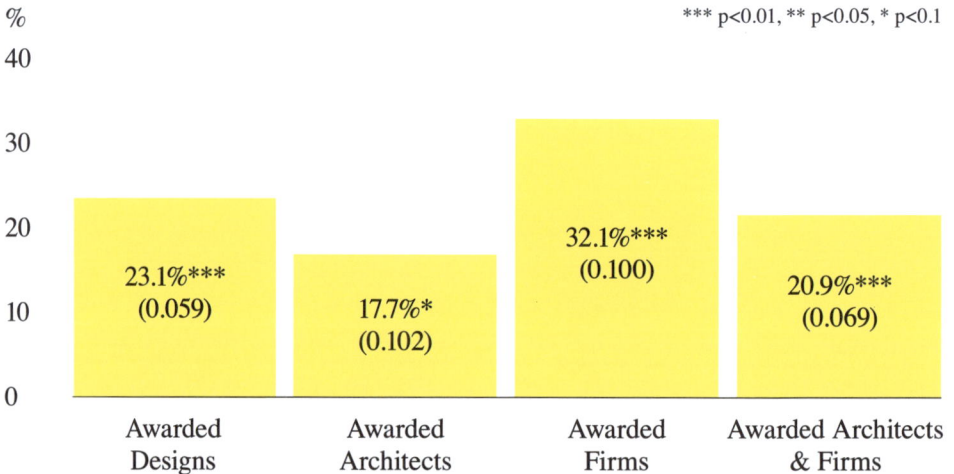

%

*** p<0.01, ** p<0.05, * p<0.1

40

30

20

10

0

23.1%*** (0.059) — Awarded Designs

17.7%* (0.102) — Awarded Architects

32.1%*** (0.100) — Awarded Firms

20.9%*** (0.069) — Awarded Architects & Firms

Note: The regression model controls for location and transaction time, building features (age, number of floors, building area, property area, building class, renovation, and walk score), and transaction features (buyer type, seller type, and lender type.) The results explain 90.6% of the variation in the logarithm of transaction price with an adjusted R-squared of 90%. Buildings designed by award-winning architects are sold with a 23.1% premium compared buildings by non-award-winning architects with positive and significant coefficients. Buildings designed by the laureates of the Lifetime Achievement Awards and emerging architect categories were traded with a 17.7% premium. The AIA Firm Award winners' designs recorded a higher premium at 32.1%, and the buildings designed by firms included in all categories showed a sales premium of 20.9%

threshold, Mies van der Rohe's Seagram Building, for example, recorded the highest transaction premium of 60.6% with a p-value less than 0.001. A p-value serves as a statistical measure to support a hypothesis with the observed data. The lower the p-value, the higher the statistical significance of the hypothesis. Typically, a p-value of 0.05 or less is considered statistically significant. Although the Seagram Building was considered an outlier and discounted in the regression model, it recorded a significantly higher transaction premium rate than the other sample buildings. When completed, the architecture community recognized the building with the highest accolades and achieved commercial success, making it the most admired property for elite investment firms and law offices.

The building's physical aspects, as the architect envisioned, undoubtedly contributed to the continued success of the building. Before the Seagram Building, the idea of an open plaza providing public space amidst the density of Manhattan was unprecedented. Mies van der Rohe meticulously designed every detail of the building, implementing the latest architectural inventions at the time, from its bronze skin exterior to the customized bathroom doorknobs. However, applying the same design strategy of the Seagram Building to other buildings, even if the same architect had designed them, would not necessarily yield the same result.

Due to the complexity of the construction process and the numerous stakeholders who influence the project's design and functionality, a building cannot be seen as the architect's sole work of imagination. In the case of the Seagram Building, the owner's commitment to creating the best spatial experience was apparent on multiple levels throughout the planning and construction phases, as well as after the building's completion. Several noteworthy aspects include the owner's efforts to ensure the architect's vision was consistently realized, the substantial financial investments made to construct the most expensive commercial building ever, and the deliberate curation of space usage and ambiance within the building. These achievements were ultimately the result of collaborative work involving the owner, engineers, and consultants from different disciplines. All the things mentioned above may contribute to the 23.1% premium observed between design quality and real estate value. However, this one numeric result represents a compressed measurement of a variety of design parameters, each of which may have its own impact on pricing.

4.2 New Design Metrics

It may appear counterintuitive to attempt to quantify design—a field often seen as highly subjective and qualitative. The endeavor to measure design is rooted in two primary challenges. The first pertains to the absence of a unanimous definition of what "design" entails for buildings. The second arises even if a consensus on the definition of "design" is reached among architects, urban planners, designers, and real estate developers; the initiative is still in its infancy concerning data collection on design features. Both hurdles are paramount to advancing the discourse on the value of design, for assessing value necessitates measuring the elements we aim to value. To propel this dialogue forward, exploring and employing the methodologies of those who have attempted to measure design in the past could be insightful.

In the design realm, there is a general reluctance to quantify qualitative aspects, and while design and empirical research intersect, the field remains unstructured. The empirical studies on design's influence on real estate value vary in defining "design," from unique architectural features to representations of historical styles. As previously discussed, studies with different measurements—award-winning, expert evaluation, construction, and operation costs—continuously confirm design's impacts on a building's economic values. However, the positive link between design excellence and real estate value reveals the complexity of evaluating the intricate interplay of qualitative design aspects in real estate's economic contexts and compels researchers and professionals to take a more fine-grained examination of design and its relationships with economic impacts.

Architecture and design graphics writer Francis Ching has distilled complex architectural design language into basic compositional features by examining how form and space are ordered in the built environment. Spatial concepts such as surface, solid and void, light, views, openings, and enclosures are among the rudimentary vocabulary of design that can be organized in the development of the design concept of a building.[23]

Likewise, in his dissection of design into 15 primary components of architecture fundamentals, such as walls, floor, ceiling, and corridor, for the 2014 Venice Architecture Biennale,

---

23   Francis D. K. Ching, *Architecture: Form, Space, & Order* (New York: John Wiley & Sons, 2014).

Rem Koolhaas presented design as a combination of tangible elements. Without question, these works are canons within the field of contemporary architecture that set the basic explanations for the organization of space.

In this book, we understand design as a set of physical, aesthetic, performative, and functional aspects integrated into a building's spatial organization. These features and elements, through their distinct arrangements and combinations, shape the overall aesthetics, experience, and utility of the building. To measure the value of design, we established a catalog of "measurable" design features. These features can be grouped into two categories: (1) building design elements, which shape a building's physical form and (2) building design performance, which describes a building's qualitative and performative features. For each feature, we also propose methods for measurement that would allow practitioners and researchers to begin to think about ways in which "design data" can be created. `Fig. 33, 45`

Fig. 33   **Building Design Elements Metrics**

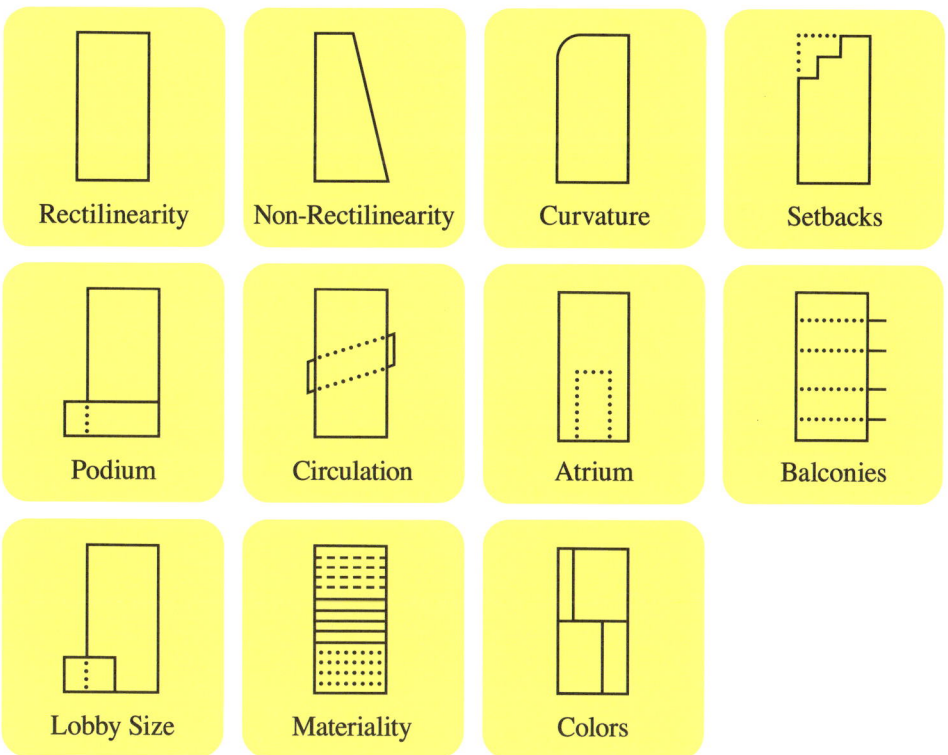

Rectilinearity   Non-Rectilinearity   Curvature   Setbacks

Podium   Circulation   Atrium   Balconies

Lobby Size   Materiality   Colors

Fig. 34 **The Seagram Building, Ludwig Mies van der Rohe, 1958, New York**

Rectilinearity

From an urban planning perspective, the gridded layout that has dominated city planning from antiquity to the contemporary era restricts the shape of the building footprint to a rectangular plot. Manhattan perhaps best illustrates the impact of such an imposed grid on its city form. Its extremity has contributed to the recognizable image of New York City. However, certain geographical features break up the rigidity of the gridiron plan by diagonally cutting through the grid, producing non-orthogonal plots of land that challenged architects to create creative designs to extend the intersection's unique shape into the sky. Fig. 34

Suggestion for Measurement

– Create a dummy variable to check whether a building's footprint is rectilinear in shape

Non-Rectilinearity and Non-Orthogonality

"There are 359 other angles. Why would you insist on this
single, solitary one?"
— Daniel Libeskind, 2005.[24]

Why are most buildings rectangular and orthogonal? Such a simple yet fundamental question is rarely asked. Planning and architecture scholar Philip Steadman attributes the wide popularity of the rectilinear form to "the superior flexibility of dimensioning allowed by rectangular packing."[25] From an architectural perspective, when rooms of varying sizes are stacked in plan, rectangular shapes minimize the chances for unusable spaces such as interstices, while reserving the maximum functionality and flexibility for interior layouts. For most buildings, an exception to the rule often occurs along the outer edge of the building which leads to more unique exterior façades that give off an impression of free-form design, while the rooms located closer to the core remain orthogonal and rectilinear in plan. Even Frank Gehry's renowned Guggenheim Museum in Bilbao follows such logic. Fig. 35

Suggestion for
Measurement

- Create a dummy variable to check whether a building's footprint features one or more non-90-degree angles
- Measure the degree of non-orthogonality by calculating the sum of the angles of the building footprint

24 Daniel Libeskind, *Breaking Ground: An Immigrant's Journey from Poland to Ground Zero* (New York: Penguin Press, 2005).
25 Philip Steadman, "Why Are Most Buildings Rectangular?," *Arq: Architectural Research Quarterly* 10, no. 2 (June 1, 2006): 119–30.

Fig. 35 The Flatiron Building, Daniel Burnham and Frederick P. Dinkelberg, 1902, New York

Lipstick Building, John Burgee and Philip Johnson, 1986, New York

Fig. 36

Curvature

While most buildings follow a rectilinear footprint, or in some cases a triangular footprint due to the urban layout, many incorporate curvilinearity in the overall massing, especially in prestigious works designed by famous architects that intend to create fluidic and organic forms that blend with surrounding landscapes and nature. According to Pythagoras, a building's physical characteristics directly impact its aesthetics, whose beauty can be measured mathematically by assessing the relationship, proportions, and ratios between its constituent architectural elements.[26] For instance, the golden ratio is scientifically proven to be aesthetically pleasing, inspiring many 20th century artists and architects to use it to proportion their works.

In many other adjacent design fields, from industrial design to interior design, curved forms have been considered as "more harmonious, relaxing, or pleasant—and more in consonance with nature than straight or broken lines."[27] Studies deriving from various disciplines collectively show that people prefer curved-contoured objects for their sense of pleasantness and harmony, suggesting curvature found in the built environment are design decisions with a tangible impact on peoples' preferences and choices in consumer and social contexts. In architecture, the emergence of organic architecture claims that free-flowing form is more compatible with the human body.[28] Its popularity is increasingly enabled by advancements in computer-aided design (CAD) and CNC construction techniques that fully unleash architects' ability to experiment with parametric modeling of curvilinear forms and to follow structural inspiration from biological precedents and complex natural forms. In contrast to rectilinearity purported by modernists, which lacks spatial sense in human terms, buildings that share formal qualities with natural forms are said to be subconsciously and psychologically perceived as more comfortable.[29] Fig. 36

Suggestion for Measurement	– Create a dummy variable to check whether a building's plan, section, or elevation feature curvilinearity – Measure the amount of curvilinearity based on the curve radii

26 Gardner Murphy, "Historical Introduction to Modern Psychology," *Journal of the American Medical Association* 141, no. 15 (December 10, 1949): 1107.
27 Gerardo Gómez-Puerto, Enric Munar, and Marcos Nadal, "Preference for Curvature: A Historical and Conceptual Framework," *Frontiers in Human Neuroscience* 9 (January 12, 2016).
28 David Pearson, *New Organic Architecture: The Breaking Wave*, (Berkeley: University of California Press, 2001).
29 Christopher Alexander, Sara Ishikawa, and Murray Silverstein, *A Pattern Language: Towns, Buildings, Construction* (New York: Oxford University Press, 1977). Nikos Angelos Salingaros, "A Scientific Basis for Creating Architectural Forms," *Journal of Architectural and Planning Research* 15, no. 4 (December 1, 1998): 283–94.

Setbacks

"The New York zoning laws protecting property rights, light,
and air have encouraged a new art by reason of the very
restrictions they contain."
—Ely Jacques Kahn, 1926.[30]

Building setbacks refer to the terrace-like, wedding-cake form in the upper portions of multilevel structures. The setbacks' initial appearance dates to ancient times when builders used them out of structural necessity to provide load-bearing functions in tall masonry buildings, such as the step pyramids of Mesopotamia and Ancient Egypt. In contemporary architecture, the "setback style" refers to a style of skyscrapers popularized in New York City during the mid-1920s in response to the Zoning Ordinance of 1916. Although the invention of the steel frame in the late 19th century removed the structural requirement for setbacks, new land use regulations mandated the use of setbacks in the upper portions of skyscrapers to ensure adequate daylight and air for all buildings in the densely built-up urban areas.[31] The principle of the zoning envelope was applied to all commercial high-rise buildings.

The numerous permutations of the formula provided by different widths of the street encouraged building owners to adopt the "wedding cake" setbacks to exploit the maximum volume allowed for the lot. As much as the predefined zoning envelope effectively predesigned the shape of the building, pioneering projects such as the Shelton Hotel and the Barclay-Vesey Telephone Building explored progressive design ideas by simplifying the number of setbacks and emphasizing the power of simple, sculptural, and pyramidal mass. The terraces also allowed for designs of outdoor spaces, which were gradually adopted by developers and building owners to maximize the usage of amenity space for commercial usage on the upper levels of the property. Even when the zoning ordinance was superseded by the 1961 Zoning Resolution, the setback style lived on as a stylistic design choice consciously made by architects and designers. Fig. 37

| Suggestion for Measurement: | – Create a dummy variable to check whether a building includes the feature of setbacks |
| | – Summation of total surface area lost to setbacks relative to surface area of the entire building |

30 Ely Jacques Kahn, "Our Skyscrapers Take Simple Forms," *New York Times*, May 2, 1926, 22.
31 Federico Mazzolani and Victor Gioncu, *Behaviour of Steel Structures in Seismic Areas* (Boca Raton: CRC Press, 1995).

Fig. 37   **120 Wall Street, Ely Jacques Kahn,
1930, New York**

The Essex, Handel Architects, 2019, New York

Fig. 38

Podium Extrusion

Traditionally, a classical skyscraper consists of a base, a shaft, and a crown. But a podium differs from a base in that it is a taller, occupiable horizontal volume less than six stories tall that incorporates commercial programs, such as conference halls or shops, at the street level. The introduction of the podium greatly enhanced skyscrapers' connection to the street and the pedestrian experience at street level. In the context of New York, the podium feature is an outcome of the updated Zoning Ordinance of 1961. The concept of floor area ratio (FAR) was introduced to limit the height of the building based on lot size, which allowed for variations to the wedding cake setback style from the previous era. However, the podium feature has become a common architectural feature used globally in tall building designs due to their flexibility in accommodating mixed-use functions. Fig. 38

Suggestion for Measurement

- Create a dummy variable to check whether a building has a podium
- Measure the relative size of the podium by calculating the ratio of volume of the podium to the volume of the rest of the building

Circulation

A building's internal circulation is an integration of multiple metrics: general experience, walkability, wayfinding, and safety. Apart from qualitative research studies involving human subjects, a number of studies also attempted to quantify the experiences of building form and spatial configurations through computational methods such as "space syntax"and the 2D isovist approach.[32] An enhanced version of the 2D isovist approach is the 3D isovist technique, which looks at perspectival drawings of interior spaces to evaluate the viability of wayfinding.[33] Fig. 39

Suggestion for Measurement

– Measure the feasibility of wayfinding in internal spaces using recently developed image recognition technology

32 John Peponis et al., "On the Description of Shape and Spatial Configuration inside Buildings: Convex Partitions and Their Local Properties," *Environment and Planning B: Planning and Design* 24, no. 5 (January 1, 1997): 761–81; Alasdair Turner, "Analysing the Visual Dynamics of Spatial Morphology," *Environment and Planning B: Planning and Design* 30, no. 5 (October 1, 2003): 657–76; Michael Batty, "Exploring Isovist Fields: Space and Shape in Architectural and Urban Morphology," *Environment and Planning B: Planning and Design* 28, no. 1 (February 1, 2001): 123–50.
33 Shashank Bhatia, Stephan K. Chalup, and Michael J. Ostwald, "Wayfinding: A Method for the Empirical Evaluation of Structural Saliency Using 3D Isovists," *Architectural Science Review* 56, no. 3 (August 1, 2013): 220–31.

The New School University Center, SOM, 2014, New York

Fig. 39

Fig. 40   **The Ford Foundation, Kevin Roche John Dinkeloo and Associates, 1967, New York**

Atrium

An "atrium" is defined as a large indoor open space that visually connects the building to its outside environment. It was first used in the Roman house for a large central space open to the sky that featured a grand entrance space, a focal courtyard, and a sheltered semi-public area. In the 20th century, revolutionary changes in architectural construction technology enabled longer spans without columns and better enclosure of interior spaces, which allowed for the wide adoption of large atrium spaces inside commercial buildings of modern architecture. Atriums can be found either on the ground level to connect the lobby of the building with the public realm outside or at higher levels of skyscrapers with large open spaces featuring generous skylights.[34] An atrium brings benefits on many fronts. A well-designed atrium enhances visual comfort, increases energy efficiency, and introduces rich daylight into the building. Prior studies show that commercial buildings featuring atriums charge noticeably higher rents, perhaps due to a combination of these reasons.[35] Fig. 40

Suggestion for Measurement

- Create a dummy variable to check whether a building has an atrium
- Measure the relative size of the atrium by calculating the ratio of volume of the atrium to the volume of the entire building

---

34 W.T. Hung and Wan Ki Chow, "A Review on Architectural Aspects of Atrium Buildings," *Architectural Science Review* 44, no. 3 (September 1, 2001): 285–95.
35 Hung and Chow, "A Review on Architectural Aspects of Atrium Buildings," 285–95.

Balconies

Balconies are platforms projected from the outside of buildings enclosed by balustrades or walls that provide access to the exterior from the interior of a building. A balcony provides an extension of the private space to the exterior suspended above the ground. Its origin traces back to circa 1308 in religious and military architecture that served to balance safety and engagement with the public realm below.[36] Its wide applicability makes it a popular feature used on buildings worldwide, with evolving styles that reflect changes in construction technology and building materials, structural design, and stylistic preferences. In contemporary architecture, balconies present unique design opportunities that become an integral part of signature façade design. For many real estate products, unique balcony designs are marketed as an added amenity that enhances a property's overall value, especially for residential properties in dense urban developments.[37] In Hong Kong, this price premium brought about by balconies for residential properties can be as high as 4%.[38] Given the high-density development and increasing vertical construction in Hong Kong, this result may not be surprising since there is diminishing connection to outdoor public spaces on the ground level, which gives higher values to private outdoor space. Another known benefit of balconies is noise screening and noise reduction, whose performance is dependent on the materiality of the front panel of the balcony.[39] Fig. 41

Suggestion for Measurement

– Create a dummy variable to check whether a building features balconies
– Measure the relative size of the balconies by calculating the ratio of the total surface area of balconies to the total surface area of the building

36 Rem Koolhaas et al., *Elements of Architecture: Corridor* (Venice: Marsilio, 2014).
37 Kwong Wing Chau, Siu Kei Wong, and Cy Yiu, "The Value of the Provision of a Balcony in Apartments in Hong Kong," *Social Science Research Network* (January 1, 2004).
38 Wadu Mesthrige Jayantha and Cheng Ka, "Do Buyers Value a Balcony as a Green Feature? An Empirical Analysis of the Hong Kong Residential Property Market," *Journal of Real Estate Practice and Education* 20, no. 1 (January 1, 2017): 27–49.
39 Shiu Keung Tang, "Noise Screening Effects of Balconies on a Building Façade," *Journal of the Acoustical Society of America* 118, no. 1 (July 1, 2005): 213–21.

Fig. 41   **100 United Nations Plaza, Der Scutt Architects, 1987, New York**

**World Trade Center, Minoru Yamasaki,
1973, New York**

Fig. 42

Lobby Size

The term "lobby" is derived from the Latin word "lobium," which means a covered walk or portico. It is a space found near the main entrance to a building that is used for access, circulation, space for administrative check-ins or a waiting area. It can be applied to a variety of building types, including residential towers, hotels, hospitals, and museums. Research from environmental psychology finds a significant relationship between appealing design features in hotel lobbies and customer behaviors.[40] However, little is known about how lobbies impact a property's economic value. To study a lobby's physical characteristics and its impact on property price, a possible approach is to examine the size or volume of the lobby. Lobbies with generous volumes can potentially provide room for unique design features as well as introducing ample daylight. However, a potential trade-off for developers is that large lobbies may take away rentable or usable areas across multiple floors. The balance between making room for a large lobby and maximizing usable square footage presents strategic decisions that would imply economic consequences for developers. Fig. 42

Suggestion for
Measurement

– Measure the relative size of the lobby by calculating the ratio of the volume of the lobby to the volume of the entire building

---

40 Dhiraj Thapa, "Hotel Lobby Design: Study of Parameters of Attraction" (Masters thesis, Texas Tech University, 2007).

Materiality

A building's materials—both exterior and interior—complement the impacts of formal and spatial design and greatly influence how the building is experienced and perceived. Much attention has been paid in the past to the ties between materiality and different political, social, and cultural transformations.[41] Over the last decade, a rising trend in materiality research has emerged to study the impact of innovative material application on building design and construction, and possibilities for new forms of interactivity. And even more recently, the rise of image recognition technology has led to explorations of studying building materiality through computational fractal analysis to assess the visual complexity of a building's exterior appearance.[42] However, this method mixes materiality with the building's overall appearance, which includes geometric information and ornamentation rather than studying it in isolation, thus the impacts of specific materials in social and economic terms remain underexplored. Fig. 43

Suggestion for Measurement

– Identify the primary materials used for a building's facades. Large-scale calculations on exterior materials could be performed using state-of-the-art computer vision techniques to analyze street-view images

41 Serena Love, "Architecture as Material Culture: Building Form and Materiality in the Pre-Pottery Neolithic of Anatolia and Levant," *Journal of Anthropological Archaeology* 32, no. 4 (December 1, 2013): 746–58.
42 Michael J. Ostwald and Özgür Ediz, "Measuring Form, Ornament and Materiality in Sinan's Kılıç Ali Paşa Mosque: An Analysis Using Fractal Dimensions," *Nexus Network Journal* 17, no. 1 (October 22, 2014): 5–22.

Fig. 43 **Building Textures, Generated by Midjourney**

William Beaver House, Tsao & McKown, 2008, New York

Fig. 44

Color

For humans, color is a sensory perception that influences both our psychological and physiological experience. The use of color in architecture does not only have aesthetic significance, but symbolic and emotional effects.[43] Architects are tasked with understanding the impacts of colors and designing for the appropriate visual stimulation for different programmatic functions, such as medical facilities, office buildings, and educational facilities whose varied functions may call for different visual treatment and psychosomatic effects. Fig. 44

Suggestion for Measurement

- Create a dummy variable to check whether a building's façade uses colors which depart from its actual materiality
- Identify building façades through computer vision algorithms and calculate RGB value range of primary building façade color

---

43 Donald N. Wilber, "The Role of Color in Architecture," *Journal of the American Society of Architectural Historians* 2, no. 1 (January 1, 1942): 17–22.

Fig. 45 **Building Design Performance Metrics**

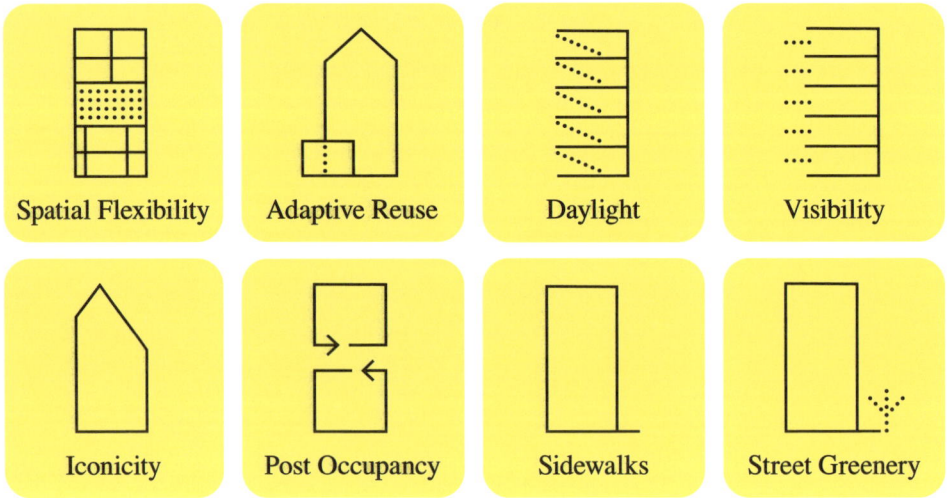

Spatial Flexibility	Adaptive Reuse	Daylight	Visibility
Iconicity	Post Occupancy	Sidewalks	Street Greenery

Spatial Flexibility

Spatial flexibility, which refers to the transformative quality of a space to assume more than a single function, has been an enduring inspiration for architects. It has been appreciated as a cost-effective response to the changing needs of the users and a crucial factor in increasing a building's longevity.[44] For office spaces, "flexible space" has been used to describe a number of office types used by occupants to increase portfolio flexibility, foster collaboration among different teams, and reduce occupancy costs. Among these office types, co-working spaces and incubators are the most prevalent and increasingly well-adopted solutions to enhance spatial flexibility. Fig. 46

Suggestion for Measurement

– Measure the total surface area of a building which has more than one programmatic function

---

44 E. Sarah Slaughter, "Design Strategies to Increase Building Flexibility," *Building Research and Information* 29, no. 3 (May 1, 2001): 208–17.

Fig. 46   **Open Plan Office Interior**

Tammany Hall, Thompson, Holmes & Converse and Charles B. Meyers, 1929, New York

Fig. 47

Adaptive Reuse Buildings

Relating to spatial flexibility is adaptive reuse. Since it is unlikely that a building will retain the same function throughout time, adaptive reuse becomes a necessary transformative process that allows for economical retrofitting of old structures for new uses. Originally developed as a way of protecting historic buildings from demolition, adaptive reuse has successfully transformed many industrial structures into office or residential buildings while allowing them to retain their historical value. This process supports a circular economy that presents solutions to both architectural obsolescence and the housing market shortage, helping to revitalize declining neighborhoods and bringing environmental advantages that benefit surrounding contexts beyond the building itself. Fig. 47

Suggestion for Measurement

– Measure how many prior uses that a building has had
– Create a dummy variable to check whether a building has had a prior use

Daylight

The immense benefit of natural light, or daylight, to human health and sustainable development has been well-studied and documented. For architects, the design for daylight has become an integrated lighting strategy used to achieve environmentally sustainable design, such as reduced energy losses and natural ventilation. For buildings with deep plans, design elements such as atriums are a main source of daylight that increases solar gain. The maturity of simulation tools has allowed for a more systematic way of measuring daylight at an urban level. Our recent research measures daylight in office spaces by calculating a building plan's spatial daylight autonomy (sDA), which is the percentage of the floor area that receives a sufficient amount of ambient natural light. `Fig. 48`

Suggestion for Measurement

—   Calculate spatial daylight autonomy (sDA) through urban scale daylight simulation. Qualitatively, sDA is a measure that describes the extent to which a space is naturally illuminated

Fig. 48   New York Times Building, Renzo Piano, 2007, New York

Fig. 49   **Washington St, Brooklyn, New York**

Visibility

Visibility refers to how far, how much, or both, a viewer may perceive visually from a set viewpoint in the urban environment. The isovist method used to assess circulation is also a common method used to study visibility.[45] Another method to calculate visibility is using the viewshed analysis approach, which records the number of grid cells in the line of sight to a viewpoint within a specified distance. Since 3D representations of the urban environment became increasingly prevalent, researchers also began measuring solid and void volumes in 3D virtual environments to analyze urban visibility. Fig. 49

Suggestion for Measurement

– Conduct viewshed analysis using high-resolution aerial images and airborne LiDAR data
– Conduct 3D isovist analysis or Spatial Openness in virtual urban model
– Conduct visibility analysis through trained image recognition algorithm and Google street-view GSV data

45 Clifford R.V. Tandy, "The Isovist Method of Landscape Survey," ed. A.C. Murray, Symposium: *Methods of Landscape Analysis*, ed. A.C. Murray (London: Landscape Research Group, 1967), 9-10; Michael Benedikt, "To Take Hold of Space: Isovists and Isovist Fields," *Environment and Planning B: Planning and Design* 6, no. 1 (January 1, 1979): 47-65.

Iconicity

Buildings gain iconicity when they gain significant recognition. They become landmarks or are assigned symbolic values by the public. Iconic buildings gain recognizability when their appearance stands out from their peer building stock, which often means they adopt customized and non-standard materials or construction techniques. Although this would typically lead to higher development and construction costs, iconic architecture is associated with positive economic impact through increased tourists spending as well as enhanced social capital and consumer optimism through image effects and increased civic pride.[46] As multiple scholars point out, iconic architectural projects designed by awarded architects generate a real estate value premium for both residential and commercial properties, and may even drive prices up for nearby building valuations.[47] Fig. 50

Suggestion for Measurement

- Create a dummy variable to check whether a building has received an award or has been designed by an awarded architect
- Crowdsource public opinions from online platforms by scrapping and analyzing publicly available comments (e.g., posts, tweets, messages) or through surveys
- Document and count the number of mentions by established media news outlet and design magazines

46   Gabriel Ahlfeldt and Alexandra Mastro, "Valuing Iconic Design: Frank Lloyd Wright Architecture in Oak Park," Housing Studies 27, 8 (2012): 1079-1099.
47   Minkoo Kang, "Dancing with the Stars: The Value of Design in Real Estate Development," Masters thesis, Massachusetts Institute of Technology, 2019); Hough and Kratz, "Can 'Good' Architecture Meet the Market Test," 40-54; Vandell and Lane, "The Economics of Architecture and Urban Design: Some Preliminary Findings," 235-60.

Empire State Building, Shreve, Lamb & Harmon, 1931, New York

Fig. 50

Fig. 51 731 Lexington Avenue (Bloomberg Tower), César Pelli & Associates, 2004, New York

Post Occupancy Analysis

How does a building perform once it is constructed? How does it affect the productivity and performance of the users inside? Three primary Workplace Performance Benchmarks have been developed by Gensler, Steelcase, and Leesman to measure employee engagement and workplace satisfaction, which slightly differ in their approaches of measuring workplace performance and experience. The Workplace Performance Index (WPI) by Gensler emerged as part of a 10-year Workplace Survey research effort. The WPI online survey tool is a proprietary tool developed by the architecture firm which sampled over 4,000 office workers in 11 industries in the United States. The survey provides insights on "how and where work is happening today, how effectively the workplace supports that work, and how the workplace environment impacts overall employee experience."[48] This approach finds high value in spaces that foster innovation and collaboration. On the other hand, the Employee Engagement and Global Workplace Study developed by Steelcase, a U.S.-based global leader in office furniture, focused on measuring employee engagement and workplace satisfaction. The survey reached 12,480 participants in 17 countries. Key questions posed include "Can the office be used as a strategic lever to impact engagement?" and "What kinds of changes to the work environment will make the biggest impact?" Lastly, the Leesman Index (Lmi) used survey data gathered from corporate workplaces in 63 countries to measure workplace effectiveness, which focuses on workplace activities in addition to the physical features and facilities and services which support these activities. This approach provides insights on the correlation between the performance of office environments based on the dimensions of design, activity, physical features and service features, and employee collaboration, productivity, pride, and effectiveness. All three approaches reach the consensus that firms are more successful when the design of their workplace and office environment promote collaboration among employees and choice over how and where employees work. Fig. 51

Suggestion for Measurement	–	Survey of employee engagement and workplace satisfaction to assess individual's pre- and post-occupancy experiences

---

48   Gensler Research Institute, "Gensler Experience Index," *Gensler*, December 1, 2017, accessed December 30, 2022, https://www.gensler.com/doc/gensler-experience-index-2017.

Sidewalks

In the built environment, the street is a political site of both public engagement and contestation, and space for building trust and inclusion, which according to Jane Jacobs, "...must not only defend the city against predatory strangers, they must also protect the many, many peaceable and well-meaning strangers who use them, ensuring their safety too as they pass through."[49] In particular, sidewalks are gaining traction in the present discussion of building healthy and walkable cities as a fundamental element of transportation infrastructure next to more popular mobility topics such as innovations in public transit.[50] Jacobs points to the trust that overtime gets built from "many, many little sidewalk contacts," which together with sidewalk safety, is able to "thwart segregation and racial discrimination."[51] More recent research from the AARP further enumerates the benefits associated with well-maintained sidewalks and higher walkability, including crime reduction through increased pedestrian activity, encouragement of physical activity which brings benefits to health, support for local businesses in economic centers, and higher housing prices reflecting the growing preference for walkable communities.[52] Attention to measuring sidewalks was raised within the design and planning community during the COVID-19 pandemic. In 2020, New York-based design technologist Meli Harvey has developed an interactive map that shows the widths of all the sidewalks in New York City to evaluate which areas of the city provide paths wide enough for safe social distancing practice.[53] The resulting visualization unveils a highly uneven landscape of sidewalks across New York's five boroughs. Although the city of New York is hailed to be one of the most walkable cities in the world, its sidewalks are generally narrow in widths, especially in the oldest parts of Lower Manhattan. During the pandemic, sidewalks with larger widths were able to accommodate outdoor dining spaces to support local restaurant businesses, which became a crucial contribution to the economic survival of the restaurant industry. The design of sidewalks in post-pandemic urban design will become especially important to building healthier, more equitable, and more resilient cities. Fig. 52

Suggestion for Measurement	–	Calculate the width of sidewalks in front of each building using existing Open Street Map (OSM) data or data from aerial photographs

49   Jane Jacobs, *The Death and Life of Great American Cities* (New York: Random House, 1961), 36.
50   Nicholas Coppola and Wesley E. Marshall, "An Evaluation of Sidewalk Availability and Width: Analyzing Municipal Policy and Equity Disparities," *International Conference on Transportation and Development 2020*, August 31, 2020.
51   Jacobs, *The Death and Life of Great American Cities*."
52   AARP Livable Communities, "AARP Livability Fact Sheet - Sidewalks," AARP, 2013, accessed December 30, 2022.
53   Meli Harvey and NYC Open Data, eds., "Sidewalk Widths NYC," NYC Open Data, 2020, accessed December 30, 2023.

Fig. 52 **Broadway Sidewalk, New York**

West End Avenue North of 70th St, New York

Fig. 53

Street-Level Greenery

It has been widely researched that urban greenery provides immense benefits for city dwellers and the environment, including but not limited to decreased carbon footprint, increased oxygen generation, enhanced thermal comfort, increased walkability, greater health outcomes, and overall improved neighborhood satisfaction. In the realm of residential and commercial asset valuation research, plenty of evidence also points to the positive value impact street-level greenery casts on property values. Given its status as a widely studied subject across so many disciplines, urban greenery continues to see the development of novel ways of measuring and assessing its attributes both quantitatively and qualitatively. In recent times, advancements in image recognition technologies and street view imagery have led to high-resolution quantitative measurement and assessment of the Green View Index, which measures the percentage of green pixels in any taken photo. The availability of street-view imagery, such as those provided by Google Maps, also enables computation to take place on a massive scale, all while remaining efficient and cost-effective. Fig. 53

Suggestion for Measurement

– Calculate the percentage of greenery from the street level perspective using Google Street View imagery

4.3 The Ivory Tower: External Architectural Formal Features

Considering the elemental building design features we identified in the previous section, there are extensive design features that can be measured inside and outside of a building. The caveat is that internal design metrics require comprehensive floor plans and section details of each building, which are currently scattered across individual architecture firms, inconsistently collected by the planning authority, and unavailable to collect for many properties. External architectural differentiations, on the other hand, can be systematically classified and analyzed by leveraging reality-capturing technologies such as aerial surveys.

Classifying Building Exteriors

In this research, we made use of the "NYC 3D Model by Community District," available at the level of detail (LOD) one to two scale and released by the New York City Department of Information Technology and Telecommunications (DOITT), to study the external architectural nuances of the city.[54] Based on DOITT's aerial survey captured in 2014, the model stands as a comprehensive public resource, capturing every building in New York City present in 2014, meticulously illustrating roof structures and even offering intricate details for some of the city's most iconic structures.[55] We selected four external architectural elements for analysis: diagonality, setbacks, podium extrusion, and curvature. All of these can be identified through assessing the exterior base geometry of a building. Fig. 54

According to our four external architectural features, we manually classified and tagged each of the buildings in Manhattan. Using the 3D model of New York, we assigned a dummy variable of "one" to each building if it has a design feature and "zero" otherwise. A concentration of buildings with podium extrusions and setbacks is found in Midtown and Downtown Manhattan, whereas buildings that are situated on diagonal intersections or that feature curvature in their geometry are distributed throughout the city. Fig. 55

Next, we matched the building geometry of our selected sample with their geolocational attributes. We utilized New

---

54 Rong et al., "The Value of Design in Real Estate Asset Pricing," 178.
55 NYC Department of City Planning, "NYC 3D Model Download," NYC Planning, 2014, accessed December 30, 2021.

Fig. 54 **External Design Features**

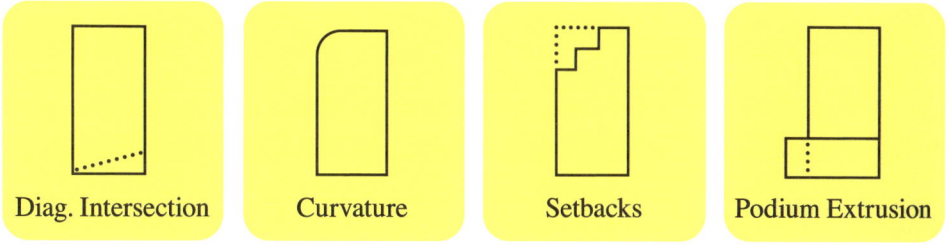

| Diag. Intersection | Curvature | Setbacks | Podium Extrusion |

Fig. 55 **Geographic Variation of External Architectural Design Features**

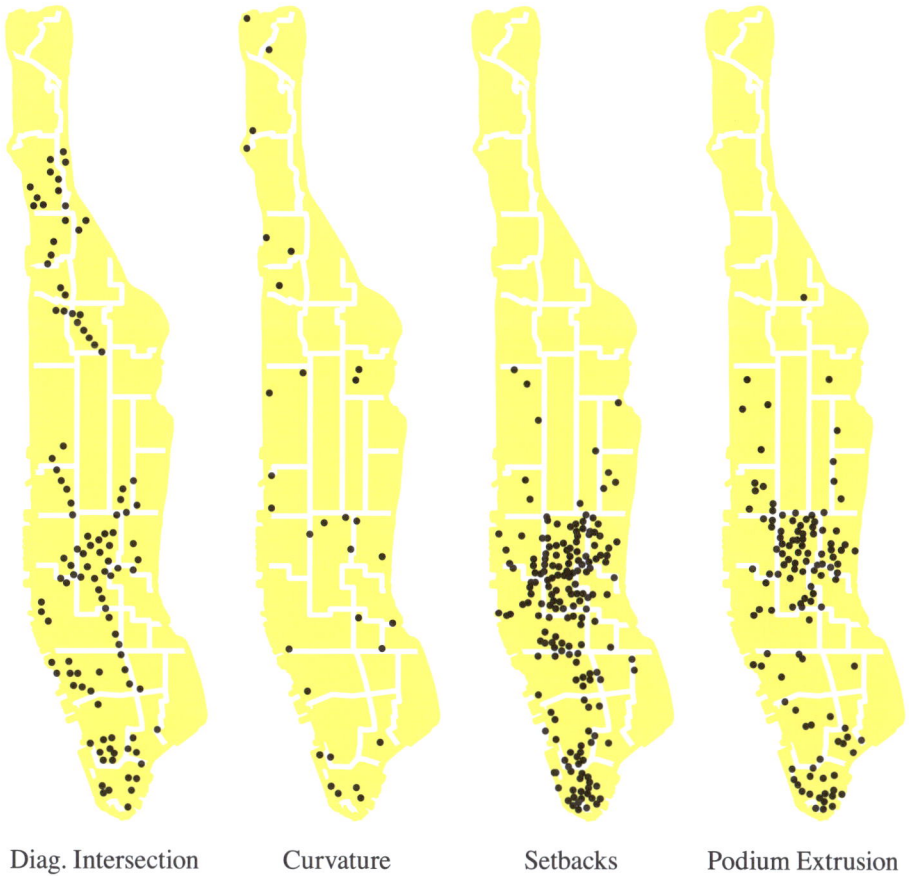

Diag. Intersection   Curvature   Setbacks   Podium Extrusion

Note: Geographic variation of external architectural design features. Buildings with diagonal intersection, curvature, setbacks, and podium extrusions highlighted on a map of Manhattan, New York.

York City's geocoding tool, GeoBat, as well as the Geosupport Desktop Edition provided by the NYC Department of City Planning, which allowed us to identify unique Building Identification Numbers (BIN). We subsequently paired the BINs from the 3D models with our building dataset, assigning a variable to each design metric. We then integrated this newly formulated design data with the commercial building transaction data from RCA (2000 - 2017), building features, and rental contract data from Compstak (2003 - 2016), as well as the dataset on the statuses of awarded designs described in the previous research. This process resulted in a comprehensive list of hedonic variables for our transaction and rental pricing models, which we tested in New York City.

After removing observations with missing data for this particular research, we were left with 3,037 observations, down from the initial 3,318 observations. Of the 3,037 observations in our dataset, 198 were situated on diagonal roads or intersections, 26 featured a curvature, 740 possessed setbacks, and 194 had podium extrusions. It's noteworthy that several observations exhibited more than one design feature: 51 observations combined setbacks with diagonal intersections; 26 had both setbacks and podium extrusions; 8 featured curvature and podium extrusions; 13 at diagonal intersections also had podium extrusions; 2 observations showcased both curvature and setbacks; 1 observation integrated curvature, setbacks, and a podium extrusion; and 2 observations on diagonal intersections also possessed setbacks and podium extrusions. To ensure that our regression analysis accurately captured the effect of each design metric on price rather than their combined effects, we further categorized our samples to focus on buildings with singular design features. This allowed for a more precise statistical evaluation of the influence of each design feature on the transaction price. Consequently, 128 observations were exclusively located on diagonal roads, 14 solely featured a curvature, 618 had only setbacks, and 135 possessed just podium extrusions. Fig. 56

Characteristics of Buildings with Exterior Design Features

An analysis of our building sample reveals interesting insights into their external design features. Notably, buildings designed by award-winning architects or firms are scarce throughout the entire sample. However, there's a significant correlation of about 49% with buildings that feature curvature. On average, buildings with design features tend to be taller than those without—referred to as the "control buildings"—the only exception being buildings with curvature.

Fig. 56

Incidence of External Architectural Design Features

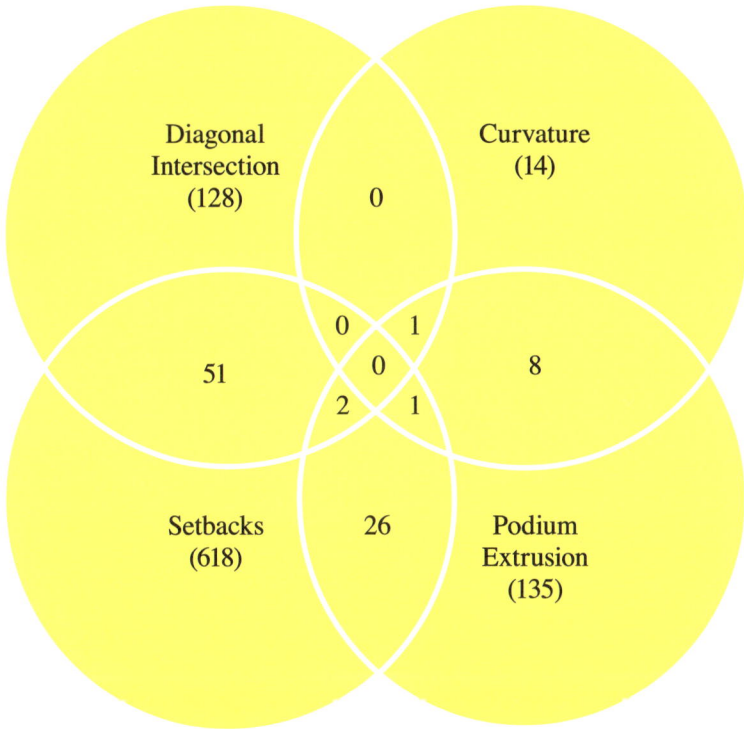

Diagonal Intersection (128)

Curvature (14)

0

51

0   1

0

2   1

8

Setbacks (618)

26

Podium Extrusion (135)

Curvature + Setbacks = 2
Diagonal   + Podium   = 13

Most buildings with design features fall into Class A or B, mirroring the control buildings. The exceptions here are buildings with curvature and podiums, which predominantly belong to Class A. Given Manhattan's highly connected urban environment, all building samples exhibit comparable walk scores. In terms of age, buildings with setbacks and podiums average 69.9 years and 41.8 years, respectively—both younger than the control sample's average of 82.7 years. Intriguingly, nearly 20% of buildings with setbacks were constructed in the last 50 years, long after the 1916 Zoning Ordinance gave way to the 1961 Zoning Resolution. New constructions built after 2000 still incorporate podiums. This suggests that architects continue to favor setbacks and podiums as stylistic choices. Regarding ownership, our data indicates that the majority of buyers (41%) are real estate private companies, a trend consistent across both design feature buildings and control samples. Specifically, 37.5% of buyers of buildings at diagonal intersections are private companies. While only 28.5% of buyers of buildings with curvature are private companies, this still represents the most significant buyer segment.

Similarly, private companies emerge as the predominant sellers in both building categories. They account for 27.5% of design-feature buildings and 30.9% of control buildings. However, their representation is lower when selling buildings with specific design features: 16.4% for diagonal intersections, 14.3% for curvature, 23.8% for setbacks, and 17% for podium extrusions.

In the area of lending, our data presents a varied picture. Buildings with curvature attract a mix of lenders spanning four categories: Commercial Mortgage-Backed Security (CMBS), international banks, national banks, and regional and local banks, closely mirroring the lender mix for control buildings. Yet, buildings with other design features show a pronounced leaning toward CMBS lenders, with a notably reduced presence of regional and local banks.

The Value of External Architectural Features

Through the hedonic regression analysis, we assessed the statistical influence of the four exterior design features on the transaction price and rental income of commercial buildings in Manhattan. After adjusting for various factors, including building attributes, neighborhood characteristics, contract details, and awarded design features, the model explained 88% of the variation in transaction price and 62% of the variance in rental income. Two distinct features, diagonality and podium extrusion, stood out for their positive impact on the transaction price. They were associated with an estimated premium of 12.4% and 9.7% respectively for transaction price, and 2% and 3.5% respectively for rental income, compared to buildings without these design elements. Although the hedonic regression model cannot give us a qualitative analysis of the results, what can be speculated from such results is that the public benefits enhanced amenities via new extensions at the street level provided by these two design features might offer a rationale for their marked positive influence on transaction values. The unique six-way "bowtie" design of diagonal street intersections provides expansive public open spaces. These spaces likely enhance the overall urban vitality of their neighborhoods, leading to tangible and measurable financial returns. The podium intervention further amplifies this effect by increasing public access to street-level commercial activities. Such observations align well with the "street vitality" concepts prevalent in urban research and design domains. Unlike roads, which primarily facilitate traffic, urban streets play a pivotal role in fostering social interactions, serving as bustling hubs for entertainment, communication, and engagement. Scholars like Mehta argue that vibrant streets are marked by consistent social activities, drawing large crowds and fostering participation. This, in turn, can be an indicator of street vitality.[56] Viewing it from this angle, buildings are not merely stand-alone structures restricted to their plot boundaries. Instead, they play a vital role in enhancing and diversifying the social functions that bring life to our streets. Fig. 57-58

Conversely, buildings with curvature did not show any significant statistical or economic distinction from either a transactional or rental price standpoint. This outcome could be closely related to the small sample size, the strong association of curvature with other design features, or the pronounced correlation of curvature with recognized design awards. In contrast, setbacks returned a statistically significant and negative result, causing a 10% deduction in transaction price and a 2.4% decrease in rents. Given that rents for these buildings are consistently negative throughout the study period, this may be due to the fact that the terrace-like form for the upper portion of tall buildings reduces saleable and rentable building footprints significantly and further adds difficulty to floor plan layouts. Unlike buildings with podiums, buildings with setbacks lose square footage without providing enough mixed-use commercial amenities to balance the loss in transaction or rental price.

While the study's findings shed light on the direct economic implications of certain exterior design features, it's essential to contextualize these results within the broader architectural discourse. Established research underscores the pivotal role of tectonic structures in determining a building's aesthetic appeal.[57] Elements such as biophilia and the deliberate disruption of monolithic rectangular forms, amplify a building's visceral appeal. This inherent aesthetic appeal may, in turn, influence its economic value, bridging the empirical data with overarching architectural principles. As previously noted, however, the confluence of design and finance as a

56 Vikas Mehta, "Lively Streets," *Journal of Planning Education and Research* 27, no. 2 (December 1, 2007): 165–87.
57 Nikos A. Salingaros, "The Biophilic Healing Index Predicts Effects of the Built Environment on Our Wellbeing," *Journal of Biourbanism* 8, no. 1 (2019): 13–34.

Fig. 57

Impact of External Design Features on Transaction Prices

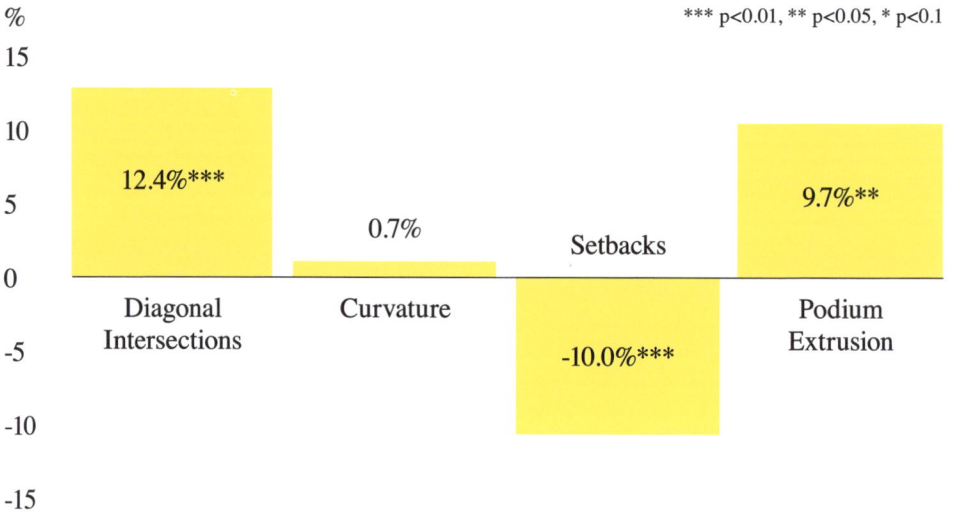

%

15

10

5

0

-5

-10

-15

12.4%***

0.7%

Setbacks

9.7%**

Diagonal
Intersections

Curvature

-10.0%***

Podium
Extrusion

Note: Hedonic regression results - transaction prices of buildings with architectural design features with dependent variable: logarithm of transaction price. External design features can either positively or negatively impact transaction and rent prices.

Fig. 58

Impact of External Design Features on Rents

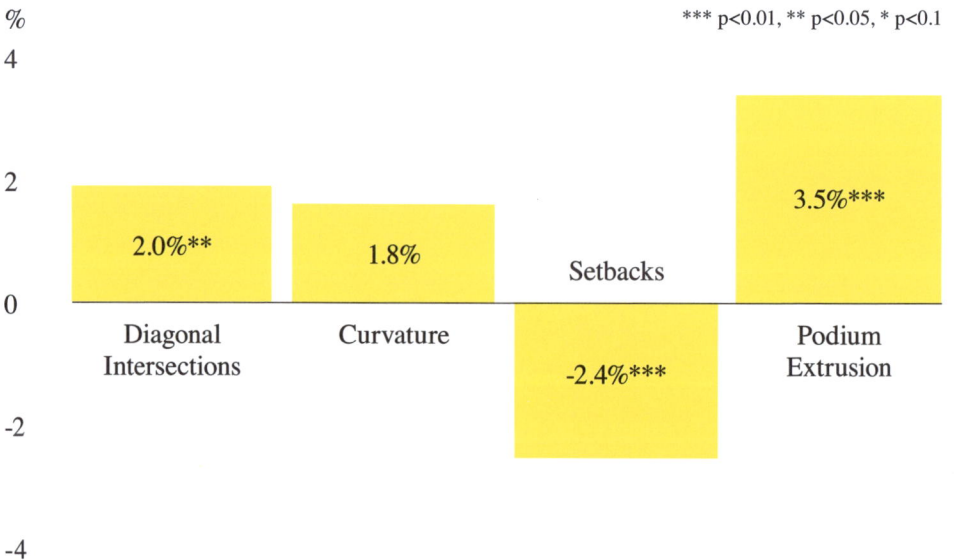

%

4

2

0

-2

-4

2.0%**

1.8%

Setbacks

3.5%***

Diagonal
Intersections

Curvature

-2.4%***

Podium
Extrusion

Note: Hedonic regression results - rental prices of buildings with architectural design features with dependent variable: logarithm of rental price

research arena is still in its infancy. There's a pressing need for more in-depth studies to address data paucity, enhance 3D modeling accuracy, and standardize methods for collecting architectural data. The evolution of architectural design into a fresh frontier of data science is gaining momentum, especially as big data and quantitative strategies gain traction and computational methods become ubiquitous in the domain. Embracing innovative technologies and methodologies will be increasingly crucial. This includes exploring algorithmic quantification of 3D complexities and leveraging computer vision to detect the presence of greenery or identify building materials—some of which subsequent sections begin to delve deeper into.[58]

4.4 Daylight and Views

In tall buildings, features like increased access to daylight and views, directly correlate to financial performance. Consider, for example, exposure to natural daylight in the workplace. It does not merely provide illumination; it contributes notably to the physiological and psychological well-being of those working.[59] In a similar vein, having an outdoor view from one's workspace extends beyond its aesthetic appeal. Evidence suggests that access to views can alleviate stress, enhance focus, and stimulate creativity, thereby increasing overall productivity. Furthermore, these factors have implications that resonate on both social and economic dimensions. A workforce that experiences better health and satisfaction due to access to daylight and views will likely have lower instances of medical leave, which consequently leads to cost savings for the organization.

There has been a significant distinction in justifying why buildings need daylight or views. In fact, these dynamic outcomes from architectural practice are decreasingly seen as

58 Gordon R. Little et al., "Measuring geometric complexity of 3d models for feature recognition," *International Journal of Shape Modeling* 03, no. 03n04 (September 1, 1997): 141–54.

59 Yousef Al Horr et al., "Occupant Productivity and Office Indoor Environment Quality: A Review of the Literature," *Building and Environment* 105 (August 1, 2016): 369–89; Myriam Aries, Jennifer A. Veitch, and Guy R. Newsham, "Windows, View, and Office Characteristics Predict Physical and Psychological Discomfort," *Journal of Environmental Psychology* 30, no. 4 (December 1, 2010): 533–41; Monika Joanna Frontczak, and Paweł Wargocki, "Literature Survey on How Different Factors Influence Human Comfort in Indoor Environments," *Building and Environment* 46, no. 4 (April 1, 2011): 922–37; Anca D. Galasiu and Jennifer A. Veitch, "Occupant Preferences and Satisfaction with the Luminous Environment and Control Systems in Daylit Offices: A Literature Review," *Energy and Buildings* 38, no. 7 (July 1, 2006): 728–42.

an amenity, but as part of the human experience, as well as a right and necessity. The importance of access to daylight is well-documented and today many cities across the globe are shaped by zoning policies aimed specifically at protecting both private and public rights to light.[60] In the United Kingdom, the doctrine of ancient lights—dating back to 1663 and still in effect today—protects access to light through an existing window.[61] In the United States, litigation and regulation in a number of states protect building occupants' right to light. Zoning ordinances are commonly employed to regulate access to light and air for solar energy systems, shifting the responsibility from individuals to the public sector, though they lack permanence. States like New Mexico have enacted statutes declaring solar energy use as a property right; as of 1980, following Colorado's 1975 Solar Easement Law, 15 states passed laws to support express easements to ensure unobstructed solar access, especially effective in moderate-density residential areas.[62] Most notably, in New York City, the zoning regulations of 1916 and 1961 aimed to minimize shading and ensure that daylight reaches pedestrians on the street by stipulating rules about the exterior massing of buildings, which, as noted previously, has had a tremendous impact on their financial performance.[63]

When we look at the historical development of views as a metric, there is less to substantively dissect from a policy perspective. Principally, views are not protected through regulation-like daylight. In architectural studies, determining views is typically accomplished using either geometric simulations or computer vision techniques. Much of the former approach originates from research in the landscape and environmental planning domains. Surveyor and landscape architect Clifford Tandy introduced the concept of an isovist—also known as a viewshed or visibility polygon—which is a 2D representation of the visible area from a particular viewpoint.[64] This geometric methodology allows the identification of everything within

60 Howard Davis, "The Future of Ancient Lights," *Journal of Architectural and Planning Research* 6, no. 2 (1988): 132–53.
61 Robert Malcolm Kerr, *On Ancient Lights and the Evidence of Surveyors Thereon: With Tables for the Measurement of Obstructions* (Oxford: John Murray, 1865); Davis, "The Future of Ancient Lights," 132-53.
62 Sophia Douglass Pfeiffer, "Ancient Lights: Legal Protection Of Access to Solar Energy," *American Bar Association Journal* 68, no. 3 (1982): 288–91.
63 Carol Willis, *Form Follows Finance: Skyscrapers and Skylines in New York and Chicago* (New York: Princeton Architectural Press, 1995).
64 Tandy, "The Isovist Method of Landscape Survey," 9-10.

a line-of-sight from any given location, and it was later incorporated in the studies of space syntax.[65]

Technology applications, such as the Ladybug Grasshopper plug-in, utilize ray-tracing-based isovist analysis.[66] Similarly, recent research has proposed that this type of analysis could be employed to investigate lines-of-sight for high-rises in New York, in an effort to efficiently address client requests for maximized view quality.[67] Alternatively, image-based view analysis has become increasingly prevalent in evaluating constructed environments.[68] In essence, methods of view analysis, including both geometric and image-based, persist in evolving in the spheres of professional application and academic research.[69]

Developing Metrics

To develop daylight and view metrics, we focused on luminance and view potential rather than on the quality of daylight or views. In this way, we did not impose a normative design judgment on the spaces but focused on the existence of daylight or views and measured the variation of the existence of daylight or view potential from spaces. We thereby continued our positivist application in the measurement of design so that it can be translated into events and further events that can be correlated with financial outcomes.

Daylight:
Measuring
Luminance

To predict how much daylight a space will get—or daylight autonomy—we first measured the total amount of direct and scattered light landing on a specific surface at a certain moment. This measurement process happened for every part of the floor across all 8,760 hours of the year. The research used special climate-based programs to model daylight—Radiance, DAYSIM, and DIVA.[70] These programs consider both the position of the sun and the sky conditions at the

65   Bill Hillier, *Space Is the Machine: A Configurational Theory of Architecture* (Cambridge: Cambridge University Press, 1996).
66   Mostapha Sadeghipour Roudsari, Michelle Pak, and Anthony Viola, "Ladybug: A Parametric Environmental Plugin for Grasshopper to Help Designers Create an Environmentally-conscious Design," *Building Simulation Conference Proceedings*, August 28, 2013.
67   Harish Doraiswamy et al., "Topology-Based Catalogue Exploration Framework for Identifying View-enhanced Tower Designs," *ACM Transactions on Graphics* 34, no. 6 (November 2, 2015): 1–13.
68   Wenting Li and Holly Samuelson, "A New Method for Visualizing and Evaluating Views in Architectural Design," *Developments in the Built Environment* 1 (February 1, 2020): 100005.
69   Doraiswamy et al., "Topology-Based Catalogue Exploration Framework for Identifying View-Enhanced Tower Designs," 1-13; Studio Gang, "Aqua Tower," 2017, accessed December 15, 2022, https://vimeo.com/175563995.
70   Greg Ward, "Radiance," Software, 2016, https://www.radiance-online.org/about; Christoph Reinhart, "DAYSIM," Software, 2017, https://daysim.software.informer.com/; Solemma, "DIVA-for-Rhino," Software, 2017, https://www.solemma.com/diva.

specific place.[71] With this information, we calculated a floor's spatial daylight autonomy (sDA), which is a way of showing what percentage of the floor area gets enough natural light. In simple terms, sDA tells us how well a space is lit naturally. The Illuminating Engineering Society of North America (IESNA) defines "enough" light as 300 lux for 50% of all the hours a space is used (sDA300/50%).[72] We took the hours of use to be regular office hours from 8 a.m. to 6 p.m., Monday to Friday. Both the LEED and WELL building certification systems use this sDA300/50% threshold, which is also widely regarded as a best practice in the industry.[73] Fig. 59

Views: Measuring View Potential[74]

Measuring the hedonic response of individuals is a complex and interesting problem. Economists would suggest that such a measure is outlined in what one is willing to pay. However, a pecuniary abstraction to decipher what one sees may perhaps even further mediate quality. Our objective in developing a view metric was to develop one that highlights the potential for a view to exist. Further, our focus was on documenting what the view is composed of, categorizing the view into its components, and understanding view variation.

We designed two interconnected metrics to model views: Minimum View Potential (MVP) and Spatial View Access (sVA). These metrics helped us understand view access from both a single viewpoint and throughout an entire space.

Minimum View Potential (MVP) calculates the proportion of the total rays originating from a specific point that intersect with chosen outdoor view elements, giving us a percentage (0–100%). It allows us to determine the amount of the outside view relative to a viewer's full field-of-view at a specific location. Spatial View Access (sVA), on the other hand, identifies the fraction of the total

71 John Mardaljevic, "Examples of Climate-Based Daylight Modelling," *CIBSE National Conference*, January 1, 2006, 1–11.
72 Illuminating Engineering Society of North America, "Approved Method: IES Spatial Daylight Autonomy (sDA) and Annual Sunlight Exposure (ASE)," *Illuminating Engineering Society*, January 1, 2012, accessed January 10, 2022.
73 U.S. Green Building Council, *LEED Reference Guide for Building Design and Construction*, V4, 2013.
74 To build up the metrics of daylight and potential views mentioned previously, we pulled together property and building data for the sample from multiple sources: A city-wide 3D geometric model from New York City's Department of Information Technology and Telecommunications; property information from the city's Department of Planning; rental contract data from CompStak; sustainable building certifications from Green Building Information Gateway; telecommunications data from Geotel; green space and hydrography data from the New York City OpenData online portal (run by the NYC Department of Information Technology and Telecommunications); and landmark sites from the publication Curbed New York. From all the data, we gathered information on 6,267 office spaces within buildings with lease contracts signed between 2010 and 2016. The spaces are located on 5,154 floors throughout Manhattan.

Fig. 59 **Floor-by-floor Daylight Simulation Workflow**

Collect data for 5,154 floors across 905 Manhattan buildings.

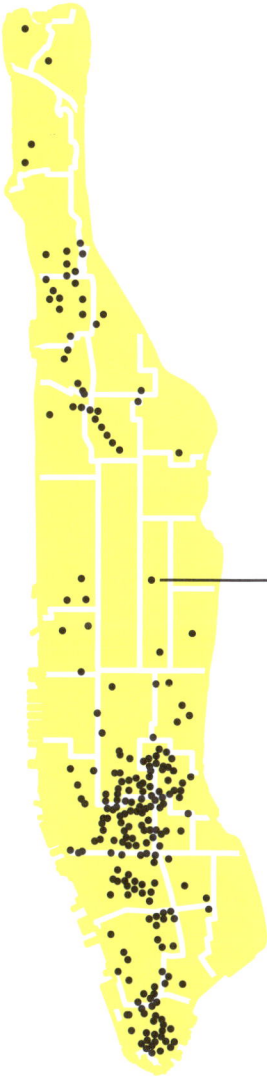

Create a Manhattan-block-size 3D model of 800ft² (244m by 244m), including adjacent buildings, for daylight simulations. Simulate hourly illuminance and calculate floor-wide Spatial Daylight Autonomy (sDA) for each floor plate of itnerest.

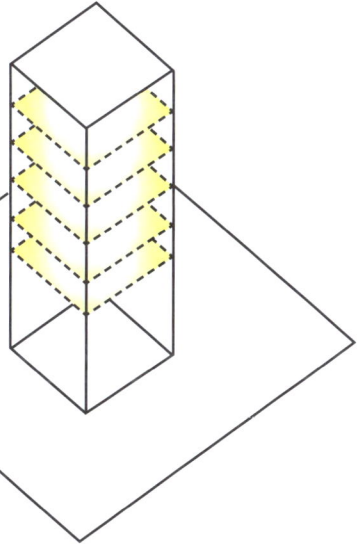

0%   100%

Percentage of hours that receive enough daylight to count toward the Spatial Dayligt Autonomy (sDA) metric.

Note: Each selected building is then segmented along with its immediate environment to construct a Radiance model, which is essential for conducting daylight evaluations. The analysis involves computing the light distribution across the floor space for every hour throughout the year. Subsequently, these light exposure levels are used to determine the spatial daylight autonomy, a yearly measure ranging from 0 to 100%, reflecting the extent to which areas of the floor receive sufficient natural light during hours of occupancy.

area of the floor-wide analysis grid that meets a minimum MVP value (at least 3%). It measures the sufficiency of MVP viewing potential throughout a space by showing the percentage of the analysis area with a minimum viewing potential.

The MVP metric is based on the understanding that a view is not about a few selected objects in the surrounding landscape but rather the entire composition within one's frame of view. The aim here is not to judge the aesthetic value of a view. Instead, it assesses the potential to have any view at all, assuming the quality of views to be a matter of personal preference that varies widely from person to person.

We calculated sVA based on the distribution of view potential, meaning we considered the potential views in an entire space, not just from every single point within the space. This approach was especially relevant for open-floor plans. It accounted for the fact that even if an occupant cannot see the view from every spot, they can see that a part of the floor has views of the outdoors. Our method involved tracing rays from each viewpoint within a 120-degree field of vision. Some of these rays intersected with the indoor space, while others passed through the window opening to the outside. `Fig. 60-61`

When measuring the views, all objects in our urban model that are accessed by the view were labeled with a view type (landmark, green space, neighboring buildings, water and greater metropolis, ground, and sky), following a similar approach to Kevin Lynch's taxonomy of visualized urban form.[75] We recorded the intersecting object and its distance for each ray cast. Although rays reaching the sky were documented in the simulation output, they were not included in the view metric to separate views from daylight access. We assumed that rays reaching the sky represent direct access to daylight. `Fig. 62`

Combined, these metrics help us estimate the total potential views in a space. We established the minimum MVP threshold, which is the smallest proportion of total rays cast from one origin point that intersect with selected outdoor view elements, contributing to the floor-wide sVA value. This MVP threshold was specifically designed to be used alongside daylight analysis, employing standard computational daylight modeling techniques.[76]

---

75 Kevin Lynch, *The Image of the City* (Cambridge: MIT Press, 1960).
76 According to the Illuminating Engineering Society, the MVP threshold, set at 3%, is specifically created to complement daylight analysis. This threshold shares similarities with the minimum daylight threshold set by the spatial daylight autonomy metric, which requires a certain light level—300 lux, for example—to be met for at least half the hours a space is occupied.

Fig. 60   Rays Projection From an Individual Viewpoint

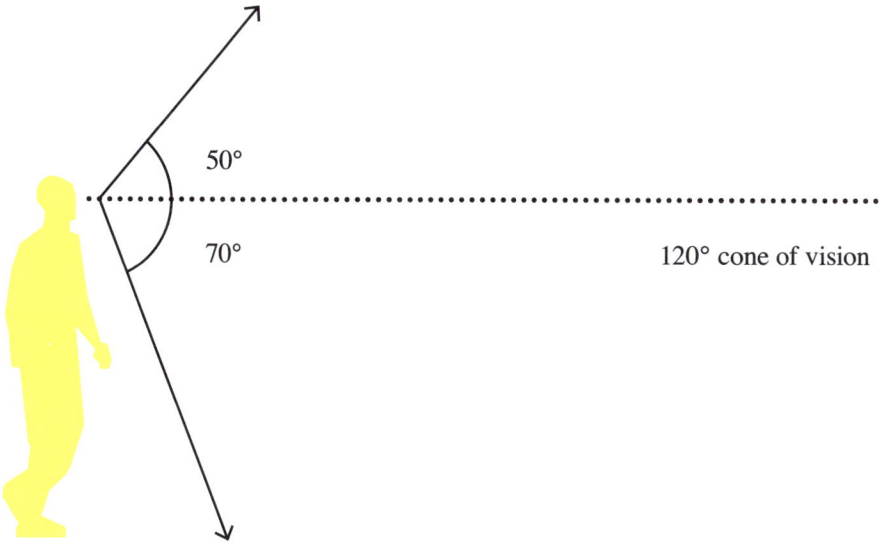

50°

70°

120° cone of vision

Note: 120-degree cone of vision at the eye-level viewpoint, used to construct a spatial grid of viewpoints.

Fig. 61   Rays Projection From a Single Viewpoint in an Open Plan

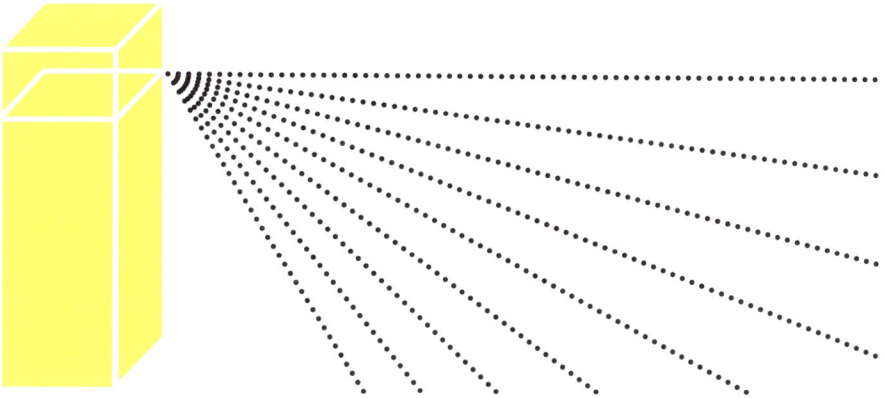

Note: Image showing how rays are projected from a single viewpoint on the 32nd floor of 17 State Street in New York. Black dots on the graphic represent a spatial grid of viewpoints. From one of these dots, the colored lines represent the type of view element that the ray intersects with in the environment around the building.

Fig. 62 **View Elements in the 3D Model**

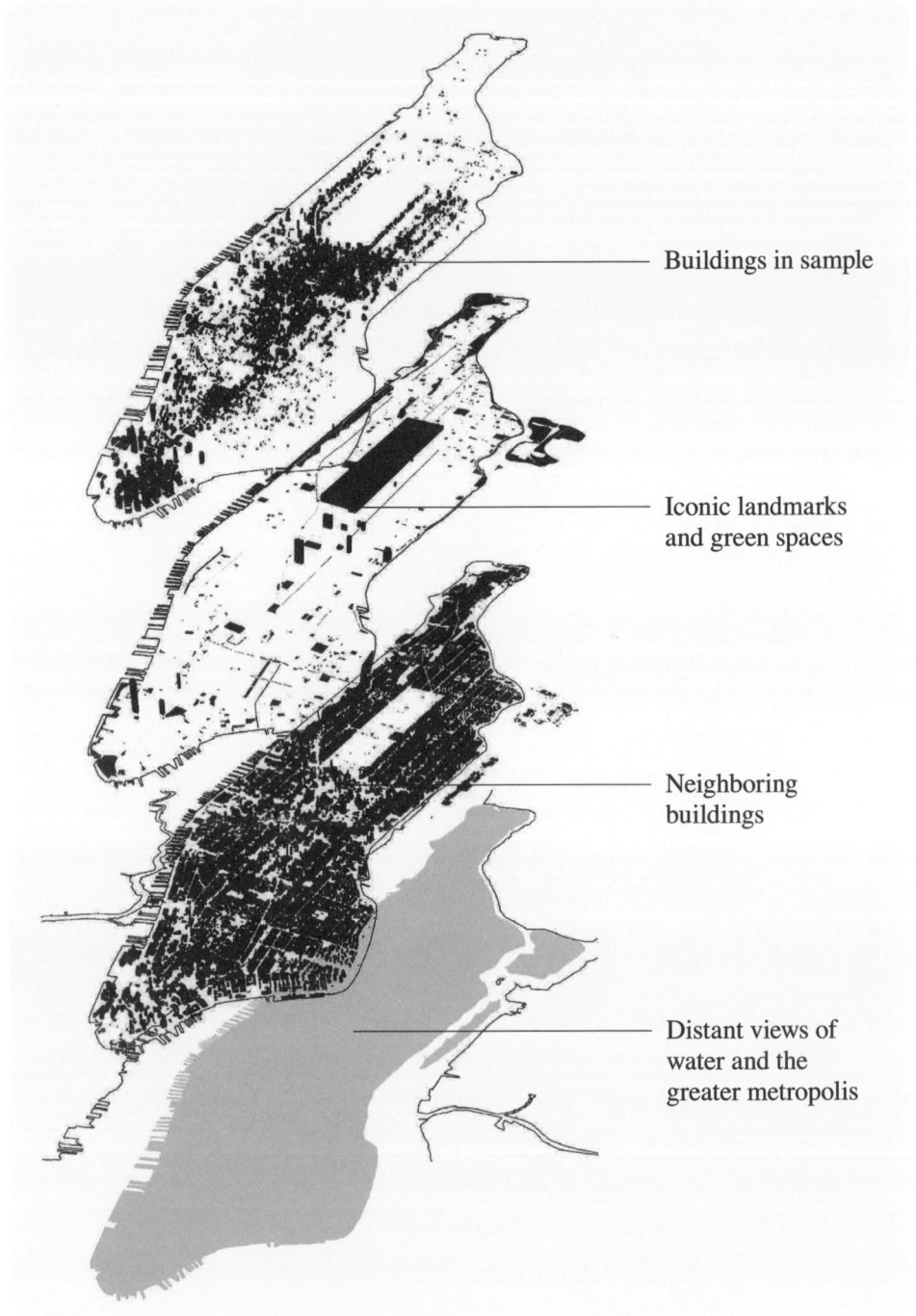

Buildings in sample

Iconic landmarks and green spaces

Neighboring buildings

Distant views of water and the greater metropolis

Note: The sample includes a variety of structures such as renowned landmarks and parks, adjacent buildings, expansive views of water bodies and the broader metropolitan region, as well as the skyline.

The Financial
Performance of
Views and Daylight

To assess the financial impact of daylight or views, we turned to the commercial office market where daylight and view potential may have an impact on the value of space. From financial literature, we have evidence that tenants prefer certain characteristics and vary what they are willing to pay for them. The marginal implicit price of the characteristics can be estimated as a multi-variable regression with prices as the outcome to which preferences vary and the different bundles of building, contractual, and neighborhood characteristics as the features of revealed preferences.[77]

For this study, our hedonic pricing model took into account the various characteristics of a commercial office building, such as building amenities, architectural design, and technology infrastructure; the unique aspects of how space gets rented—such as, variations in contract agreements between a tenant and landlord—urban features in the surrounding environment, and so forth. Since daylight and views are included, we used this model to figure out how much someone is willing to pay for each individual feature of office space in New York.

As previously described, we evaluated view potential and daylight in the offices and correlated these with the 6,267 office spaces. Our results showed that spaces with high access to views (10–100% sVA) have a 6% premium over spaces with low access to views. This financial impact is independent of other value drivers, like daylight.

However, if we consider that daylight and views are interconnected factors, how does the blend of these two factors affect prices? Our research showed that properties offering both high daylight and high view access command a 6.5% premium. This is very similar to the impact of just having good views. When we look at a model with both high daylight (sDA) and view access, we find similar results to a model that only considers daylight. In other words, having both features, daylight and views, is valuable but it does not necessarily mean having both is more valuable than having either one individually.

77   Andrea Chegut, Piet Eichholtz, and Nils Kok, "Supply, Demand and the Value of Green Buildings," *Urban Studies* 51, no. 1 (May 16, 2013): 22–43; Andrea Chegut, Piet Eichholtz, and Paulo Rodrigues, "Spatial Dependence in International Office Markets," The Journal of Real Estate Finance and Economics 51, (November 9, 2015): 317-350; Franz Fuerst and Jorn van de Wetering, "How Does Environmental Efficiency Impact on the Rents of Commercial Offices in the UK?," *Journal of Property Research* 32, no. 3 (June 22, 2015): 193–216; Piet Eichholtz, Nils Kok, and John M. Quigley, "Doing Well by Doing Good? Green Office Buildings," *The American Economic Review* 100, no. 5 (December 1, 2010): 2492–2509; Annika Feige, Patrick McAllister, and Holger Wallbaum, "Rental Price and Sustainability Ratings: Which Sustainability Criteria Are Really Paying Back?," *Construction Management and Economics* 31, no. 4 (April 1, 2013): 322–34.

Spaces with high daylight (55-75% sDA300/50%) garner a 5.3% higher price compared to spaces with low daylight. Spaces with very high daylight (75-100% sDA300/50%) even achieve a 6.4% premium compared to spaces with low daylight. Regarding view access, spaces with high view access (10-100% sVA3) have a 6.3% higher price over spaces with low view access (0-10% sVA3), when taking into account daylight's impact on net effective rent.[78] To put these percentages into perspective, imagine a typical office space with low daylight and view access being sold for $50.00 per square foot ($538.20 per square meter). If the same space has high daylight but low view access, it would sell for 5.3% more, or $52.60 per square foot ($566.19 per square meter), all other things being equal. Conversely, the same space with high view access but low daylight would sell for 6.4% more, or $53.20 per square foot ($572.64 per square meter), all other factors being equal.[79]

Daylight and views significantly contribute to architectural design, shaping the perception of a space, and they carry substantial financial value, which is often overlooked. Recognizing the concrete financial impact of daylight and views is crucial, not only because it can balance costs involved in optimizing these features during the design and construction phases but also because it can guide equitable building and planning policies. By understanding the tangible value these elements provide, developers and designers can justify the initial construction costs by incorporating quantifiable daylight levels and view quality into financial valuation models during all stages of a building's development.

It is important to note that while the 5–6% premium identified in our study pertains to Manhattan's commercial office market, similar trends likely exist in major office markets around the globe. Previous research has identified common value trends related to specific factors across different cities, indicating that the positive relationship between daylight and rent prices could be a global phenomenon. We hope our work inspires further improvements in daylight and view quality in the design of office spaces.

---

78 These findings hold true regardless of the building's height. One might assume that taller structures are the only way to guarantee daylight and views. However, our research reveals that different levels of daylight and views are achievable at various building heights, and each of these combinations can command a premium.

79 However, while our hedonic model explains a significant portion of office rent prices in Manhattan, around 40% of the price remains undetermined, emphasizing the influence of qualitative features.

4.5 Productive Buildings

In the built environment, one of the hardest metrics to measure is human, or user, productivity. Stakeholders want to connect the features of urban design, architectural design, interior design, and even industrial design to productive outcomes. However, productivity is a nebulous and moving target and defining productivity is complicated. How do we conclude if a human has been productive or not? This question relates to what a subject was doing, how they were doing it, when they were doing it, and—relevant to our research—where they were doing it.

Productivity of Space

There is a large and growing body of literature that aims to deconstruct what it is that we do when we do a job.[80] Very simply, in the market system, a job is broken down into a collection of coordinated tasks. In this way, some jobs have more measurable numeric outcomes and others have more categorical outcomes. Factors that can measure the productivity of space are varied. Health outcomes, absenteeism, presentism, the quantity of things finished, and surveys of employee satisfaction are all means that studies have used to assess whether people are productive.[81] A diverse group of spatial features have also been linked to productivity. For example, studies have measured the negative and positive impact of indoor air quality on the effects upon absenteeism and presenteeism in the working environments.[82] For adults, the most solid evidence we have on the effects of space on productivity is based on call center research. The features and elements of call centers that principally lead to enhanced worker productivity relate back to air quality and room configuration. However, most agree that this is a poor performance indicator of the average office worker's productivity.

---

80   Karim Chandrasekar, "Workplace Environment and Its Impact on Organisational Performance in Public Sector Organisations," *International Journal of Enterprise Computing and Business Systems* 1, no. 1 (January 2011): 1-19.
81   Michael H. Brill, "Workspace Design and Productivity," *PubMed* 35, no. 5 (August 6, 1992): 51, 53; Adrian Leaman and Bill Bordass, "Building Design, Complexity and Manageability," *Facilities* 11, no. 9 (September 1, 1993): 16–27; Rick Mohr, "Office Space Is a Revenue Enhancer, Not an Expense, " National Real Estate Investor, July 1, 1996, accessed January 10, 2022; Alex Bryson, John Forth, and Lucy Stokes, "Does Worker Wellbeing Affect Workplace Performance?," Social Science Research Network, January 1, 2015.
82   Juan Palacios, Piet Eichholtz, and Nils Kok, "Moving to Productivity: The Benefits of Healthy Buildings," Social Science Research Network, January 1, 2020.

Our lack of understanding may in fact be due to an unacknowledged tension. Designers rarely engage in post-occupancy analysis of spaces. Such analyses measure the impact of architectural and urban designs on the human experiences it was designed for. The reasons for this rarity are manifold. Firstly, there is the risk of litigation exposure and legal complexities surrounding access rights, which can deter designers from undertaking these analyses. Secondly, the design process involves a complex array of design professionals, from architects and interior designers to industrial and landscape architects, further complicating the analysis. Additionally, the potential discontinuous involvement of designers throughout a project's lifespan may complicate the continuity required for effective evaluation. Ultimately, the statistical "identification problems"—referring to the challenges in determining a clear cause-and-effect relationship within a set of data—arises in attributing productivity or financial performance outcomes directly to specific designs or designers, making such linkages tenuous at best. More specifically, the problem implies that the observed outcomes could be influenced by multiple factors, and isolating the effect of a single variable is problematic. In our study, this means that while we can observe correlations between design features and productivity measures, asserting causation is complicated. External variables such as employee behavior, organizational culture, or even external economic conditions can confound the results, making it hard to attribute productivity changes to design elements alone. Consequently, linking productivity or their financial performance outcomes back to an individual designer is tenuous.

Workplace Performance Indicators

Workplaces are more than just physical spaces—they encompass both the tangible and intangible aspects of the work environment. Comfort plays a vital role in measuring productivity.[83] Studies have revealed that when workplaces are appropriately designed, they contribute to increased engagement, satisfaction, happiness, and overall well-being.[84] Moreover, in a service-oriented economy, where knowledge-based businesses thrive, talent

83   Demet Leblebici, "Impact of Workplace Quality on Employee's Productivity: Case Study of a Bank in Turkey," *Journal of Business Economics and Finance* 1, no. 1 (2012): 38–49; Virangi Mendis, "Workplace Design and Job Performance: A Study of Operational Level Employees in the Apparel Industry of Sri Lanka," *International Journal of Scientific and Research Publications* 6, no. 12 (2016): 148–53.
84   Meredith Wells, "Office Clutter or Meaningful Personal Displays: The Role of Office Personalization in Employee and Organizational Well-being," *Journal of Environmental Psychology* 20, no. 3 (September 1, 2000): 239–55; Richard J. Pech and Bret Slade, "Employee Disengagement: Is There Evidence of a Growing Problem?," *Handbook of Business Strategy* 7, no. 1 (January 1, 2006): 21–25.

scarcity is a reality, which highlights the immense importance of workplace design in attracting and retaining skilled workers.[85]

Many corporate real estate developers recognize the link between workplace design and business success, and acknowledge the power of productivity in their rental market competitiveness.[86] Yet, the direct connection between workplace environment and individuals' performance is difficult to quantify. Groundbreaking research conducted by leaders in the interior design industry and the furniture sector has shed light on the powerful connections between workplace design, employee engagement, and performance. Industry surveys have shown that the physical workplace environment is intimately linked to "workplace experiences"—from social interactions and productivity to employee health and well-being.

Workplace performance benchmarks like Gensler's Workplace Performance Index (WPI[SM]), Leesman's Lmi, and Steelcase's Employee Engagement and Global Workplace metrics, use a combination of physical and well-being metrics in addition to now accepted employee performance drivers like motivation, satisfaction, and engagement in order to measure workplace performance feedback.[87] Leesman, Gensler, and Steelcase use different approaches toward measuring workplace performance. While Steelcase's approach has employee engagement in the workplace as its focus, Gensler finds high value in spaces that fostered innovation and collaboration. Leesman, meanwhile, found data that supported the notion that workplace designs that supported varied workplace activities increased staff collaboration, productivity, pride, and effectiveness. On the other hand, all three approaches agree that organizations are successful when their workplace design and environment promote collaboration, choice, and control over how and where employees work.

85 James Bessen, "Employers Aren't Just Whining – the 'Skills Gap' Is Real," *Harvard Business Review*, August 15, 2014.

86 Norm Miller, "Collaborative, Productive and Innovative Workspaces: Implications for Future Office Demand Telecommuting Will Kill," Slideshow, February 13, 2014, https://www.normmiller.net/?edmc=463.

87 Gensler, "U.S. WORKPLACE SURVEY 2016," 2016, accessed July 23, 2017, https://www.gensler.com/workplace-surveys/us/2016. The "WPI[SM]" research has been renamed as "WPIx." For more information, see: https://www.gensler.com/workplace-performance-index. However, it is important to note that our research was conducted in 2017 and thus we still adopt the original name "WPI[SM]" in this publication for consistency and clarity.; Leesman, "Are Your Workplaces the Best Places to Work?," Leesman Index, accessed July 23, 2017, https://www.leesmanindex.com/; Steelcase, "Engagement and the Global Workplace," Steelcase Global Report (Steelcase, 2016), accessed July 23, 2017, https://www.steelcase.com/eu-en/research/reports/engagement-global-workplace/. Steelcase, "Engagement and the Global Workplace," Steelcase Global Report, 2017, accessed July 23, 2017, https://info.steelcase.com/global-employee-engagement-workplacereport.

Financial	The connection between financial performance and workplace

Financial
Performance
of Workplace
Performance
Indicators

The connection between financial performance and workplace design remains largely unexplored, offering vast opportunities for research. To study the quality of workspace design and its contribution to the value growth of commercial buildings, we investigated the correlation between workplace designs that enhance employee performance—as measured by benchmarks like Gensler's WPI^{SM}—and the financial value these workplaces generate, as reflected by effective rental prices.

Gensler's WPI^{SM} is an occupancy evaluation tool that scores workplaces based on the level of employee workplace performance that those spaces support. Gensler has surveyed a sample of over 4,000 US, 1,200 UK, and 2,000 Asian office workers in 11 industries using their proprietary WPI^{SM} platform, an online survey tool, which is built upon a core set of validated questions gauging workplace effectiveness and functionality that have been used and refined from late 2000 to 2016s.[88] The survey analysis results in each space being given a WPI^{SM} Score.

The survey findings offer valuable perspectives on current work patterns, the effectiveness of the workplace in supporting these patterns, and its influence on the overall employee experience.[89] The data reveals a significant connection between the workplace's quality and its functionality and the innovation level employees attribute to their firms. Furthermore, the research highlights innovation as a key indicator of employee achievement. Gensler has translated this data into an innovation rating for workplaces. Workplaces with elevated WPI^{SM} ratings also boast higher innovation ratings. Innovators display greater autonomy in their work, are more adept at working in settings that best fit them, and utilize a diverse range of spaces.

To identify correlations between design and financial performance in real estate, we linked WPI^{SM} scores for individual spaces to CompStak's database of Manhattan effective rents over the 2005 to 2015 period. In New York City, we found 139 buildings with spaces that have a WPI^{SM} score and effective rent contracts. In total, this led to 1,137 leases, of which 70 leases have WPI^{SM} scores broken down across quantiles—above average, average, and below average, and the remaining contracts are used as the control samples. This data was then used in a quasi-natural experiment regression model, where we looked

---

88   The survey outcomes are measured by a series of indicators, such as critical time spent in the office, layout, light, air, storage, furniture, privacy, and access.
89   Gensler, "U.S. WORKPLACE SURVEY 2016."

closely at how different office designs within the same building affect its value. We compared offices with different designs (our focus group) against other offices in the same building that didn't have these designs (our comparison group). This way, we could pinpoint whether the design of an office has an impact on the building's overall value. We made sure to account for other factors that could affect the building's value, like its location or features that are the same for the whole building, to ensure that any differences we saw were truly due to the office design itself. As a result, any remaining differences in the rental prices per square foot could be due to the quality of the tenants, the specifics of the lease agreements, or the workplace performance design, which would be the main focus of our study. Fig. 63

Workplace Indicators Impact on Financial Performance

Our findings revealed intriguing insights into the relationship between workplace performance and effective rents in Manhattan's office market, highlighting both the benefits of high-performing workplaces and the consequences of below-average performance. We found that spaces occupied by below-average-performing workplaces experienced a notable decline in effective rents, approximately 10% lower compared to similar non-treated leases. This translates to a marginal reduction in effective rents per square foot, approximately $5.50 less when compared to similar spaces in the same building.

High-performing workplaces significantly influence Manhattan's office market's effective rents, particularly for leases qualified for the WPI[SM] scoring. Even after accounting for factors such as neighborhood locations and the start date of the lease, there is a 12.7% premium on rents for WPI[SM]-scored leases compared to those that are not scored. Conversely, leases with Below-Average WPI[SM] scores have rents that are 15.2% lower. It is clear that the impact of top-performing workplace leases is linked to market variables like specific sub-market locations, contract details such as lease durations and types, and other unique features. When these factors are considered, the rent premiums for top-performing workplaces can vary in size.

These findings have important implications for organizations looking to optimize their workplace environments and achieve better business outcomes. The results highlight the financial benefits of investing in workplaces that foster enhanced performance. By prioritizing design interventions that promote productivity and well-being, organizations

Fig. 63   **Buildings with WPI-Scored Spaces in New York City**

●   Buildings with WPI-scored spaces

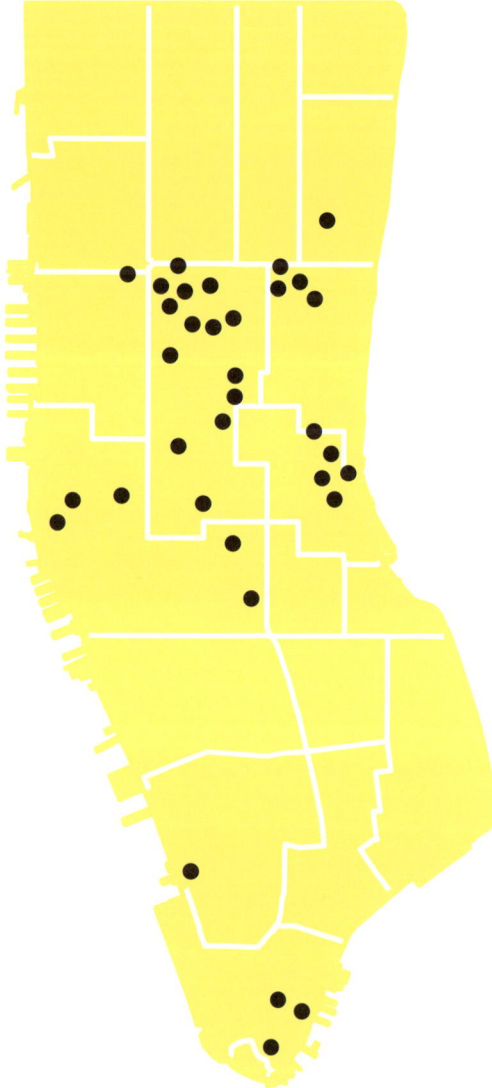

Market Stats	Sample: 1,137 Leases, 139 Locations Rent: $55 PSF/YR AVG, $144 PSF/YR PRIME
Findings: WPI Rents	Low WPI vs non-scored: Below average performing WPI-scored leases command marginal effective rent discounts, provided the former achieve 50 or lower WPI^{SM} score: -10%

can create spaces that are valued by tenants seeking to rent office space. This emphasizes the potential return on investment that can be achieved through thoughtful workplace design. However, the study design does have its limitations. Our objective was not to learn the drivers of workplace design that correlate with value, but rather to understand the financial incentive for landlords to invest in productive, healthy, and engaging spaces. To this end, the study links occupancy analysis of office spaces as captured in a survey-based score index for the Manhattan market to effective rents. As evident from the literature, a direct connection between workplace environment and work performance has been difficult to quantify and this study does not infer causality to support this. Although 27 industry-led studies have repeatedly shown that the physical quality of workplaces influence employee productivity, our study is a first step toward linking workplace performance to effective rents to highlight the financial implications of developing high performing workplaces.[90]

4.6 Urban Greenery

In a high-density city like New York, buildings are tightly integrated into the urban environment, making access to outdoor urban spaces an impactful factor for the value of a building. Access to public parks is a privilege for many residents who live in green space deserts. Greenery—trees, flowers, and shrubs—on the streets becomes an indispensable component of creating micro green spaces in the city, especially in the post-pandemic era when people are increasingly aware of the significance of outdoor spaces for physical and mental health. Such street-level greenery is one of the most prevalent and tangible urban design elements in today's cities. However, improving and maintaining street-level greenery is never a favored job for the private sector. In New York City, the Department of Parks & Recreation (NYC Parks) and other non-profit local community organizations currently take charge of maintaining street plants, but only a few private actors are part of the effort. How may society create more incentives for private entities to help improve street-level

---

90 Results of this analysis suggest that spaces that have below average WPI scores, earn effective rents that are 10% or $5.50 per square foot less than a comparable rented space within the same building's control group. This signals that spaces that are not competitively designed for workplace performance receive a discount as measured by effective rents in the marketplace.

greenery? To answer this question, we explored the economic values of street-level greenery in New York City.

What about the Urban Greenery?

Urban greenery is an indispensable part of today's cities and closely aligned with quality of life. Studies have shown a significant impact on public health and wellness—from enhanced cognition to increased perceived mental health and decreased all cause-mortality—and the presence of urban greenery simply enhances the attractiveness of cities to residents, employees, tourists, investors, and firms.[91] Moreover, urban greenery delivers significant environmental benefits, including the reduction of carbon footprint and the promotion of oxygen generation.[92] In densely populated cities affected by the heat island effect, the presence of urban greenery is particularly crucial, as it helps improve thermal comfort for its residents.[93]

However, most studies on urban greenery tend to focus on measuring land use designated to green spaces, such as parks and urban greenways, rather than the more prevalent green features on the street. Most of this research also shares a common focus on the residential property market, rather than commercial real estate, in cities across the globe.[94] In general, the

---

91   Gregory N. Bratman et al., "The Benefits of Nature Experience: Improved Affect and Cognition," *Landscape and Urban Planning* 138 (June 1, 2015): 41–50; Katia Perini and Adriano Magliocco, "Effects of Vegetation, Urban Density, Building Height, and Atmospheric Conditions on Local Temperatures and Thermal Comfort," *Urban Forestry & Urban Greening* 13, no. 3 (January 1, 2014): 495–506; S.M.E. Van Dillen et al., "Greenspace in Urban Neighbourhoods and Residents' Health: Adding Quality to Quantity," *Journal of Epidemiology and Community Health* 66, no. 6 (June 29, 2011): e8; M.M.H.E. Van Den Berg et al., "Health Benefits of Green Spaces in the Living Environment: A Systematic Review of Epidemiological Studies," *Urban Forestry & Urban Greening* 14, no. 4 (January 1, 2015): 806–16; Yuhao Kang et al., "A Review of Urban Physical Environment Sensing Using Street View Imagery in Public Health Studies," *Annals of GIS* 26, no. 3 (July 2, 2020): 261–75; Paschalis Arvanitidis et al., "Economic Aspects of Urban Green Space: A Survey of Perceptions and Attitudes," *International Journal of Environmental Technology and Management* 11, no. 1/2/3 (January 1, 2009): 143.

92   Wendy Y. Chen, "The Role of Urban Green Infrastructure in Offsetting Carbon Emissions in 35 Major Chinese Cities: A Nationwide Estimate," *Cities* 44 (April 1, 2015): 112–20; David J. Nowak, Robert E. Hoehn, and Daniel E. Crane, "Oxygen Production by Urban Trees in the United States," *Arboriculture and Urban Forestry* 33, no. 3 (May 1, 2007): 220–26.

93   Briony A. Norton et al., "Planning for Cooler Cities: A Framework to Prioritise Green Infrastructure to Mitigate High Temperatures in Urban Landscapes," *Landscape and Urban Planning* 134 (February 1, 2015): 127–38.

94   This unbalanced focus on residential properties is understandable due to the sheer size and value of the residential real estate market, which the 2018 US Census estimates at 89 million owner occupied units and Zillow values at about $31.8 trillion. However, per unit commercial buildings have a larger role to play as they shelter the collective workforce's productivity. The Commercial Buildings Energy Consumption Survey (CBECS) estimates 5.6 million commercial building units, and the National Association of Real Estate Investment Trusts (NAREIT) estimates the total commercial real estate stock in the United States is worth about $16 trillion. This suggests that the per-unit value of commercial real estate is higher and changes to each building are immense.

---

access to green spatial features, such as parks and greenways, has been correlated with higher residential property values, and, as previously noted, research results have documented that street-level greenery has a positive value impact on residential properties. The proximity to green spaces results in an increase in residential property values ranging from 3% to over 20% depending on the specific types of green space and the urban context in comparison.[95] Also, using over 800 samples from the city of Castellón, Spain, researchers found that every 100 meters further away from a green area equated to a drop of approximately $2,000 in the average home's price.[96] According to evidence from Indianapolis, Indiana, and Austin, Texas, urban green trails also bring up real estate property values, ranging from 2.4% to 20.2%.[97]

New Data: Green View Index (GVI)

In recent years, the advancement of image recognition technology has enabled researchers to measure street-level greenery. In this research, we computed a Green View Index (GVI) using Google Street View images to measure Manhattan's street-level greenery. The GVI measures the visually perceived density of greenery on the street. The index provides an alternative measurement of the quality of urban greenery that is different from calculating such features as park areas, vegetation types, and the number of trees.

The first use of the term "Green View Index" dates to 2009. A group of researchers took color images captured from four directions as representative of human perception from the street level to measure the visibility of surrounding urban greenery. The emergence of street view images—available from the 2010s on—provides a novel data source for characterizing the urban landscape. Integration of street view images at a large data scale and image recognition algorithms allows for a new approach to measuring street greenery at the human scale. Fig. 64

More nascent research has been conducted on the relationship between street-level greenness and housing prices using GVI calculated through street-view images. The results

95   Sarah Nicholls and John L. Crompton, "The Impact of Greenways on Property Values: Evidence From Austin, Texas," *Journal of Leisure Research* 37, no. 3 (September 1, 2005): 321–41.

96   Aurelia Bengochea Morancho, "A Hedonic Valuation of Urban Green Areas," *Landscape and Urban Planning* 66, no. 1 (December 1, 2003): 35–41.

97   Greg Lindsey et al., "Public Choices and Property Values: Evidence from Greenways in Indianapolis," *Center for Urban Policy and the Environment Publications*, Indiana University (January 1, 2003); John L. Crompton, "The Impact of Parks on Property Values: Empirical Evidence From the Past Two Decades in the United States," *Managing Leisure* 10, no. 4 (October 1, 2005): 203-218.

Fig. 64

GVI Captures the Visually Perceived Density of Greenery at the Street Level

Note: GVI captures the visually perceived density of greenery at the street-level. Top: Street-level images, high to low, bottom: Processed images, high to low.

show that visible street greenery and street accessibility in cities across the globe have a positive economic impact, with a significant positive coefficient for housing prices.[98] Fig. 65

Using this method, we were able to calculate the GVI for specific buildings in New York. We then paired the GVI data with over 1,400 rental transaction data and over 7,400 sale transaction data, and found that offices located in "low," "medium," and "high" street-level greenness obtained a 10.5%, 10%, and 8.5% price premium for sale transactions, and a 7.8%, 4.1%, and 5.6% price premium for leasing transactions, respectively, compared to those offices that were spatially correlated with virtually no greenery.[99] Fig. 66-67

98 Yonglin Zhang and Rencai Dong, "Impacts of Street-Visible Greenery on Housing Prices: Evidence From a Hedonic Price Model and a Massive Street View Image Dataset in Beijing," *ISPRS International Journal of Geo-Information* 7, no. 3 (March 14, 2018): 104; Yu Ye et al., "Daily Accessed Street Greenery and Housing Price: Measuring Economic Performance of Human-Scale Streetscapes via New Urban Data," *Sustainability* 11, no. 6 (March 22, 2019): 1741; Fu Xiao et al., "Do Street-level Scene Perceptions Affect Housing Prices in Chinese Megacities? An Analysis Using Open Access Datasets and Deep Learning," *PLOS ONE* 14, no. 5 (May 30, 2019): e0217505.

99 This group of data is labeled as the "very low" level of greenness in the regression results.

Fig. 65 **GVI Identification Process**

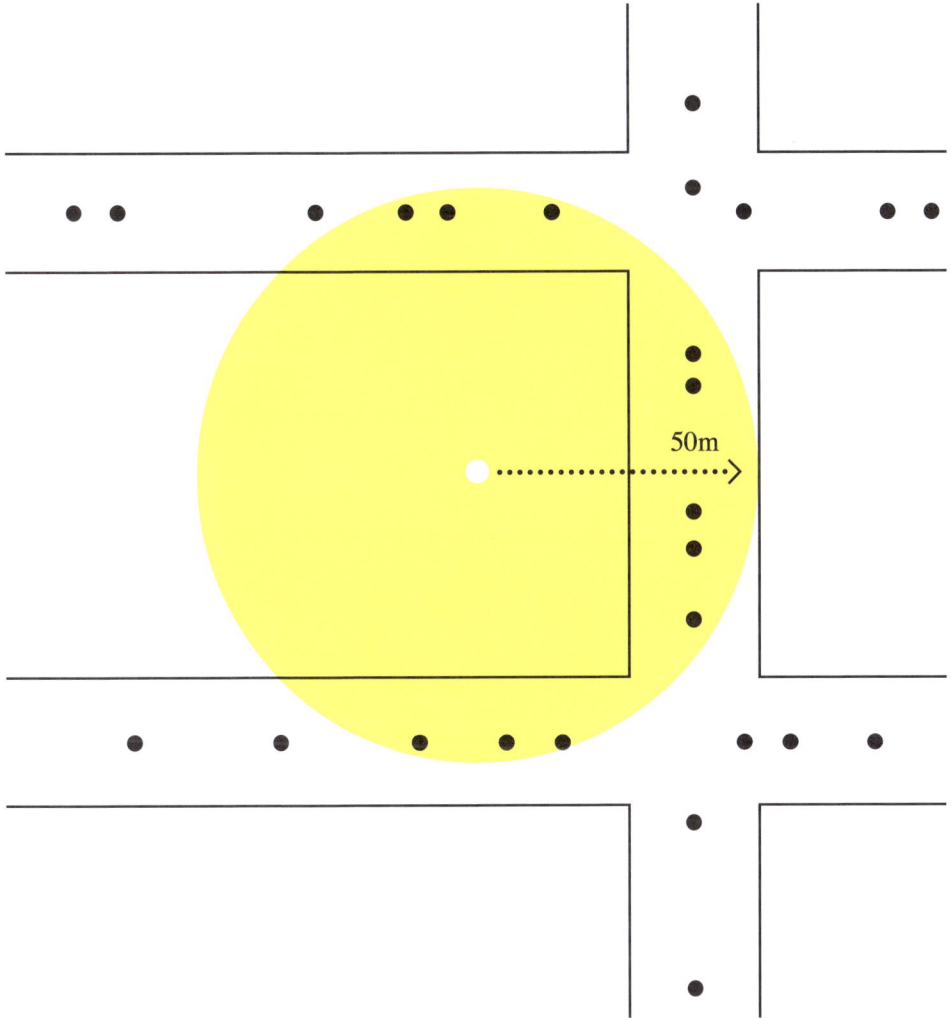

50m

● GSV Coordinate

Note: Collect street-level images within 50m from the target building coordinates. For each street view panorama, there are four images, on each of which we will calculate the green view index. At each assigned coordinate, we calculated the average percentage of green pixels from collected street view images that were taken from April to October in New York City. Address: 979 3rd Ave, Building Address ID: 1038623

Fig. 66

Greenery Positively Influences Building Transaction Price

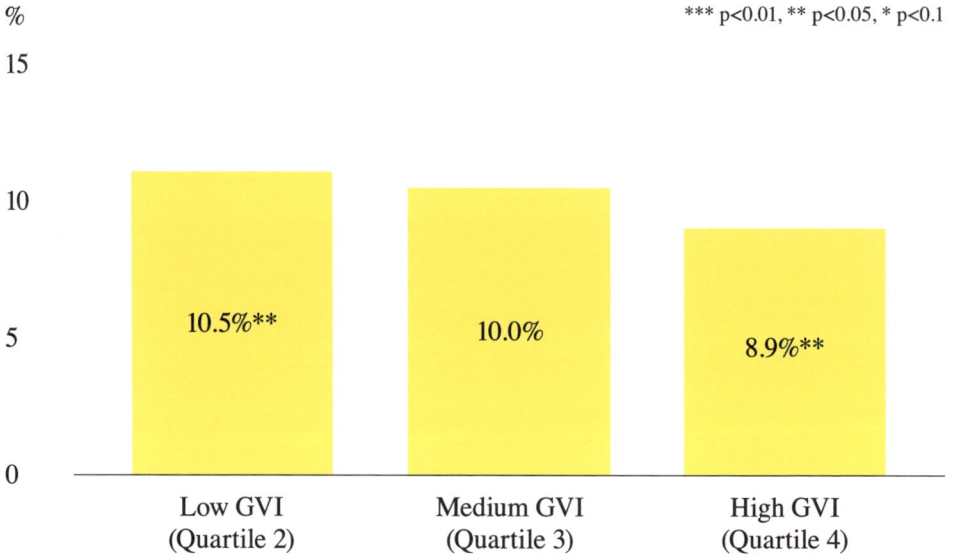

%

*** p<0.01, ** p<0.05, * p<0.1

15

10

5

10.5%**   10.0%   8.9%**

0

| Low GVI (Quartile 2) | Medium GVI (Quartile 3) | High GVI (Quartile 4) |

Note: Transaction prices of buildings with different levels of GVI with dependent variable: logarithm of transaction price.

Fig. 67

Greenery Positively Influences Rents, But to a Smaller Degree

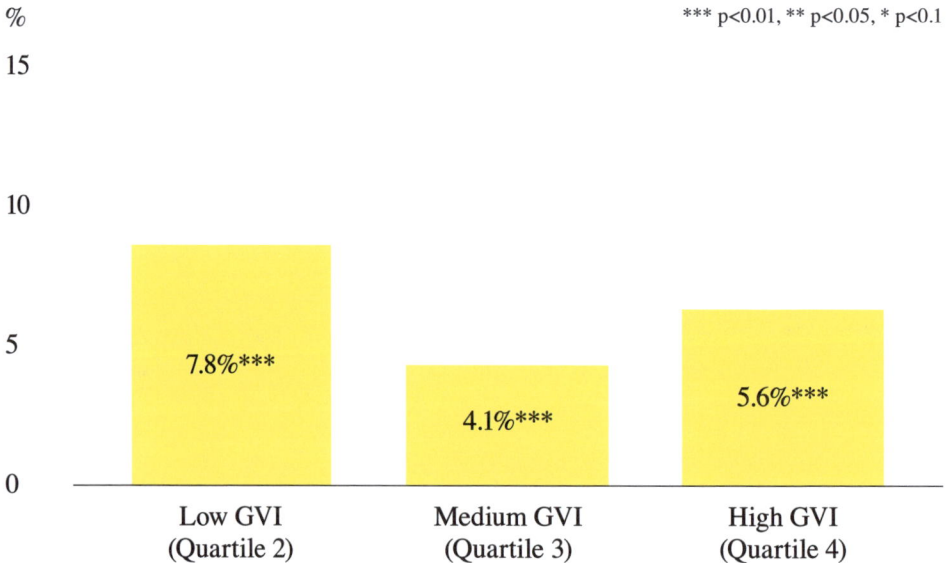

%

*** p<0.01, ** p<0.05, * p<0.1

15

10

5

7.8%***   4.1%***   5.6%***

0

| Low GVI (Quartile 2) | Medium GVI (Quartile 3) | High GVI (Quartile 4) |

Note: Rental prices of buildings with different levels of GVI with dependent variable: logarithm of rental price.

Commercial Real Estate and Street-level Greenery

Within commercial markets there is evidence of a correlation between green building practices, as measured by BREEAM, LEED, or Energy Star labels, and positive transaction prices.[100] However, none of the research to date has assessed the impacts of urban greenery on the commercial real estate market. This suggests that the per-unit value of commercial real estate is higher and changes to each building are immense. A better understanding of this relationship would serve as a crucial supplement to urban planning and design and investments in urban greenery.

Our findings suggest that offices associated with higher levels of street-level greenery acquire a positive premium (between 8.9% and 10.5%) for sales price and a positive premium (between 4.1% and 7.8%) for leasing price. In other words, the 736 buildings with at least a medium level of GVI acquired an average of $11.73 million more per transaction and rented for an average of $2.59 per square meter more per lease, ceteris paribus, than those buildings with virtually no street-level greenery.

This research helps to not only align urban residents but also incentivize institutional investment stakeholders and urban planners to improve street-level greenery. By shedding light on the influence of greenery on commercial building valuations, we hope to provide a comprehensive understanding of its impact on urban environments and the economic significance of landscape architecture, planning, and development in cities. In the meantime, through comparing GVI distribution and neighborhood income levels, we also found that variation in access to trees is a signal of inequality in social outcomes and racism. Studies have shown that lower income neighborhoods frequently have fewer green spaces, while the provision of more greenery has been tied to increased satisfaction and equity between neighborhoods.[101] Efforts devoted to improving and maintaining the quality of street-level greenery are a

100 Franz Fuerst and Patrick McAllister, "New Evidence on the Green Building Rent and Price Premium," *Social Science Research Network*, January 1, 2009; Franz Fuerst and Patrick McAllister, "Green Noise or Green Value? Measuring the Effects of Environmental Certification on Office Values," *Real Estate Economics* 39, no. 1 (December 1, 2010): 45–69; Eichholtz, Kok, and Quigley, "Doing Well by Doing Good? Green Office Buildings," 2492-2509. Nils Kok and Maarten Jennen, "The Impact of Energy Labels and Accessibility on Office Rents," *Energy Policy* 46 (July 1, 2012): 489–97; Piet Eichholtz, Nils Kok, and John M. Quigley, "The Economics of Green Building," *The Review of Economics and Statistics* 95, no. 1 (March 1, 2013): 50–63; Yongheng Deng and Jing Wu, "Economic Returns to Residential Green Building Investment: The Developers' Perspective," *Regional Science and Urban Economics* 47 (July 1, 2014): 35–44; Chegut, Eichholtz, and Kok, "Supply, Demand and the Value of Green Buildings," 22-43. Turan et al., "The Value of Daylight in Office Spaces."
101 Christopher L. Ambrey and Christopher Fleming, "Public Greenspace and Life Satisfaction in Urban Australia," *Urban Studies* 51, no. 6 (July 18, 2013): 1290–1321.

critical step for achieving social equity and economic development goals.

Street-level greenery, as a prominent element of urban design, noticeably influences the prices of commercial real estate. This practical implication emphasizes the interconnectedness between corporate and institutional investment portfolios in office real estate and the endeavors of landscape architecture and urban planning experts to improve this valuable urban feature. Real estate developers are motivated to collaborate with these professionals to make the most of the value-enhancing potential of urban greenery.

4.7   The Challenges of Being Green

By 2100, 190 million people in major cities around the world will be living on land below the high tide.[102] This means that cities will receive both major and non-major storm events with increasing frequency. More specifically, this will affect trillions in residential and commercial real estate and cast an untold impact on our human experience, the likes of which we are not prepared for and don't truly yet understand the ramifications.

The real estate and construction industries are responsible for producing approximately 40% of carbon emissions of the total emissions expelled by our collective economic functioning.[103] The provision of residential and commercial buildings is responsible for over one-third of global energy use and energy-related greenhouse gas emissions. This is partly due to the manufacturing of building materials like concrete, brick, steel, and other materials, which accounted for 11% of global energy- and process-related GHG emissions in 2018.[104]

Green Buildings

Our ability to address the current climate crisis is high. However, our willingness to act has been low. In the past 25 years, for major global markets that experienced a significant building boom, there has been substantially limited growth in the building technology industry that addresses the issue of climate change. For context, 13–15% of the new building

102 Scott Kulp and Benjamin Strauss, "New Elevation Data Triple Estimates of Global Vulnerability to Sea-level Rise and Coastal Flooding," *Nature Communications* 10, no. 1 (October 29, 2019): 1-12.

103 David Carlin, "40% of Emissions Come From Real Estate; Here's How the Sector Can Decarbonize," *Forbes*, April 5, 2022.

104 Xiaoyang Zhong et al., "Global Greenhouse Gas Emissions From Residential and Commercial Building Materials and Mitigation Strategies to 2060," *Nature Communications* 12, no. 1 (October 21, 2021): 6126.

stock in the United States has been thoughtfully cared for, with respect to design and technology interventions that are able to lower carbon emissions, abate electricity consumption, reduce waste, and minimize the wasteful use of water.[105] The vast majority of buildings in the U.S. will remain for the next 50 to 60 years. In this way, the attention to green design interventions is paramount and its attention has actually increased in the past decade. Since the 2000s, there has been growing attention to developing and building more sustainable buildings within the mainstream institutional building industry.

More than a century ago, ideas around green building began to address the health and safety issues of buildings in cities such as London and New York City. Over time, attention shifted from understanding how buildings function to how building structures and building technologies can interact with the human experience. An interest in the sustainability and productivity of buildings first peaked in the 1970s and then again in the 2000s. This transformation has led to a continued focus on the energy consumption of buildings, how buildings themselves contribute to climate change, and how the wasteful use of resources in the development and production of buildings negatively impacts the built environment.

In recent times, designers and developers have assembled a cadre of tools to construct a more sustainable and less resource-intensive building stock. Considering the current debate on the global climate crisis, policymakers, corporations, and institutional investors consider buildings to represent one of the most crucial vehicles for achieving energy efficiency, carbon abatement, and corporate social responsibility. Such a shift in perspective and understanding moves the commercial real estate market toward increased levels of energy efficiency and sustainability.

As researchers and practitioners venture into the realm of green design and building technology innovations, several questions arise: How do we transform a building to have lower energy consumption? How can we minimize the use of water in buildings? How can buildings themselves decrease waste disposal? These questions and their potential associated incentives align with a broader movement toward net zero use of energy. From a technical perspective, it is possible to achieve fully operational buildings that are zero carbon-emitting

105 Rogier Holtermans and Nils Kok, "International Green Building Adoption Index 2018," CBRE and Maastricht University, January 1, 2018.

owing to advancements in material science, building technology design, and computational understanding of buildings.

Classifying Green Buildings

Researchers around the globe have demonstrated through empirical analysis that there is indeed a significant financial performance premium for commercial properties with a "green" certification. Environmental certifications such as Leadership in Energy and Environmental Design (LEED) and Energy Star labeling have become standard ways of measuring how buildings address the issues of carbon, energy, water, waste, transportation, materials, health, and indoor environmental quality. In the United States, the Green Business Certification Inc (GBCI) is responsible for reviewing and verifying projects and awarding them points that correspond to a level of LEED certification, which ranges from Certified (40–49 points) to Silver (50–59 points), Gold (60–79 points), and Platinum (80+ points).

Methodologically, researchers use hedonic regression models to assess how well buildings with green certifications perform financially when compared with buildings that do not have such certifications. In some instances, researchers not only examine buildings that have earned green certifications through featuring design and technological interventions that reduce energy consumption, but also their neighboring structures and buildings that were constructed around the same time, to take into account the spatiotemporal effects of green building construction. What we can conclude from these studies is that there is ultimately a significant financial performance differential between different types of buildings, as judged by their transaction prices and rental values. Across the globe, the transaction prices for green buildings that are certified have a price differential between 13.3–36.5% compared to buildings that are not certified.[106] This suggests that buildings which contribute to the combat of climate change are not only environmentally sustainable but also economically valuable.

In categorizing whether a building is "green" or not, the finance literature emphasizes a strict assessment of identification that is based on quantifiable metrics. The initial effort of measuring the value of green buildings began with

---

106 Eichholtz, Kok, and Quigley, "Doing Well by Doing Good? Green Office Buildings," 2492-2509; Eichholtz, Kok, and Quigley, "The Economics of Green Building," 50-63; Fuerst and McAllister, "Green Noise or Green Value? Measuring the Effects of Environmental Certification on Office Values," 45-69; and Chegut, Eichholtz, and Kok, "Supply, Demand and the Value of Green Buildings," 22-43.

Miller, Spivey, and Florance's seminal work on "Does Green Pay Off?" (2008) and Eichholtz, Kok, and Quigley's work on "Doing Well by Doing Good? Green Office Buildings" (2010).[107] Both efforts attempted to provide empirical evidence derived from market transactions using real estate databases on the economic value of green-labeled buildings that are certified by third party groups such as LEED, Energy Star, or GreenStar. In essence, these certifications serve as proxies to indicate whether a building has actually undergone a production or construction process that makes it more energy efficient and environmentally sustainable. Without these certification schemes, it is practically impossible to know whether a building is effectively addressing our shared climate goals in its technology and design. This is a critical step toward an industry-wide collection of and dissemination of data and data science and data frameworks within the architecture and design practice.

Challenge to Building Green

Within architecture practice today, the green building certification marks one of the initial steps in documenting building design and construction prescriptions and whether these prescriptions meet the goals of minimizing energy use, enhancing daylight, or fulfilling other performance criteria, which we have discussed throughout this chapter. Although the green labeling system is far from flawless, it is nonetheless bringing together, for the first time, the previously siloed industries of design and finance. For the first time, investors are able to understand the economic value of green buildings through empirical and quantifiable evidence presented at the portfolio level and at the city level that proves green buildings can transact and rent at a premium compared to their non-green counterparts. This has ultimately created mutual dialogue and incentive alignment between financiers and designers and thus helped accelerate the adoption of green building technologies more widely. Another way to understand this situation is that buildings that did not incorporate green building technologies received a discount from the marketplace for not engaging in society's net-zero targets and our common goals of reducing energy consumption and carbon emissions in the built environment. This perspective calls for enhanced coordination and

---

107 Norman G. Miller, Jay Spivey, and Andrew Florance, "Does Green Pay Off?," *The Journal of Real Estate Portfolio Management* 14, no. 4 (January 1, 2008): 385–400; Eichholtz, Kok, and Quigley, "Doing Well by Doing Good? Green Office Buildings," 2492-2509.

engaged efforts amongst designers, planners, engineers, and technologists to innovate around the construction process of green buildings and understand how these buildings can ultimately make a difference.

However, there are still many challenges and caveats to the production of green buildings. Although there is a notable trend toward adopting green buildings with the rise of ESG and the proliferation of energy consumption measurement tools and standards, it nevertheless takes a long time for architecture, development, and investment firms to collectively accept such green practices as the mainstream standard. Market data from CBRE shows that environmentally certified buildings represent only 5.4% of the commercial office stock, and even less so in other sectors like retail and industrial buildings.[108] Although green construction is generally gaining traction and market share, new construction and building refurbishment remain mostly conventional. Principally, there is uncertainty around green buildings' design and construction process due to a lack of coordination effort and knowledge sharing amongst designers, developers, policymakers, and investors. A prior lack of measurement and pricing standards led to a slowed fusion for those who are engaged in the actual financing and construction of buildings. In addition, there is also limited transparency about how energy efficiency is effectively priced using post-occupancy evidence. The slow take-up of green construction could be due to construction costs that are higher than the marginal benefits resulting from having green labels. Given that green building construction is relatively new in the field, developers are uncertain about the marginal cost of such innovative building practices relative to traditional property development. These combined factors lead to a slowed diffusion of energy-efficient and sustainable building practices, and thereby the necessary reduction of the carbon externality from the built environment.

Measuring Construction Cost of Green Buildings

Prior literature has focused mostly on comparing a small handful of green buildings to conventional counterfactuals without properly and rigorously controlling for other features of the construction process such as construction costs. To address this gap in research, we looked at the input cost

---

108 CBRE and Maastricht University, "National Green Building Adoption Index 2015," CBRE and Maastricht University, 2014, accessed June 1, 2021, https://www.corporatesustainabilitystrategies.com/cbre-real-green-research-index/.

of building green buildings to investigate whether this poses a potential barrier of green building adoption.[109] While the majority of the work we have introduced thus far in this book focused on the commercial property market in New York, this example case study is based on an empirical analysis on the largest commercial property market in the United Kingdom. In this work, we came across the Royal Institution of Chartered Surveyors' elemental construction cost database—The Building Cost Information Services (BCIS)—that gave us some notion of how much it costs to build buildings in the context of London. This is the largest non-proprietary dataset that provides information on project cost, project duration, and contract data for individual construction projects in the U.K. What is unique about this dataset is that it is fully crowdsourced. Subscribers input information about their projects, such as the cost incurred in the development process of their building, and get access to everyone else's submissions and be able to check the cost of future projects. In this way, the crowdsourcing of information democratizes the data collection process by addressing the problem of information asymmetry that we currently face in the general economy.

These data were linked to the BREEAM label from the Building Research Establishment (BRE) database, which represents the most widely adopted green building certification in the U.K. Using the statistical method of propensity score matching, we assessed the marginal construction cost for a set of 336 BREEAM-certified buildings, matching projects on location and construction period with a set of control group samples that consists of 2,060 non-certified construction projects that were built between 2003 and 2014. We then calculate a statistically significant difference in total construction cost between green (BREEAM-certified) buildings and conventional (non-certified) buildings. We found that the average difference in costs for this is 6.5%, after controlling for factors such as property type, building owner category, and construction contract, and tendering characteristics.

Highlights from this study shows that the higher overall costs for more efficient, green buildings stem from a specific set of construction cost elements, such as design,

---

109 Andrea Chegut, Piet Eichholtz, and Nils Kok, "The Price of Innovation: An Analysis of the Marginal Cost of Green Buildings," *Journal of Environmental Economics and Management* 98 (November 1, 2019): 102248.

preliminaries, substructure, external work, and finishings.[110] The next question we asked was: what is the contribution of each of these elements to the total construction cost? After controlling for building and contract characteristics, only design fees, building fittings, and finishes appear to be significantly correlated with the degree of a building's sustainability; green building design costs are 32% more than the design costs of conventional building design and fittings and finishes costs are 32% and 28% higher, respectively.[111] For the most advanced green buildings (i.e., the BREEAM Outstanding buildings), design fees can be as high as 150% higher than the design fees for non-certified buildings.[112] Fig. 68

In addition to construction cost, another factor that is weighed highly by the developer is the development time because longer construction periods can significantly increase the burden of construction loans and reduce the return on the developer's equity investment. To account for this, we also assessed the duration of the construction projects and found that more efficient, green buildings take significantly longer to complete, after controlling for factors that could impact project duration. Green buildings take about 11% more time to complete than their non-green counterparts, and this difference is even higher for the most energy-efficient buildings.[113]

The key takeaway from these findings is that the average marginal cost of green-labeled construction projects is smaller than the value premiums documented in the literature, which provides evidence for advocating for more green construction even from an economic and financial perspective. The energy-efficiency gap in real estate may be due to both a market barrier and a market failure, which ultimately explain the slow adoption and diffusion of green buildings in the industry. The

---

110 Costed elements in the Preliminaries and Summary sections, omitting the contractor's markup for profit and overheads, may encompass: administrative personnel, initial site setup, provisional utilities, safeguarding measures, health and environmental safety provisions, regulation safeguarding, mechanical equipment, interim constructions, documentation of site activities, site tidiness and maintenance, and load bearing framework of a building. This work refers to ground—including road—and external ventilation-related infrastructure of a building. For more information, see: Chegut, Eichholtz, and Kok, "The Price of Innovation: An Analysis of the Marginal Cost of Green Buildings," 5.

111 "Design fees" mostly refer to design consultant's fees and contractor's design fees; "Building fittings" refers to fittings, fixtures, furniture, non-mechanical and electrical equipment; "Finishes" refers to work and finishes to surfaces of indoor vertical surfaces. For more information, see: Chegut, Eichholtz, and Kok, "The Price of Innovation: An Analysis of the Marginal Cost of Green Buildings," 17.

112 See Table 5 in Chegut, Eichholtz, and Kok, "The Price of Innovation: An Analysis of the Marginal Cost of Green Buildings," 15.

113 Chegut, Eichholtz, and Kok, "The Price of Innovation: An Analysis of the Marginal Cost of Green Buildings," 16.

Fig. 68

Elemental Costs for BREEAM-Certified and Non-Certified Buildings

%

*** p<0.01, ** p<0.05, * p<0.1

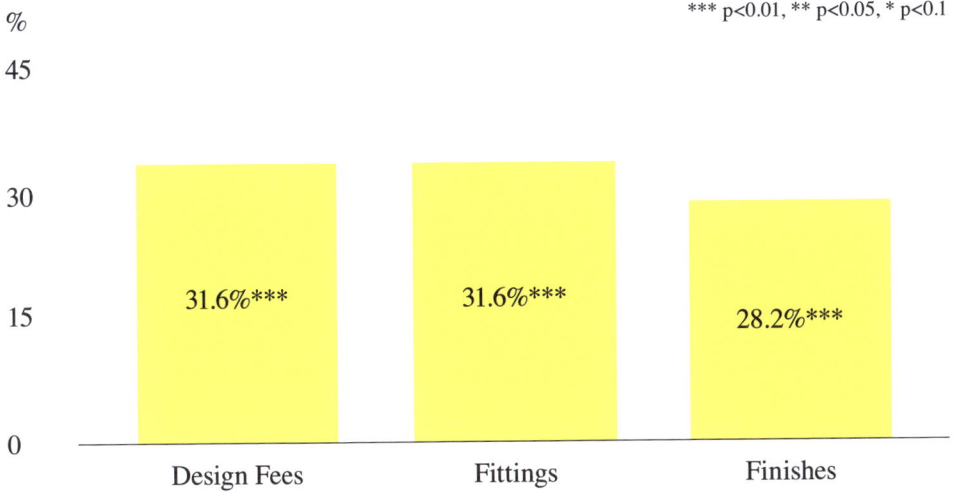

Note: Elemental costs for BREEAM-certified and non-certified buildings with dependent variable: logarithm of transaction price.

market barrier is effectively the long construction time. The project length essentially increases the uncertainty of total project costs and ultimately the uncertainty around the developer's expected return on equity. However, this additional time required to construct green buildings will reduce with time as both developers and construction companies become more experienced with green building construction.

On the other hand, the higher construction cost elements related to design, fittings, and finishes discourage decision-making developers who must make the upfront payment from their equity.[114] Although these cost elements on aggregate represent a small proportion of total costs and are presumably capitalized into the price at which the developer can sell an asset, they accrue to a group of stakeholders making decisions that impact the lifecycle value of the entire building. Importantly, even though design fees are only 3% of overall costs, these fees are investments with a significant risk, since fees are paid during a phase when developers still face fundamental uncertainty regarding the success of their project.

114 David Geltner et al., *Commercial Real Estate Analysis and Investments* (Nashville: Southwestern Educational Publishing House, 2006), 777.

These fees can thus be regarded as the premium a developer has to incur for the option to develop a building. The fact that the results show design fees that are more than 150% higher for the most advanced green buildings reduces the likelihood that developers engage in the option to develop such projects. Fittings and finishes are implemented later in the development process, but if lenders are unwilling to provide additional financing for more sustainable, green buildings, these additional costs might prohibit green construction.

For the first time, we are able to systematically present evidence to show potential barriers to green building adoption, which primarily consist of high upfront design costs and long construction times. However, we can see that the marginal benefits of green construction in the long run outweigh the marginal costs, making a case for green building adoption not only from an environmental sustainability perspective but also from a financial sustainability perspective.

Augmenting the existing quality of a product or process often requires a significant amount of effort, which leads to the "slow diffusion problem" that we see with green building adoption in the building design and construction industry. Changing the way we do things costs time and effort that many building practitioners are unwilling to spend. However, innovation comes in iterative waves as forward-thinking designers and developers continue to create products that disrupt conventional practices which ultimately help move forward the standards and qualities of our products. Eventually, we arrive at a steady state in which new standards are established and acknowledged as accepted practice, and from which the cycle of innovation and disruption repeats. It is important to understand how we move from these innovative design approaches to normalizing them as new standards that could help us solve greater societal challenges such as climate change, an effort that requires a productive coalition between designers, developers, researchers, and policymakers.

Epilogue

This book is one of the early exploratory works to bridge the gap between design and finance in architecture and real estate by harnessing the availability of big urban data and sensing technologies. We delve into the intricacies of the fields of real estate analytics and architecture and urban design to understand their unique language and evaluation techniques and to find a common ground where they could meet.

Acknowledging the limitations in evaluating design through descriptive anecdotes, we shift our focuses to computational techniques and data technologies. Conceptually, building upon studies by Ching and Koolhaas, we consider design as a unique combination of physical, aesthetic, performative, and functional considerations in the process of constructing buildings.[1] Statistically, our research and analysis delve into the physical and performative aspects of architectural design language, identifying and turning specific design features into quantitatively measurable variables. These features include formal components on the building's appearance, functional components that shape interior experiences, and the buildings' surrounding urban environments. In this way,

---

1   Frank Ching, *Architecture, Form, Space & Order* (New York: John Wiley & Sons, 1979); Rem Koolhaas et al., *Elements of Architecture* (Los Angeles: TASCHEN, 2018).

our studies and discussions point toward a more data-driven perspective that differentiates from previous perspectives that associated real estate value with an architect's accolades or expert scoring and a more nuanced approach that no longer relies on crude classification of buildings. With some novel insights on the relationships between design and their economic values, we anticipate there may be further exploration relying on robust statistics and nuanced surveying methods to understand not only design, but also design's wide impacts on other socioeconomic activities.

Evidence for the Values of Design

Our studies provide pieces of evidence of design's economic impacts on real estate pricing. The prestige of its architect and the awards of the design have a demonstrable impact on its economic value. Buildings crafted by award-winning architects or with an award-winning design command a significant premium in the real estate market. This premium is not uniform but varies according to the accolade. Designs by AIA Firm Award winners attract the highest premiums, highlighting the value that the market places on renowned architectural expertise.[2]

2   Kang, "Dancing With the Stars : The Value of Design in Real Estate Development," 68-70.

The external architectural features of a building also play a crucial role in its economic performance in the market.[3] For a unique urban environment like Manhattan, certain design features like building's diagonality and podium extrusion not only influence the transaction price but also affect rental income positively. It is likely that these features enhance the street-level experience by providing amenities and facilitating social interactions, which in turn contribute to the economic premium on such properties. Conversely, other design elements such as setbacks can have a negative economic impact, suggesting that while certain design innovations are favored, others may be detrimental to value.

Functional design attributes within buildings also influence real estate pricing. The intrinsic qualities of daylight and view access in office spaces are more than just aesthetic concerns – they carry a significant economic premium. High levels of natural light and open views are associated with increased transaction prices.[4] This underlines the importance of integrating these elements into the design and development of office buildings as they are not only desirable for the well-being and productivity of the occupants but also for their potential to yield financial

3   Rong, "The Value of Design in Real Estate Asset Pricing," 17-18.
4   Turan et al., "The Value of Daylight in Office Spaces," 8-10; Turan et al., "Development of View Potential Metrics and the Financial Impact of Views on Office Rents," 5-10.

returns. In addition, the quality of the workplace environments, as measured by the Workplace Performance Index (WPI[SM]), also correlates with higher effective rents.[5] This suggests that there is a market acknowledgment of the link between the physical quality of interior workplace design and employee productivity, even though it may be difficult to quantify. In adjacency to buildings, the presence of urban greenery has been recognized as a contributing factor to higher transaction and leasing prices for commercial buildings. This observation encourages urban planners and real estate developers to invest in street-level greenery, aligning urban environmental benefits with economic incentives.[6]

Collectively, these insights underline the significant economic impacts of design choices in today's urban environment. They highlight a growing acknowledgment in real estate studies and practices of the value added by both aesthetic and functional design features, which can manifest in considerable economic premiums for properties that embody these characteristics.

The convergence of architectural design with financial analysis heralds a transformative period where the value of design transcends aesthetics and utility. In this era, the marriage of a building's

5   Puri, John, and Chegut, "Does Work Performance Design Impact Value? Linking Design Metrics to Financial Performance in Cities," 20-25.
6   Yang et al., "The Financial Impact of Street-Level Greenery on New York Commercial Buildings," 7-8.

form and real estate financial modeling is no longer a distant ideal but a practical reality. Holistic valuation practices now recognize the qualitative, and sometimes subjective, impact of design on social and environmental outcomes. This paradigm shift is reflected in how buildings designed with resiliency, equity, health, and wellness in mind begin to command not only admiration but also tangible financial premiums. As seen in New York City's real estate market, features that enhance public amenities or workplace environments are directly linked to economic returns, demonstrating that design excellence and financial success are not mutually exclusive but rather interdependent.

New York City's dynamic and diverse urban ecosystem has long served as an incubator for groundbreaking approaches to urban development. It acts as a laboratory where the integration of design and finance is rigorously applied and continuously evolved. However, the principles and strategies that prove successful in New York have implications far beyond its borders. They serve as a template for global urban development, adaptable to the varied contexts of cities worldwide. There is an enduring imperative to extend this spirit of innovation and to continually challenge and refine the integration of design with financial viability. The call to action extends to all stakeholders in the urban development process: to harness the momentum generated within the pages of research and the frameworks established by forward-thinking cities like New York and to drive socially responsible and economically viable design strategies across the globe.

Social and Environmental Benefits

The significant relationship between design and economic value creation is garnering the attention of key stakeholders and decision-makers who influence the built environment. This book operates under the premise that design transcends mere aesthetics or compliance; it is a potent source of tangible economic, social, and environmental value in contemporary society. To fully appreciate design's impact, a holistic perspective is crucial—even if the focus is on a singular value among the three.

As indicated in some of our research projects, there is an emerging shift toward socially responsible and sustainable designs to balance investor returns and the public good. The industry is witnessing a transformative approach where design not only adheres to zoning laws and investment returns but also proactively contributes to community resilience, social equity, health, and individual well-being. Such a realization echoes the ethical imperative that intersects deeply with social welfare and environmental preservation. In real estate development and building construction, design strategies are propelled by a collective realization that buildings can and should serve the greater good. Such a nuanced appreciation for design's role in environmental and social sustainability has been reinforced in the post-pandemic era. The health crisis has further underscored the urgency for adaptive and responsive urban spaces, highlighting the need for designs that accommodate shifted living and working paradigms. Evidently, high-quality public spaces, amenities with access to the outdoors, and the presence of greenery have become critical features to attract urban dwellers in the post-pandemic real estate market. The future of real estate development hinges on the ability to anticipate and respond to evolving lifestyle demands, with a renewed focus on human-oriented design.

While long-term socially beneficial design may enhance market-capturable economic value, stakeholders involved in construction may lack this farsighted vision, focusing instead on immediate market prices. The public sector and conscious designers face the challenge of balancing and capturing the long-term social benefits of design without significantly compromising the economic value for developers. It is incumbent upon architects, urban planners, developers, and associated professionals to unite in a concerted effort to embed sustainable and socially responsible principles into the fabric of our urban environments. By harnessing collective expertise and vision, these professionals can craft spaces that do more than function—they can inspire, support, and sustain the community and environmental health.

Bibliography

AARP Livable Communities. "AARP Livability Fact Sheet - Sidewalks." AARP, 2013. Accessed December 30, 2022. https://www.aarp.org/content/dam/aarp/livable-communities/livable-documents/documents-2014/Livability%20Fact%20Sheets/Sidewalks-Fact-Sheet.pdf.

Adams, Nicholas. *Gordon Bunshaft and SOM: Building Corporate Modernism.* New Haven: Yale University Press, 2019.

Ahlfeldt, Gabriel M. and Alexandra Mastro. "Valuing Iconic Design: Frank Lloyd Wright Architecture in Oak Park, Illinois." *Housing Studies* 27, no. 8 (November 1, 2012): 1079–99. https://doi.org/10.1080/02673037.2012.728575.

Alexander, Christopher, Sara Ishikawa, and Murray Silverstein. *A Pattern Language: Towns, Buildings, Construction.* New York: Oxford University Press, 1977.

Ambrey, Christopher L., and Christopher Fleming. "Public Greenspace and Life Satisfaction in Urban Australia." *Urban Studies* 51, no. 6 (July 18, 2013): 1290–1321. https://doi.org/10.1177/0042098013494417.

American Institute of Architects (AIA). "1950 Survey of the Architectural Profession: Progress Report." *The Survey of Education and Registration.* American Institute of Architects, 1951.

American Planning Association. "Broadway: New York, New York." 2014. https://www.planning.org/greatplaces/streets/2014/broadway.htm.

Architectural Forum. "Seagram's Bronze Tower." July 1958.

Aries, Myriam, Jennifer A. Veitch, and Guy R. Newsham. "Windows, view, and office characteristics predict physical and psychological discomfort." *Journal of Environmental Psychology* 30, no. 4 (December 1, 2010): 533–41. https://doi.org/10.1016/j.jenvp.2009.12.004.

Arvanitidis, Paschalis, Konstantinos Lalenis, George Petrakos, and Yannis Psycharis. "Economic Aspects of Urban Green Space: A Survey of Perceptions and Attitudes." *International Journal of Environmental Technology and Management* 11, no. 1/2/3 (January 1, 2009): 143. https://doi.org/10.1504/ijetm.2009.027192.

Babin, Janet. "Luxury Condos Help Fuel NYC Construction Boom." *WNYC*, October 23, 2014. http://www.wnyc.org/story/luxury-condos-help-fuel-construction-boom/.

Bagli, Charles. "G.M. Building Sells For $1.4 Billion, A Record." *New York Times*, August 30, 2003. https://www.nytimes.com/2003/08/30/nyregion/gm-building-sells-for-1.4-billion-a-record.html.

Barr, Jason. "The Economics of Skyscraper Construction in Manhattan: Past, Present, and Future." *International Journal of High-Rise Buildings* 5, no. 2 (2016): 137–44.

———. "Manhattan Profits (Part II): Return on Investment for a Superslim Skyscraper - Building the Skyline." *Building the Skyline - The Birth & Growth of Manhattan's Skyscrapers* (blog), November 26, 2017. https://buildingtheskyline.org/manhattan-profits-2-roi/

Batty, Michael. "Exploring Isovist Fields: Space and shape in architectural and urban morphology." *Environment and Planning B: Planning and Design* 28, no. 1 (February 1, 2001): 123–50. https://doi.org/10.1068/b2725.

Benedikt, Michael. "To take hold of space: isovists and isovist fields." *Environment and Planning B: Planning and Design* 6, no. 1 (January 1, 1979): 47–65. https://doi.org/10.1068/b060047.

Berg, Eric N. "Citicorp Selling Part Offers Headquarter." *New York Times*, October 3, 1987.

Bessen, James. "Employers Aren't Just Whining – the 'Skills Gap' Is Real." *Harvard Business Review*, August 15, 2014. Accessed January 20, 2021. https://hbr.org/2014/08/employers-arent-just-whining-the-skills-gap-is-real.

Bhatia, Shashank, Stephan K. Chalup, and Michael J. Ostwald. "Wayfinding: a method for the empirical evaluation of structural saliency using 3D Isovists." *Architectural Science Review* 56, no. 3 (August 1, 2013): 220–31. https://doi.org/10.1080/00038628.2013.811635.

Bille, Mikkel, and Tim Flohr Sorensen, eds. *Elements of Architecture: Assembling Archaeology, Atmosphere and the Performance of Building Spaces.* London: Routledge, 2016.

Board of Governors of the Federal Research Systems. "Financial Stability Report - May 2023." *The Federal Reserve*, 2023. https://www.fcderalreserve.gov/publications/2023-may-financial-stability-report-purpose-and-framework.htm.

Borges, Jorge Luis. *Collected Fictions.* New York: Peguin Books, 1999.

Boysen, Ryan. "The Priciest Lease in NYC History May Have Just Been Signed." *BISNOW*, February 17, 2016. https://www.bisnow.com/new-york/news/office/the-priciest-lease-in-nyc-history-may-have-just-been-signed-56099.

Bratman, Gregory N., Gretchen C. Daily, Benjamin J. Levy, and James J. Gross. "The Benefits of Nature Experience: Improved Affect and Cognition." *Landscape and Urban Planning* 138 (June 1, 2015): 41–50. https://doi.org/10.1016/j.landurbplan.2015.02.005.

Brenzel, Kathryn. "NYC's 10 Most Active Developers of 2020." *The Real Deal*, December 28, 2020.

Brill, Michael H. "Workspace Design and Productivity." *PubMed* 35, no. 5 (August 6, 1992): 51, 53. https://pubmed.ncbi.nlm.nih.gov/10121434.

Bryson, Alex, John Forth, and Lucy Stokes. "Does Worker Wellbeing Affect Workplace Performance?" *Social Science Research Network*, January 1, 2015. https://doi.org/10.2139/ssrn.2655044.

Carlin, David. "40% of Emissions Come From Real Estate: Here's How the Sector Can Decarbonize." *Forbes*, April 5, 2022. https://www.forbes.

com/sites/davidcarlin/2022/04/05/40-of-emissions-come-from-real-estate-heres-how-the-sector-can-decarbonize/?sh=606dcdd263b7.

CBRE. "2019 H2 Manhattan Office Market Review." *CBRE*, January 1, 2020.

— — —. "Office Buildings Hardest Hit by Pandemic Share Common Characteristics." CBRE, April 04, 2023. https://www.cbre.com/insights/viewpoints/office-buildings-hardest-hit-by-pandemic-share-common-characteristics.

CBRE and Maastricht University. "National Green Building Adoption Index 2015." CBRE. CBRE and Maastricht University, 2014. Accessed June 1, 2021. https://www.corporatesustainabilitystrategies.com/cbre-real-green-research-index/.

Chandrasekar, Karim. "Workplace environment and its impact on organisational performance in public sector organisations." *International Journal of Enterprise Computing and Business Systems* 1, no. 1 (January 2011): 1-19. https://www.ijecbs.com/January2011/N4Jan2011.pdf.

Chau, Kwong Wing, Siu Kei Wong, and Cy Yiu. "The value of the provision of a balcony in apartments in Hong Kong." *Social Science Research Network*, January 1, 2004. https://papers.ssrn.com/sol3/Delivery.cfm/SSRN_ID1465195_code537855.pdf?abstractid=1465195&mirid=1.

Chegut, Andrea, Piet Eichholtz, and Nils Kok. "Supply, Demand and the Value of Green Buildings." *Urban Studies* 51, no. 1 (May 16, 2013): 22–43. https://doi.org/10.1177/0042098013484526.

— — —. "The Price of Innovation: An Analysis of the Marginal Cost of Green Buildings." *Journal of Environmental Economics and Management* 98 (November 1, 2019): 102248. https://doi.org/10.1016/j.jeem.2019.07.003.

Chegut, Andrea, Piet Eichholtz, and Paulo Rodrigues. "Spatial Dependence in International Office Markets." *Journal of Real Estate Finance and Economics* 31, no. 2 (November 9, 2014): 317–50. https://doi.org/10.1007/s11146-014-9484-x.

Chen, Stefanos. "The Decade Dominated by the Ultraluxury Condo." *New York Times*, January 10, 2020. https://www.nytimes.com/2020/01/10/realestate/new-york-decade-real-estate.html.

Chen, Stefanos, and Sydney Franklin. "New York Rents Continue to Slide, While Sales Rebound in Brooklyn." New York Times (italicized), January 14, 2021.

Chen, Wendy Y. "The Role of Urban Green Infrastructure in Offsetting Carbon Emissions in 35 Major Chinese Cities: A Nationwide Estimate." *Cities* 44 (April 1, 2015): 112–20. https://doi.org/10.1016/j.cities.2015.01.005.

Cheshire, Paul, and Gerard Dericks. "'Iconic Design' as Deadweight Loss: Rent Acquisition by Design in the Constrained London Office Market." *RePEc: Research Papers in Economics*, January 23, 2014.

Ching, Francis. *Architecture, Form, Space & Order.* 1st ed. New York: John Wiley & Sons, 1979.

Chupin, Jean-Pierre, Carmela Cucuzzella, and Georges Adamczyk. *The Rise of Awards in Architecture.* 1st ed. Vernon Press, 2022.

Clough, Shepard Bancroft. *A Century of American Life Insurance: A History of the Mutual Life Insurance Company of New York, 1843-1943.* New York : Columbia University Press, 1946.

Coppola, Nicholas, and Wesley E. Marshall. "An evaluation of sidewalk availability and width: Analyzing municipal policy and equity disparities." *International Conference on Transportation and Development 2020*, August 31, 2020. https://doi.org/10.1061/9780784483152.002.

Council, U.S. Green Building. *LEED Reference Guide for Building Design and Construction, V4*, 2013.

Coxe, Weld, Nina F. Hartung, Hugh H. Hochberg, Brian J. Lewis, Maister, Robert F. Mattox, and Peter A. Piven. "Charting Your Course." *Architectural Technology* 5 (1982): 52–58. http://davidmaister.com/wp-content/themes/davidmaister/pdf/ChartingYourcourse750.pdf.

Crompton, John L. "The Impact of Parks on Property Values: Empirical Evidence From the Past Two Decades in the United States." *Managing Leisure* 10, no. 4 (October 1, 2005): 203–18. https://doi.org/10.1080/13606710500348060.

Davis, Brian. "On Broadway, Tactical Urbanism." *faslanyc: Speculative Histories, Landscapes and Instruments, and Latin American Landscape Architecture* (2010).

Davis, Howard. "The Future of Ancient Lights." *Journal of Architectural and Planning Research* 6, no. 2 (1988): 132–53. https://www.jstor.org/stable/43028917.

De Certeau, Michel, and Pierre Mayol. *The Practice of Everyday Life: Living and Cooking. Volume 2.* U of Minnesota Press, 1998.

Deng, Yongheng, and Jing Wu. "Economic Returns to Residential Green Building Investment: The Developers' Perspective." *Regional Science and Urban Economics* 47 (July 1, 2014): 35–44. https://doi.org/10.1016/j.regsciurbeco.2013.09.015.

Derrington, Patrice. *Built Up: An Historical Perspective on the Contemporary Principles and Practices of Real Estate Development.* London: Routledge, 2021.

Doraiswamy, Harish, Nivan Ferreira, Marcos Lage, Huy T. Vo, Luc Wilson, Heidi Werner, Muchan Park, and Cláudio Silva. "Topology-based Catalogue Exploration Framework for Identifying View-enhanced Tower Designs." *ACM Transactions on Graphics* 34, no. 6 (November 2, 2015): 1–13. https://doi.org/10.1145/2816795.2818134.

Douglas Elliman Inc. "The Douglas Elliman Report, 2001-2010." *Miller Samuel*, 2011. https://millersamuel.com/files/2011/10/MMR10.pdf.

Drew, J.E. "The Economic Value of Design." New Orleans, United States of America, June 25, 1959. Quoted in Nicholas Adams. *Gordon Bunshaft and SOM: Building Corporate Modernism.* New Haven: Yale University Press, 2019.

Eichholtz, Piet, Nils Kok, and John M. Quigley. "Doing Well by Doing Good? Green Office Buildings." *The American Economic Review* 100, no. 5 (December 1, 2010): 2492–2509. https://doi.org/10.1257/aer.100.5.2492.

———. "The Economics of Green Building." *The Review of Economics and Statistics* 95, no. 1 (March 1, 2013): 50–63. https://doi.org/10.1162/rest_a_00291.

Ennis, Thomas W. "Company Edifices 'Sell' Products: Businesses Find That It Pays to Advertise With Good Architecture." *New York Times*, August 7, 1960.

Esri, "ArcGIS: The Foundation for Digital Twins," 2021.

Ewing, Reid, and Susan Handy. "Measuring the Unmeasurable: Urban Design Qualities Related to Walkability." *Journal of Urban Design (Abingdon)* 14, no. 1 (February 1, 2009): 65–84. https://doi.org/10.1080/13574800802451155.

Ewing, Reid, Susan Handy, Ross C. Brownson, Otto Clemente, and Emily Winston. "Identifying and Measuring Urban Design Qualities Related to Walkability." *Journal of Physical Activity & Health* 3, no. s1 (February 1, 2006): S223–40. https://doi.org/10.1123/jpah.3.s1.s223.

Faria e Castro, Miguel and Samuel Jordan-Wood. "Commercial Real Estate: Where Are the Financial Risks?" *Economic Research Federal Reserve Bank of St. Louis*, 2023. https://research.stlouisfed.org/publications/economic-synopses/2023/11/17/commercial-real-estate-where-are-the-financial-risks.

Feige, Annika, Patrick McAllister, and Holger Wallbaum. "Rental Price and Sustainability Ratings: Which Sustainability Criteria Are Really Paying Back?" *Construction Management and Economics* 31, no. 4 (April 1, 2013): 322–34. https://doi.org/10.1080/01446193.2013.769686.

Fernandez, Rodrigo, Annclore Hofman, and Manuel B. Aalbers. "London and New York as a Safe Deposit Box for the Transnational Wealth Elite." *Environment and Planning A: Economy and Space* 48, no. 12 (2016): 2443–61.

Ferriss, Hugh. *The Metropolis of Tomorrow*. Mineola: Dover Publications, 2005.

Fishman, Robert, ed. *The American Planning Tradition: Culture and Policy*. Washington D.C.: Woodrow Wilson Center Press, 2000.

Frank, Robert. "Manhattan Real Estate Prices Reach Record as Buying 'frenzy' Takes Hold," CNBC (italicized), July 2, 2021.

Freeman, Lance, Kathryn M. Neckerman, Ofira Schwartz-Soicher, James W. Quinn, Catherine Richards, Michael Bader, Gina S. Lovasi, et al. "Neighborhood Walkability and Active Travel (Walking and Cycling) in New York City." *Journal of Urban Health* 90, no. 4 (September 1, 2012): 575–85. https://doi.org/10.1007/s11524-012-9758-7.

Frontczak, Monika Joanna and Paweł Wargocki. "Literature survey on how different factors influence human comfort in indoor environments." *Building and Environment* 46, no. 4 (April 1, 2011): 922–37. https://doi.org/10.1016/j.buildenv.2010.10.021.

Fuerst, Franz and Jorn Van De Wetering. "How Does Environmental Efficiency Impact on the Rents of Commercial Offices in the U.K.?" *Journal of Property Research* 32, no. 3 (June 22, 2015): 193–216. https://doi.org/10.1080/09599916.2015.1047399.

Fuerst, Franz and Patrick McAllister. "New Evidence on the Green Building Rent and Price Premium." *Social Science Research Network*, January 1, 2009. https://doi.org/10.2139/ssrn.1372440.

———. "Green Noise or Green Value? Measuring the Effects of Environmental Certification on Office Values." *Real Estate Economics* 39, no. 1 (December 1, 2010): 45–69. https://doi.org/10.1111/j.1540-6229.2010.00286.x.

Fuerst, Franz, Patrick McAllister, and Claudia Murray. "Designer Buildings: Estimating the Economic Value of 'Signature' Architecture." *Environment and Planning A: Economy and Space* 43, no. 1 (January 1, 2011): 166–84. https://doi.org/10.1068/a43270.

Galasiu, Anca D. and Jennifer A. Veitch. "Occupant preferences and satisfaction with the luminous environment and control systems in daylit offices: a literature review." *Energy and Buildings* 38, no. 7 (July 1, 2006): 728–42. https://doi.org/10.1016/j.enbuild.2006.03.001.

Geltner, David, Norman G. Miller, Jim Clayton, and Piet Eichholtz. *Commercial Real Estate Analysis and Investments*. 2nd ed. Nashville: Southwestern Educational Publishing House, 2006.

Gensler. "U.S. WORKPLACE SURVEY 2016," 2016. Accessed July 23, 2017. https://www.gensler.com/workplace-surveys/us/2016.

Gensler Research Institute. "Gensler Experience Index." *Gensler*, December 1, 2017. Accessed December 30, 2022. https://www.gensler.com/doc/gensler-experience-index-2017.

Giovanetti, Erika. "Review of Historical Mortgage Rates: See Averages and Trends by Decade." *US News*, November 22, 2023. https://money.usnews.com/loans/mortgages/articles/historical-mortgage-rates.

Glaessgen, Edward and David Stargel. "The digital twin paradigm for future NASA and US Air Force vehicles." In *53rd AIAA/ASME/ASCE/AHS/ASC structures, structural dynamics and materials conference 20th AIAA/ASME/AHS adaptive structures conference 14th AIAA*, 2012.

Goldberger, Paul. "New York and the New Urbanism: Congress for the New Urbanism, New York, NY." *Lectures*, June 9, 2001. https://www.paulgoldberger.com/lectures/new-york-and-the-new-urbanism/.

Goldfield, David R. and Blaine A. Brownell. *Urban America: A History*. New York: Houghton Mifflin, 1990.

Gómez-Puerto, Gerardo, Enric Munar, and Marcos Nadal. "Preference for curvature: a historical and conceptual framework." *Frontiers in Human Neuroscience* 9 (January 12, 2016): 1. https://doi.org/10.3389/fnhum.2015.00712.

Grant, Jill. "The Dark Side of the Grid: Power and Urban Design." *Planning Perspectives* 16, no. 3 (January 1, 2001): 219–41. https://doi.org/10.1080/02665430152469575.

Grieves, Michael. "Digital twin: manufacturing excellence through virtual factory replication." *White paper* 1, no. 2014 (2014): 1-7.

Grieves, Michael and John Vickers. "Digital Twin: Mitigating Unpredictable, Undesirable Emergent Behavior in Complex Systems." In *Springer eBooks*, 85–113, 2016. https://doi.org/10.1007/978-3-319-38756-7_4.

Gupta, Arpit, Vrinda Mittal, and Stijin Van Nieuwerburgh. "Work From Home and the Office Real Estate Apocalypse." *National Bureau of Economic Research*, 2022.

Haag, Matthew. "A Bleak Outlook for Manhattan's Office Space May Signal a Bigger Problem." *New York Times*, April 25, 2023.

Haag, Matthew. "How Luxury Developers Use a Loophole to Build Soaring Towers for the Ultrarich in N.Y." *New York Times*, April 20, 2019. https://www.nytimes.com/2019/04/20/nyregion/tallest-buildings-manhattan-loophole.html.

Harvey, Meli and NYC Open Data, eds. "Sidewalk Widths NYC." NYC Open Data, 2020. Accessed December 30, 2023. https://opendata.cityofnewyork.us/projects/sidewalk-widths-nyc/.

Hillier, Bill. *Space Is the Machine: A Configurational Theory of Architecture*. Cambridge: Cambridge University Press, 1996.

Hofstadtler, Richard. *The Age of Reform: From Bryan to FDR*. New York: Vintage Press, 1955.

Holtermans, Rogier and Nils Kok. "International Green Building Adoption Index 2018." *CBRE*. CBRE, January 1, 2018. https://cris.maastrichtuniversity.nl/en/publications/international-green-building-adoption-index-2018.

Holusha, John. "Office Vacancies Rise, as Do Building Prices." *New York Times*, September 15, 2002. https://www.nytimes.com/2002/09/15/realestate/office-vacancies-rise-as-do-building-prices.html.

Horr, Yousef Al, Mohammed Arif, Aditya Kaushik, Ahmed Mazroei, Martha Katafygiotou, and Esam Elsarrag. "Occupant productivity and office indoor environment quality: A review of the literature." *Building and Environment* 105 (August 1, 2016): 369–89. https://doi.org/10.1016/j.buildenv.2016.06.001.

Hough, Douglas E. and Charles G. Kratz. "Can 'good' architecture meet the market test?" *Journal of Urban Economics* 14, no. 1 (July 1, 1983): 40–54. https://doi.org/10.1016/0094-1190(83)90028-1.

Hung, W.T. and Wan Ki Chow. "A review on architectural aspects of atrium buildings." *Architectural Science Review* 44, no. 3 (September 1, 2001): 285–95. https://doi.org/10.1080/00038628.2001.9697484.

Huxtable, Ada Louise. "Park Avenue School of Architecture: Business and Its New Sleek and Shiny Temples Have Transformed a Famous Residential Street." *New York Times*, December 15, 1957.

———. *The Tall Building Artistically Reconsidered: The Search for a Skyscraper Style*. Berkeley: University of California Press, 1992.

Illuminating Engineering Society of North America. "Approved Method: IES Spatial Daylight Autonomy (sDA) and Annual Sunlight Exposure (ASE)." *Illuminating Engineering Society*, January 1, 2012. Accessed January 10, 2022. https://infoscience.epfl.ch/record/196436.

International Council of Design, "What Is Design?," n.d. https://www.theicod.org/en/professional-design/what-is-design/what-is-design.

Ivanov, Sergey, Ksenia Nikolskaya, Глеб Радченко, Leonid B. Sokolinsky, and Mikhail Zymbler. "Digital Twin of City: Concept Overview." *2020 Global Smart Industry Conference (GloSIC)*, November 17, 2020. https://doi.org/10.1109/glosic50886.2020.9267879.

Jacobs, Jane. *The Death and Life of Great American Cities*. 1st ed. New York: Random House, 1961.

Jayantha, Wadu Mesthrige and Cheng Ka. "Do buyers value a balcony as a green feature? An Empirical analysis of the Hong Kong residential property market." *Journal of Real Estate Practice and Education* 20, no. 1 (January 1, 2017): 27–49. https://doi.org/10.1080/10835547.2017.12091768.

Jones, David, Chris Snider, Aydin Nassehi, Jason Yon, and Ben Hicks. "Characterising the Digital Twin: A Systematic Literature Review." *CIRP Journal of Manufacturing Science and Technology* 29 (May 1, 2020): 36–52. https://doi.org/10.1016/j.cirpj.2020.02.002.

Kahn, Ely Jacques. "Our Skyscrapers Take Simple Forms." *New York Times* 4 (1926): 22.

Kang, Minkoo. "Dancing with the stars : the value of design in real estate development," 2019. https://dspace.mit.edu/handle/1721.1/124036.

Kang, Yuhao, Fan Zhang, Song Gao, Hui Lin, and Yu Liu. "A Review of Urban Physical Environment Sensing Using Street View Imagery in Public Health Studies." *Annals of GIS* 26, no. 3 (July 2, 2020): 261–75. https://doi.org/10.1080/19475683.2020.1791954.

Kastle, "Getting America Back to Work." 2023. https://www.kastle.com/safety-wellness/getting-america-back-to-work/.

Kayden, Jerold S. "The New York City Department of City Planning, and The Municipal Art Society of New York." *Privately Owned Public Space: The New York City Experience* (2000): 9-12.

Kempeneer, Shirley, M. Peeters, and Tine Compernolle. "Bringing the User Back in the Building: An Analysis of ESG in Real Estate and a Behavioral Framework to Guide Future Research." *Sustainability* 13, no. 6 (March 15, 2021): 3239. https://doi.org/10.3390/su13063239.

Kepos, Paula and Thomas Derdak. *International Directory of Company Histories*. Chicago: Saint James Press, 1988.

Kerr, Robert Malcolm. *On Ancient Lights and the Evidence of Surveyors Thereon: With Tables for the Measurement of Obstructions*. London: John Murray, 1865.

King, Moses, ed. *New York: The American Cosmopolis, the Foremost City of the World.* Boston: M. King, 1894.

Kok, Nils and Maarten Jennen. "The Impact of Energy Labels and Accessibility on Office Rents." *Energy Policy* 46 (July 1, 2012): 489–97. https://doi.org/10.1016/j.enpol.2012.04.015.

Kong, Lily and Orlando Woods. "The Ideological Alignment of Smart Urbanism in Singapore: Critical Reflections on a Political Paradox." *Urban Studies* 55, no. 4 (January 16, 2018): 679–701. https://doi.org/10.1177/0042098017746528.

Koolhaas, Rem. *Delirious New York: A Retroactive Manifesto for Manhattan.* Oxford: Oxford University Press, 1978.

Koolhaas, Rem, Stephan Trüby, Hans Werlemann, Kevin Mcleod, and Irma Boom. *Elements of Architecture: Corridor.* Venice: Marsilio, 2014.

Kostof, Spiro. *The Architect: Chapters in the History of the Profession.* Oxford: Oxford University Press, 1986.

Kulp, Scott and Benjamin Strauss. "New Elevation Data Triple Estimates of Global Vulnerability to Sea-level Rise and Coastal Flooding." *Nature Communications* 10, no. 1 (October 29, 2019): 3. https://doi.org/10.1038/s41467-019-12808-z.

Lambert, Phyllis. *Building Seagram.* New Haven: Yale University Press, 2013.

Landau, Sarah Bradford and Carl W. Condit. *Rise of the New York Skyscraper: 1865-1913.* New Haven: Yale University Press, 1999.

Leaman, Adrian and Bill Bordass. "Building Design, Complexity and Manageability." *Facilities* 11, no. 9 (September 1, 1993): 16–27. https://doi.org/10.1108/eum0000000002256.

Leblebici, Demet. "Impact of Workplace Quality on Employee's Productivity: Case Study of a Bank in Turkey." *Journal of Business Economics and Finance* 1, no. 1 (2012): 38–49. https://dergipark.org.tr/tr/download/article-file/374627.

Lee, Douglass B. "Requiem for Large-Scale Models." *Journal of the American Institute of Planners* 39, no. 3 (May 1, 1973): 163–78. https://doi.org/10.1080/01944367308977851.

Leesman. "Are your workplaces the best places to work?" Leesman Index. Accessed July 23, 2017. https://www.leesmanindex.com/.

Levinson, David. "425 Park Avenue." 2012.

Li, Wenting and Holly Samuelson. "A New Method for Visualizing and Evaluating Views in Architectural Design." *Developments in the Built Environment* 1 (February 1, 2020): 100005. https://doi.org/10.1016/j.dibe.2020.100005.

Life Insurance Association of America. *Life Insurance Companies as Financial Institutions: A Monograph Prepared for the Commission on Money and Credit,* 1962.

Lindsey, Greg, Seth Payton, Joyce Y. Man, and John R. Ottensmann. "Public Choices and Property Values: Evidence From Greenways in Indianapolis." *Center for Urban Policy and the Environment Publications,* January 1, 2003. https://archives.iupui.edu/handle/2450/447.

Little, Gordon R., Bob Tuttle, D. E. R. Clark, and Jonathan Corney. "Measuring Geometric Complexity of 3D Models for Feature Recognition." *International Journal of Shape Modeling* 03, no. 03n04 (September 1, 1997): 141–54. https://doi.org/10.1142/s0218654397000112.

Love, Serena. "Architecture as material culture: Building form and materiality in the Pre-Pottery Neolithic of Anatolia and Levant." *Journal of Anthropological Archaeology* 32, no. 4 (December 1, 2013): 746–58. https://doi.org/10.1016/j.jaa.2013.05.002.

Lu, Qiuchen, Ajith Kumar Parlikad, Philip Woodall, Gishan Don Ranasinghe, Xinyou Xie, Zhenglin Liang, Eirini Konstantinou, James T. Heaton, and Jennifer Schooling. "Developing a Digital Twin at Building and City Levels: Case Study of West Cambridge Campus." *Journal of Management in Engineering* 36, no. 3 (May 1, 2020). https://doi.org/10.1061/(asce)me.1943-5479.0000763.

Luckman, Charles. *Twice in a Lifetime: From Soap to Skyscrapers.* New York: W.W. Norton & Company, 1988.

Lynch, Kevin. *The Image of the City.* Cambridge: MIT Press, 1960.

Macrotrends, "Federal Funds Rate - 62 Year Historical Chart." *Macrotrends,* 2022. https://www.macrotrends.net/2015/fed-funds-rate-historical-chart.

Makielski, Stanislaw J. *The Politics of Zoning: The New York Experience.* New York: Columbia University Press, 1966.

Marcuse, Peter. "The Grid as City Plan: New York City and Laissez-faire Planning in the Nineteenth Century." *Planning Perspectives* 2, no. 3 (September 1, 1987): 287–310. https://doi.org/10.1080/02665438708725645.

Mardaljevic, John. "Examples of Climate-Based Daylight Modelling." *CIBSE National Conference,* January 1, 2006, 1–11. http://climate-based-daylighting.com/lib/exe/fetch.php?media=academic:mardaljevic_cibse_paper.pdf.

Mazzolani, Federico and Victor Gioncu. *Behaviour of steel structures in seismic areas.* Boca Raton: CRC Press, 1995.

McCain, Abby. "30 Essential Hybrid Work Statistics [2023]: The Future of Work." *Zippia,* February 20, 2023. https://www.zippia.com/advice/hybrid-work-statistics/.

McGregor, Jena. "The Key Comparison to Make With This Year's Wall Street Bonuses." *Washington Post,* December 5, 2021. https://www.washingtonpost.com/news/on-leadership/wp/2015/03/12/the-key-comparison-to-make-with-this-years-wall-street-bonuses/.

McGregor, Patrick. "Real Estate's Recovery in New York City." *PropertyShark,* April 27, 2020.

McNamara, Robert S. and Brian VanDeMark. "In retrospect: the tragedy and lessons of Vietnam." Data set. *The SHAFR Guide Online,* October 2, 2017. https://doi.org/10.1163/2468-1733_shafr_sim170060030.

McPherson, John W. "Some Economic and Legal Aspects of the Purchase and Lease of Real Estate by Life Insurance Companies." *University of Pennsylvania Law Review* 97, no. 4 (March 1949): 482. DOI.

Mehta, Vikas. "Lively streets." *Journal of Planning Education and Research* 27, no. 2 (December 1, 2007): 165–87. https://doi.org/10.1177/0739456x07307947.

Mendis, Virangi. "Workplace Design and Job Performance: A Study of Operational Level Employees in the Apparel Industry of Sri Lanka." *International Journal of Scientific and Research Publications* 6, no. 12 (2016): 148–53.

Mike, Shafto, Conroy Mike, Doyle Rich, Glaessgen Ed, Kemp Chris, LeMoigne Jacqueline, and Wang Lui. "Modeling, Simulation, Information Technology & Processing Roadmap." *National Aeronautics and Space Administration* 32, no. 2012 (2012): 1–38.

Miller, Norm. "Collaborative, Productive and Innovative Workspaces: Implications for Future Office Demand Telecommuting Will Kill." Slideshow, February 13, 2014. https://www.normmiller.net/?edmc=463.

Miller, Norman G., Jay Spivey, and Andrew Florance. "Does Green Pay Off?" *The Journal of Real Estate Portfolio Management* 14, no. 4 (January 1, 2008): 385–400. https://doi.org/10.1080/10835547.2008.12089822.

Mohr, Rick. "Office Space Is a Revenue Enhancer, Not an Expense." *National Real Estate Investor*, July 1, 1996. Accessed January 10, 2022. https://www.nreionline.com/mag/office-space-revenue-enhancer-not-expense.

Morancho, Aurelia Bengochea. "A Hedonic Valuation of Urban Green Areas." *Landscape and Urban Planning* 66, no. 1 (December 1, 2003): 35–41. https://doi.org/10.1016/s0169-2046(03)00093-8.

Mumford, Lewis. *The City in History : Its Origins, Its Transformations, and Its Prospects.* New York: Harcourt, 1961.

Murphy, Gardner. "Historical introduction to modern psychology." *Journal of the American Medical Association* 141, no. 15 (December 10, 1949): 1107. https://doi.org/10.1001/jama.1949.02910150073039.

Nancy Packes Inc. "December 2019, Market Report." *Nancy Packes Data Services*, 2020.

National Council of Architectural Registration Boards. "NBTN 2023 jurisdictions." National Council of Architectural Registration Boards Blog, August 7, 2023. Accessed December 30, 2023. https://www.ncarb.org/nbtn2023/jurisdictions.

New York Building Congress "NYC Construction Spending Reached $36 Billion in 2014; a 26 Percent Increase From 2013," April 2015. https://www.buildingcongress.com/advocacy-and-reports/reports-and-analysis/Construction-Outlook/NYC-construction-spending-reached-36-billion-in-2014-a-26-percent-increase-from-2013.html.

New York City Landmarks Preservation Commission. "Lever House." November 9, 1982.

Nicholls, Sarah, and John L. Crompton. "The Impact of Greenways on Property Values: Evidence From Austin, Texas." *Journal of Leisure Research* 37, no. 3 (September 1, 2005): 321–41. https://doi.org/10.1080/00222216.2005.11950056.

Niedens, Lyle. "Commercial Office Vacancy Rates Don›t Tell the Whole Story." *Investopedia*, June 8, 2023. https://www.investopedia.com/commercial-office-vacancy-rates-don-t-tell-whole-story-7507372.

Norton, Briony A., Andrew Coutts, Stephen J. Livesley, Richard Harris, Annie M. Hunter, and Nicholas S. G. Williams. "Planning for Cooler Cities: A Framework to Prioritise Green Infrastructure to Mitigate High Temperatures in Urban Landscapes." *Landscape and Urban Planning* 134 (February 1, 2015): 127–38. https://doi.org/10.1016/j.landurbplan.2014.10.018.

Nowak, David J., Robert E. Hoehn, and Daniel E. Crane. "Oxygen Production by Urban Trees in the United States." *Arboriculture and Urban Forestry* 33, no. 3 (May 1, 2007): 220–26. https://doi.org/10.48044/jauf.2007.026.

NYC Department of City Planning. *The Zoning Handbook.* New York: NYC Department of City Planning, 2018.

———. "NYC 3D Model Download." NYC Planning, 2014. Accessed December 30, 2021. https://www.nyc.gov/site/planning/data-maps/open-data/dwn-nyc-3d-model-download.page.

OECD, Paris. "OECD glossary of statistical terms." 2008.

Office of the State Comptroller. "The Construction Industry in New York City Recent Trends and Impact of COVID-19." Office of the New York State Comptroller. Office of the State Comptroller for the City of New York, June 2021. https://www.osc.ny.gov/reports/osdc/construction-industry-new-york-city-recent-trends-and-impact-covid-19.

Ostwald, Michael J. and Özgür Ediz. "Measuring Form, Ornament and Materiality in Sinan's Kılıç Ali Paşa Mosque: An Analysis Using Fractal Dimensions." *Nexus Network Journal* 17, no. 1 (October 22, 2014): 5–22. https://doi.org/10.1007/s00004-014-0219-3.

O'Neill, Philip. "Financial Narratives of the Modern Corporation." *Journal of Economic Geography* 1, no. 2 (2001): 181–99.

Palacios, Juan, Piet Eichholtz, and Nils Kok. "Moving to Productivity: The Benefits of Healthy Buildings." *Social Science Research Network*, January 1, 2020. https://doi.org/10.2139/ssrn.3710946.

Papp, Timea-Erika. "New York City's Recovery: Can History Help Estimate the Timeline?" *Commercial Property Executive*, April 13, 2020. https://www.commercialsearch.com/news/new-york-downturns-can-past-events-help-estimate-a-recovery-timeline/.

Park, Sun Jung Park. "Data Science Strategies for Real Estate Development." PhD diss., Massachusetts Institute of Technology, 2020.

Parker, Kim. "About a third of U.S. workers who can work from home now do so all the time." *Pew Research Center*. March 30, 2023. https://www.pewresearch.org/short-reads/2023/03/30/about-a-third-of-us-workers-who-can-work-from-home-do-so-all-the-time.

Partnership for New York City. "Return to Office Survey - June 2021." June 2021. https://pfnyc.org/research/return-to-office-survey-june-2021/.

Pearson, David. *New Organic Architecture: The Breaking Wave*. 1st ed. Berkeley and Los Angeles: University of California Press, 2001.

Pech, Richard J. and Bret Slade. "Employee Disengagement: Is There Evidence of a Growing Problem?" *Handbook of Business Strategy* 7, no. 1 (January 1, 2006): 21–25. https://doi.org/10.1108/10775730610618585.

Peponis, John, Jean Wineman, M. H. M. Rashid, S. Hong Kim, and Sonit Bafna. "On the description of shape and spatial configuration inside buildings: convex partitions and their local properties." *Environment and Planning B: Planning and Design* 24, no. 5 (January 1, 1997): 761–81. https://doi.org/10.1068/b240761.

Perini, Katia and Adriano Magliocco. "Effects of Vegetation, Urban Density, Building Height, and Atmospheric Conditions on Local Temperatures and Thermal Comfort." *Urban Forestry & Urban Greening* 13, no. 3 (January 1, 2014): 495–506. https://doi.org/10.1016/j.ufug.2014.03.003.

Pfciffer, Sophia Douglass. "Ancient Lights: Legal Protection of Access to Solar Energy." *American Bar Association Journal* 68, no. 3 (1982): 288–91. http://www.jstor.org/stable/20748462.

Piore, Adam. "Finance elite toasts Seagram Building." *The Real Deal*, October 23, 2007. https://therealdeal.com/issues_articles/finance-elite-toasts-seagram-building-2/.

Ponzini, Davide. "The Values of Starchitecture: Commodification of Architectural Design in Contemporary Cities." *Organizational Aesthetics* 3, no. 1 (January 3, 2014): 10–18.

Puri, Zoya, Suneeth John, and Andrea Chegut. "Does Work Performance Design Impact Value? Linking Design Metrics to Financial Performance in Cities." *MIT Real Estate Innovation Lab Working Paper*, 2018. https://realestateinnovationlab.mit.edu/research_article/does-work-performance-design-impact-value-linking-design-metrics-to-financial-performance-in-cities/.

Reinhart, Christoph. "DAYSIM." Software, 2017. https://daysim.software.informer.com/.

Rittel, Horst W.J. and Melvin M. Webber. "Dilemmas in a General Theory of Planning." *Policy Sciences* 4, no. 2 (June 1, 1973): 155–69. https://doi.org/10.1007/bf01405730.

Rong, Helena Hang, Juncheng Yang, Minkoo Kang, and Andrea Chegut. "The Value of Design in Real Estate Asset Pricing." *Buildings* 10, no. 10 (October 9, 2020): 178. https://doi.org/10.3390/buildings10100178.

Rosen, Sherwin. "Hedonic Prices and Implicit Markets: Product Differentiation in Pure Competition." *Journal of Political Economy* 82, no. 1 (January 1, 1974): 34–55. https://doi.org/10.1086/260169.

Rosenberg, Zoe and Tanay Warerkar. "The Stararchitect-led Projects That Will Transform NYC's Skyline, Mapped." *Curbed NY*, July 26, 2018. http://ny.curbed.com/maps/nyc-architecture-star-projects-under-construction.

Rosinsky, Alan. "Market Report: A Look at NYC Office Sales Activity From 2010 to 2020." *Metro Manhattan*, February 4, 2020. https://www.metro-manhattan.com/blog/market-report-a-look-at-nyc-office-sales-activity-from-2010-to-2020/.

Roth, Leland M. *American Architecture: A History*. London: Routledge, 2018.

Roudsari, Mostapha Sadeghipour, Michelle Pak, and Anthony Viola. "Ladybug: A Parametric Environmental Plugin for Grasshopper to Help Designers Create an Environmentally-conscious Design." *Building Simulation Conference Proceedings*, August 28, 2013. https://doi.org/10.26868/25222708.2013.2499.

Rundle, Andrew, Kathryn M. Neckerman, Lance Freeman, Gina S. Lovasi, Marnie Purciel, James W. Quinn, Catherine Richards, Neelanjan Sircar, and Christopher C. Weiss. "Neighborhood Food Environment and Walkability Predict Obesity in New York City." *Environmental Health Perspectives* 117, no. 3 (March 1, 2009): 442–47. https://doi.org/10.1289/ehp.11590.

Salingaros, Nikos A. "A scientific basis for creating architectural forms." *Journal of Architectural and Planning Research* 15, no. 4 (December 1, 1998): 283–94. http://patterns.architexturez.net/doc/az-cf-172615.

———. "The Biophilic Healing Index predicts effects of the built environment on our wellbeing." *Journal of Biourbanism* 8, no. 1 (2019): 13–34. http://zeta.math.utsa.edu/~yxk833/Biophilicindex.pdf.

———. "Neuroscience Experiments to Verify the Geometry of Healing Environments: Proposing a Biophilic Healing Index of Design and Architecture." In *Urban Experience and Design: Contemporary Perspectives on Improving the Public Realm*, edited by Ann Sussman and Justin Hollander, 1st ed., 58–72. New York: Routledge, 2021.

Samuels, David. "The Real-Estate Royals: End of the Line." *New York Times*, August 10, 1997.

Sclar, Elliott D. "The Infinite Elasticity of Air: New York City's Financialization of Transferable Development Rights." *American Journal of Economics and Sociology* 80, no. 2 (March 1, 2021): 353–80. https://doi.org/10.1111/ajes.12385.

Sclar, Elliott, Bernadette Baird-Zars, Lauren Ames Fischer, and Valerie Stahl, eds. *Zoning: A guide for 21st-century planning*. London: Routledge, 2019.

Scott, Mel. *American City Planning Since 1890: A History Commemorating the Fiftieth Anniversary of the American Institute of Planners*. Berkeley and Los Angeles: University of California Press, 1969.

Severini, Lois. *The Architecture of Finance: Early Wall Street*. Ann Arbor: UMI Research Press, 1983.

Sharp, Naomi. "New York by Design | Center for an Urban Future (CUF)." Center for an Urban Future (CUF). Accessed December 30, 2023. https://nycfuture.org/research/new-york-by-design.

Shaw, Joe. "Platform Real Estate: Theory and Practice of New Urban Real Estate Markets." *Urban Geography* 41, no. 8 (October 17, 2018): 1037–64. https://doi.org/10.1080/02723638.2018.1524653.

Shepard, Bancroft and Clough. *A Century of American Life Insurance: A History of the Mutual Life Insurance Company of New York, 1843-1943*. New York: Columbia University Press, 1946.

Siekman, Philip. «The Bronfmans: An Instinct for Dynasty," *Fortune*, Dec. 1966.

Sklair, Leslie. "Iconic Architecture and the Culture-ideology of Consumerism." *Theory, Culture & Society* 27, no. 5 (2010): 135–59. DOI.

Slaughter, E. Sarah. "Design strategies to increase building flexibility." *Building Research and Information* 29, no. 3 (May 1, 2001): 208–17. https://doi.org/10.1080/09613210010027693.

Solemma. "DIVA-for-Rhino." Software, 2017. https://www.solemma.com/diva.

Statista, "Quarterly Office Vacancy Rates in the United States from 4th Quarter 2017 to 1st Quarter 2023." *Statista*, June 29, 2023. https://www.statista.com/statistics/194054/us-office-vacancy-rate-forecasts-from-2010/.

Steadman, Philip. "Why are most buildings rectangular?" *Arq: Architectural Research Quarterly* 10, no. 2 (June 1, 2006): 119–30. https://doi.org/10.1017/s1359135506000200.

Steelcase. "Engagement and the Global Workplace." *Steelcase Global Report*. Steelcase, 2016. Accessed July 23, 2017. https://www.steelcase.com/eu-en/research/reports/engagement-global-workplace/.

Stevens, Sara. *Developing Expertise: Architecture and Real Estate in Metropolitan America*. New Haven: Yale University Press, 2016.

Strozier, Matthew. "Comparing Manhattan's Housing Market After 9/11, Lehman." *The Wall Street Journal*, September 8, 2011. https://www.wsj.com/articles/BL-DVB-20285.

Studio Gang, "Aqua Tower." 2017. Accessed December 15, 2022. https://vimeo.com/175563995.

Sun, Kevin. "How Manhattan's Office Market Responded in Previous Recessions: TRD Insights." *The Real Deal*, April 20, 2020. https://therealdeal.com/new-york/2020/04/22/how-manhattans-office-market-responded-in-previous-recessions-trd-insights/.

Tanaka, Adam. "Fiduciary Landlords: Life Insurers and Large-scale Housing in New York City." *Joint Center for Housing Studies, Working Paper, Cambridge, MA: Harvard University* (April 2017): 9-17.

Tandy, Clifford R.V. "The Isovist Method of Landscape Survey." Edited by A.C. Murray. *Symposium: Methods of Landscape Analysis*, 1967, 9–10.

Tang, Shiu Keung. "Noise screening effects of balconies on a building facade." *Journal of the Acoustical Society of America* 118, no. 1 (July 1, 2005): 213–21. https://doi.org/10.1121/1.1931887.

Tao, Fei, He Zhang, Ang Liu, and A. Y. C. Nee. "Digital Twin in Industry: State-of-the-Art." *IEEE Transactions on Industrial Informatics* 15, no. 4 (April 1, 2019): 2405–15. https://doi.org/10.1109/tii.2018.2873186.

Tarmy, James. "New York Luxury Real Estate Could Be a Bargain in 2021." *Bloomberg*, December 27, 2020.

Thapa, Dhiraj. "Hotel lobby design: Study of parameters of attraction." 2007. https://ttu-ir.tdl.org/handle/2346/9110.

The Journal News. "Lever Brothers Busy with Expansion Plans." *The Journal News*, October 5, 1949.

The New York Times. "Insurance Companies Increase Investments in Income-Producing Realty to $144,000,000." *The New York Times*, November 30, 1947.

The New York Times. "INVEST $87,000,000 in INCOME REALTY: Insurance Companies Taking Advantage of New Law as Outlet for Funds." *The New York Times*, March 30, 1947.

The New York Times. "Park Ave. To Get New Skyscraper: Seagrams Pans a Gleaming 34-Story Headquarters--Voisin to Lose Home." *The New York Times*, July 13, 1954.

The New York Times. "Metro Business: Alcoa Will Renew New York Presence." *The New York Times*, November 26, 1999.

The New York Times. "Office Vacancy Rate Climbs in New York." *The New York Times*, November 10, 2001. URL.

The White House. "ACT SHEET: Biden-Harris Administration Takes Action to Create More Affordable Housing by Converting Commercial Properties to Residential Use." October 27, 2023. https://www.whitehouse.gov/briefing-room/statements-releases/2023/10/27/fact-sheet-biden-harris-administration-takes-action-to-create-more-affordable-housing-by-converting-commercial-properties-to-residential-use/.

Tomko, Martin and Stephan Winter. "Beyond Digital Twins – a Commentary." *Environment and Planning B: Urban Analytics and City Science* 46, no. 2 (December 11, 2018): 395–99. https://doi.org/10.1177/2399808318816992.

Trager, James. *Park Avenue: Street of Dreams*. Vol. 73. New York: Scribner, 1990.

Tuegel, Eric J., Anthony R. Ingraffea, Thomas Eason, and S. Michael Spottswood. "Reengineering Aircraft Structural Life Prediction Using a Digital Twin." *International Journal of Aerospace Engineering* 2011 (January 1, 2011): 1–14. https://doi.org/10.1155/2011/154798.

Turan, Irmak, Andrea Chegut, Daniel Fink, and Christoph Reinhart. "The Value of Daylight in Office Spaces." *Building and Environment* 168 (January 1, 2020): 8-10. https://doi.org/10.1016/j.buildenv.2019.106503.

———. "Development of View Potential Metrics and the Financial Impact of Views on Office Rents." *Landscape and Urban Planning* 215 (November 1, 2021): 5-10. https://doi.org/10.1016/j.landurbplan.2021.104193.

Turner, Alasdair. "Analysing the visual dynamics of spatial morphology." *Environment and Planning B: Planning and Design* 30, no. 5 (October 1, 2003): 657–76. https://doi.org/10.1068/b12962.

Vandell, Kerry D. and Jonathan Lane. "The Economics of Architecture and Urban Design: Some preliminary findings." *Real Estate Economics* 17, no. 2 (June 1, 1989): 235–60. https://doi.org/10.1111/1540-6229.00489.

Van Den Berg, M.M.H.E., Wanda Wendel-Vos, Mireille N. M. Van Poppel, H.C.G. Kemper, Willem Van Mechelen, and Jolanda Maas. "Health Benefits of Green Spaces in the Living Environment: A Systematic Review of Epidemiological Studies." *Urban Forestry & Urban Greening* 14, no. 4 (January 1, 2015): 806–16. https://doi.org/10.1016/j.ufug.2015.07.008.

Van Dillen, S.M.E., S. De Vries, Peter Groenewegen, and Peter Spreeuwenberg. "Greenspace in Urban Neighbourhoods and Residents' Health: Adding Quality to Quantity." *Journal of Epidemiology and Community Health* 66, no. 6 (June 29, 2011): e8. https://doi.org/10.1136/jech.2009.104695.

Wainwright, Oliver. "Super-Tall, Super-Skinny, Super-Expensive: The "Pencil Towers" of New York›s Super-Rich." *The Guardian* 5 (2019). https://www.theguardian.com/cities/2019/feb/05/super-tall-super-skinny-super-expensive-the-pencil-towers-of-new-yorks-super-rich

Wan, Li, Timea Nochta, and Jennifer Schooling. "Developing a City-Level Digital Twin–Propositions and a Case Study." *International Conference on Smart Infrastructure and Construction 2019*, January 1, 2019. https://doi.org/10.1680/icsic.64669.187.

Ward, Greg. "Radiance." Software, 2016. https://www.radiance-online.org/about.

Wells, Meredith. "Office Clutter or Meaningful Personal Displays: The Role of Office Personalization in Employee and Organizational Well-being." *Journal of Environmental Psychology* 20, no. 3 (September 1, 2000): 239–55. https://doi.org/10.1006/jevp.1999.0166.

Wilber, Donald N. "The role of color in architecture." *Journal of the American Society of Architectural Historians* 2, no. 1 (January 1, 1942): 17–22. https://doi.org/10.2307/901200.

Willis, Carol. *Form Follows Finance: Skyscrapers and Skylines in New York and Chicago.* New York: Princeton Architectural Press, 1995.

Xiao, Fu, Tianxia Jia, Xueqi Zhang, Shanlin Li, and Yonglin Zhang. "Do Street-level Scene Perceptions Affect Housing Prices in Chinese Megacities? An Analysis Using Open Access Datasets and Deep Learning." *PLOS ONE* 14, no. 5 (May 30, 2019): e0217505. https://doi.org/10.1371/journal.pone.0217505.

Yamagata, Yoshiki, Daisuke Murakami, Takahiro Yoshida, Hajime Seya, and Sho Kuroda. "Value of Urban Views in a Bay City: Hedonic Analysis With the Spatial Multilevel Additive Regression (SMAR) Model." *Landscape and Urban Planning* 151 (July 1, 2016): 89–102. https://doi.org/10.1016/j.landurbplan.2016.02.008.

Yang, Juncheng, Helena Hang Rong, Yuhao Kang, Fan Zhang, and Andrea Chegut. "The Financial Impact of Street-level Greenery on New York Commercial Buildings." *Landscape and Urban Planning* 214 (October 1, 2021): 104162. https://doi.org/10.1016/j.landurbplan.2021.104162.

Ye, Yu, Hanting Xie, Fang Jia, Hetao Jiang, and Wang De. "Daily Accessed Street Greenery and Housing Price: Measuring Economic Performance of Human-Scale Streetscapes via New Urban Data." *Sustainability* 11, no. 6 (March 22, 2019): 1741. https://doi.org/10.3390/su11061741.

Zhang, Yonglin and Rencai Dong. "Impacts of Street-Visible Greenery on Housing Prices: Evidence From a Hedonic Price Model and a Massive Street View Image Dataset in Beijing." *ISPRS International Journal of Geo-Information* 7, no. 3 (March 14, 2018): 104. https://doi.org/10.3390/ijgi7030104.

Zhong, Xiaoyang, Mingming Hu, Sebastiaan Deetman, Bernhard Steubing, Hai Lin, Glenn A. Aguilar-Hernandez, Carina Harpprecht, Chunbo Zhang, Arnold Tukker, and Paul Behrens. "Global Greenhouse Gas Emissions From Residential and Commercial Building Materials and Mitigation Strategies to 2060." *Nature Communications* 12, no. 1 (October 21, 2021). https://doi.org/10.1038/s41467-021-26212-z.

Image Credits

Fig. 1 John Randel, engraved by P. Maverik, https://commons.wikimedia.org/wiki/File:Commissioners%27_Plan_of_1811_by_John_Randel_published_in_1821.jpg

Fig. 2 Commission on Building Districts, https://commons.wikimedia.org/wiki/File:Setback_tower_options,_1916.jpg

Fig. 3 https://www.loc.gov/item/2003668551/

Fig. 4 Hugh Ferriss, https://commons.wikimedia.org/wiki/File:Drawing,_Study_for_Maximum_Mass_Permitted_by_the_1916_New_York_Zoning_Law,_Stage_4,_1922_(CH_18468717).jpg

Fig. 5 Chicago Architectural Photographing Company, https://commons.wikimedia.org/wiki/File:Home_Insurance_Building.JPG

Fig. 6 Valentine's Manual, https://commons.wikimedia.org/wiki/File:Equitable_Life_Assurance_Building,_120_Broadway,_New_York_City_1870.jpg

Fig. 7 Glasshouse Images / Alamy Stock Photo, Gottscho-Schleisner Collection, March 1952, https://www.alamy.com/lever-house-53rd-street-and-park-avenue-new-york-city-new-york-usa-gottscho-schleisner-collection-march-1952-image407919393.html

Fig. 8 Alpha Stock / Alamy Stock Photo, https://www.alamy.com/seagram-building-image329066235.html

Fig. 13 MIT Real Estate Innovation Lab

Fig. 34 Ken OHYAMA, https://commons.wikimedia.org/wiki/File:Seagram_Building_(35098307116).jpg

Fig. 35 Detroit Publishing Co., ca. 1908, https://www.loc.gov/item/2016800547/

Fig. 36 Kenneth C. Zirkel, https://commons.wikimedia.org/wiki/File:Lipstick_building,_viewed_from_10th_floor.jpg

Fig. 37 Kenneth Grant / Alamy Stock Photo, https://www.alamy.com/120-wall-street-at-the-east-river-edge-of-manhattans-financial-dis-trict-has-prominent-wedding-cake-setbacks-at-its-upper-levels-image546048052.html

Fig. 38 Andre Carrotflower, https://commons.wikimedia.org/wiki/File:A_Rainy_Day_on_Delancey_Street_(featuring_The_Essex),_Lower_East_Side,_Manhattan_-_20200910.jpg

Fig. 39 Ajay Suresh, https://commons.wikimedia.org/wiki/Category:Parsons_School_of_Design?uselang=de

Fig. 40 Carol M. Highsmith, https://www.loc.gov/item/2011631191/

Fig. 41 Alyaksandr Stzhalkouski / Alamy Stock Photo, https://www.alamy.com/stock-photo-100-united-nations-plaza-building-in-manhattan-new-york-74267201.html

Fig. 42 Balthazar Korab Studios, Ltd., https://commons.wikimedia.org/wiki/File:World_Trade_Center_Interior_Large_arched_windows_-_LCCN2020714985.jpg

Fig. 43 Image generated by the author through AI generation using Midjourney

Fig. 44 King of Hearts, https://commons.wikimedia.org/wiki/File:William_Beaver_House_August_2012.jpg

Fig. 46 Hufton+Crow / Alamy Stock Photo, Port House, Antwerp, Belgium. Architect: Zaha Hadid Architects, 2016, https://www.alamy.com/stock-photo-open-plan-office-in-refurbished-fire-station-port-house-antwerp-belgium-123944990.html

Fig. 47 Loominosity Z, https://commons.wikimedia.org/wiki/File:Tammany_Hall_Building.jpg

Fig. 48 Arcaid Images / Alamy Stock Photo, https://www.alamy.com/stock-photo-the-new-york-times-building-by-renzo-piano-completed-2007-36125223.html

Fig. 49 Ajith, https://commons.wikimedia.org/wiki/File:DUMBO_Aug_2017.jpg

Fig. 50 Zoonar GmbH / Alamy Stock Photo, https://www.alamy.com/empire-state-building-image361241177.html?imageid=7CA3BC4E-E800-4513-B59D-7077D60B2635&p=64 5526&pn=2&searchId=143afc1632175534f-45957c7199bacae&searchtype=0

Fig. 51 Patrick Batchelder / Alamy Stock Photo, https://www.alamy.com/stock-photo-empty-office-building-at-night-50770923.html

Fig. 52 Momos, https://commons.wikimedia.org/wiki/File:Upper_West_Side_-_Broadway.jpg

Fig. 53 Batchelder / Alamy Stock Photo, https://www.alamy.com/empty-street-in-new-york-city-during-the-covid-19-coronavirus-pandemic-image369951656.html

Fig. 59 Irmak Turan, Andrea Chegut, Daniel Fink, and Christoph Reinhart / MIT REIL, Floor-by-floor Daylight Simulation Workflow.*

Fig. 60 Irmak Turan, Andrea Chegut, Daniel Fink, and Christoph Reinhart / MIT REIL, Rays Projection from an Individual Viewpoint.*

Fig. 61 Irmak Turan, Andrea Chegut, Daniel Fink, and Christoph Reinhart / MIT REIL, Rays Projection from a Single Viewpoint in an Open Plan.*

Fig. 62 Irmak Turan, Andrea Chegut, Daniel Fink, and Christoph Reinhart / MIT REIL, View Elements in the 3D Model.*

Fig. 63 Zoya Puri, Suneeth P. John, and Andrea Chegut / MIT REIL, Buildings with WPI-scored spaces in New York City.*

Fig. 64 MIT REIL, GVI Captures the Visually Perceived Density of Greenery at the Street Level.*

Fig. 65 MIT REIL, GVI Identification Process.*

* Diagram modified for illustrative purposes in this book

Acknowledgments

We extend our sincere gratitude to the collaborative organizations associated with the MIT Real Estate Innovation Lab for their generous support. Our thanks go to the MIT Center for Real Estate, Gensler, and Epic Games for their invaluable contributions and partnership. We are also immensely grateful to our former Lab members and friends, Daniel Fink, Erin Glennon, Irmak Turan, and Svafa Gronfeldt, for their steadfast support in editing and publishing this book. We also thank our developmental editor Julia van den Hout of Original Copy and our graphic designer Studio Lin, whose hard work has been a vital part of our journey.

In addition, we are deeply appreciative of the efforts and expertise provided by several former members and collaborators of the MIT Real Estate Innovation Lab. Their significant contributions to the research presented in Chapter 4 of this book have been instrumental. We would like to specifically acknowledge Piet Eichholtz, Daniel Fink, Suneeth P. John, Yuhao Kang, Nils Kok, Zoya Puri, Christoph Reinhart, Irmak Turan, and Fan Zhang for their contributions.

We also thank the following individuals for contributing to the last-mile fundraising effort of this project: Dr. Chegut's family—Daniel Fink, David Fink, Tamar Fink, and our dear friends and supporters— Ian D Bradley, Benjamin Breslau, Priscilla Burnsed, Francisco Caiado, Myeong Jae Choi, Hye Joo Chung, Brock DeSmit, Diego Fernandez, Yun S. Gerik, Erin Glennon, Paul Goodwin, Luke Graham, Hoon Her, Rosalynn Hillenbrand, Hyun-Joo Kang, Sangkoo Kang, Sung-Il Kang, Chaeyoung Kim, Seungyeol Kim, George Knowlton, JeHyun Lee, Jie Hwan Lee, Man Young Lee, Ok Soon Lee, Pak Wa Lim, Ryan Lovett, Paulo Mayer, Boungdoo Park, James Peraino, Zoya Puri, Ricardo Salvador Alcalde Gaytan, Weijia Song, Amina Thomas, Irmak Turan, Midori Wong, Fei Xu, Zixiao Yin, KwanSik Yoon, and Alexander Yuen. Your support and generosity are greatly acknowledged and appreciated.

Colophon

Published by Applied Research and Design
Publishing, an imprint of ORO Editions.
Gordon Goff: Publisher

www.appliedresearchanddesign.com
info@appliedresearchanddesign.com

Authors: Andrea Chegut, Minkoo Kang,
Helena Rong, Juncheng Yang
Book Design: Studio Lin
Project Manager: Jake Anderson
Developmental Editor: Julia van den Hout,
Original Copy

10 9 8 7 6 5 4 3 2 1 First Edition

ISBN: 978-1-951541-97-2

Prepress and Print work by ORO Editions Inc.
Printed in China

AR+D Publishing makes a continuous effort
to minimize the overall carbon footprint of
its publications. As part of this goal, AR+D,
in association with Global ReLeaf, arranges
to plant trees to replace those used in the
manufacturing of the paper produced for
its books. Global ReLeaf is an international
campaign run by American Forests, one of
the world's oldest nonprofit conservation
organizations. Global ReLeaf is American
Forests' education and action program that
helps individuals, organizations, agencies,
and corporations improve the local and global
environment by planting and caring for trees.